A BRIEF HISTORY

OF

EQUALITY

THOMAS PIKETTY

Translated by Steven Rendall

The Belknap Press of Harvard University Press

CAMBRIDGE, MASSACHUSETTS   LONDON, ENGLAND   2022

LIBRARY OF CONGRESS CATALOGING-IN-PUBLICATION DATA

Names: Piketty, Thomas, 1971– author. | Rendall, Steven, translator.
Title: A brief history of equality / Thomas Piketty ; translated
from the French by Steven Rendall.
Other titles: Brève histoire de l'égalité English
Description: Cambridge, Massachusetts : The Belknap Press of
Harvard University Press, 2022. | First published in French as
Une bréve histoire de l'égalité, Éditions du Seuil, 2021. |
Includes bibliographical references and index. |
Identifiers: LCCN 2021053186 | ISBN 9780674273559 (cloth)
Subjects: LCSH: Equality—History. | Social classes—History. |
Income distribution—History.
Classification: LCC HM821 .P547 2022 | DDC 305.09—dc23/eng/20211202
LC record available at https://lccn.loc.gov/2021053186

Contents

Acknowledgments

"What you write is interesting, but couldn't you make it a little shorter, so I can share your research with my friends and family?"

In part, this book is a response to this question, which has regularly been asked by readers over the years. In the course of the last two decades, I have written three works running to about a thousand pages (each!) concerning the history of inequalities: *Top Incomes over the Twentieth Century* (2001), *Capital in the Twenty-First Century* (2013), and *Capital and Ideology* (2019). These books are themselves based on a vast international program of historical and comparative research that has led to the publication of several collective reports and studies as well as to the development of the World Inequality Database (WID).[1] The volume of the documentation thereby constituted might well discourage the best-intentioned citizen. It was time for a summation. Here is the result.

However, this book is not limited to a systematic presentation of the main lessons learned from these works. By recapitulating the

---

1. The editions in English are: A. B. Atkinson and T. Piketty, eds., *Top Incomes over the Twentieth Century* (Oxford: Oxford University Press, 2007); A. B. Atkinson and T. Piketty, *Top Incomes: A Global Perspective* (Oxford: Oxford University Press, 2010); F. Alvaredo, L. Chancel, T. Piketty, E. Saez, and G. Zucman, *World Inequality Report 2018* (Cambridge, MA: Belknap Press of Harvard University Press, 2018); A. Gethin, C. Martínez-Toledano, and T. Piketty, eds., *Political Cleavages and Social Inequalities* (Cambridge, MA: Harvard University Press, 2021). Many texts and materials proceeding from this research are available on these websites: wid.world, wpid.world, and piketty.pse.ens.fr.

debates to which these questions have given rise in recent years, it provides a new perspective on the history of inequality based on a strong conviction forged in the course of my research: the advance toward equality is a battle that began long ago and needs only to be continued in the twenty-first century, provided that we all participate in it and that we break with the divisions based on racial or cultural identity and on disciplines that too often prevent us from moving forward. Economic questions are too important to be left to a small class of specialists and managers. Citizens' reappropriation of this knowledge is an essential stage in the transformation of power relationships. Naturally, I also hope to convince some of my readers to peruse, one day, the more voluminous works (which, I hasten to say, are very accessible, despite their length!). In the meantime, this short text can be read independently of the others, and I would like to take this opportunity to thank all the readers, students, and citizens who have encouraged me in this enterprise, and whose questions have enriched this work. This book is dedicated to them.

A BRIEF HISTORY OF EQUALITY

INTRODUCTION

This book offers a comparative history of inequalities among social classes in human societies. Or rather, it offers a history of equality, because, as we shall see, there has been a long-term movement over the course of history toward more social, economic, and political equality.

This is not, of course, a peaceful history, and still less a linear one. Revolts and revolutions, social struggles and crises of all kinds play a central role in the history of equality reviewed here. This history is also punctuated by multiple phases of regression and identitarian introversion.

Nonetheless, at least since the end of the eighteenth century there has been a historical movement toward equality. The world of the early 2020s, no matter how unjust it may seem, is more egalitarian than that of 1950 or that of 1900, which were themselves in many respects more egalitarian than those of 1850 or 1780. The precise developments vary depending on the period, and on whether we are studying inequalities between social classes defined by legal status, ownership of the means of production, income, education, national or ethno-racial origin—all dimensions that will interest us here. But over the long term, no matter which criterion we employ, we arrive at the same conclusion. Between 1780 and 2020, we see developments tending toward greater equality of status, property, income, genders, and races within most regions and societies on the planet, and to a certain extent when we compare these societies on the global scale. If we adopt a global, multidimensional perspective on inequalities, we can see that, in several respects, this advance toward equality has also continued during the period from 1980 to 2020, which is more complex and mixed than is often thought.

Since the end of the eighteenth century, there has been a real, long-term tendency toward equality, but it is nonetheless limited in scope. We shall see that different inequalities have persisted at considerable and unjustified levels on all these dimensions—status, property, power, income, gender, origin, and so on—and, moreover, that individuals often face inequalities in combination. To assert that there is a tendency toward equality is not to brag about success. Instead, it is to call for continuing the fight on a solid, historical basis. By examining how movement toward equality has actually been produced, we can learn precious lessons for our future and better understand the struggles and mobilizations that have made this movement possible, as well as the institutional structures and legal, social, fiscal, educational, and electoral systems that have allowed equality to become a lasting reality. Unfortunately, this process of collective learning about equitable institutions is often weakened by historical amnesia, intellectual nationalism, and the compartmentalization of knowledge. In order to continue the advance toward equality, we must return to the lessons of history and transcend national and disciplinary borders. The present work—which belongs to the domains of history and the social sciences, and is both optimistic and progressive—seeks to move in that direction.

A New Economic and Social History

It is possible to write this *Brief History of Equality* today chiefly because of the many international studies that have profoundly renewed research in economic and social history in recent decades.

In particular, I shall base my remarks on the multiple works that have provided us with a genuinely global perspective on the history of capitalism and of the Industrial Revolution. I am thinking, for example, about Ken Pomeranz's study, published in 2000, on the "great divergence" between Europe and China in the eighteenth and nineteenth centuries,[1] probably the most important and influential book on the history of the world-economy (*économie-monde*) since the publication of Fernand Braudel's *Civilisation matérielle, économie et capitalisme* in 1979 and the works of Immanuel Wallerstein on "world-systems analysis."[2] For Pomeranz, the development of Western industrial capitalism is closely linked to systems of the international division of labor, the frenetic exploitation of natural resources, and the European powers' military and colonial domination over the rest of the planet. Subsequent studies have largely confirmed that conclusion, whether through the research of Prasannan Parthasarathi or that of Sven Beckert and the recent movement around the "new history of capitalism."[3]

More generally, historians of colonial empires and slavery, along with those who study global, connected history, have made immense strides over the past twenty to thirty years, and I shall lean very heavily on their works. I am thinking in particular of the research of Frederick Cooper, Catherine Hall, Or Rosenboim, Emmanuelle Saada, Pierre Singaravelou, Alessandro Stanziani, Sanjay Subrahmanyam, and many others who will appear as the argument advances.[4] My

---

1. K. Pomeranz, *The Great Divergence: China, Europe and the Making of the Modern World Economy* (Princeton, NJ: Princeton University Press, 2000).

2. F. Braudel, *Civilization and Capitalism*, 3 vols., trans. Siân Reynold (New York: Harper and Row, 1982–1984); I. Wallerstein, *The Modern World-System*, 4 vols. (New York: Academic Press, 1974–1989).

3. P. Parthasarathi, *Why Europe Grew Rich and Asia Did Not: Global Economic Divergence 1600–1850* (Cambridge: Cambridge University Press, 2011); S. Beckert, *Empire of Cotton: A Global History* (New York: Alfred A. Knopf, 2014); S. Beckert and S. Rockman, *Slavery's Capitalism: A New History of American Economic Development* (Philadelphia: University of Pennsylvania Press, 2016); J. Levy, *Ages of American Capitalism: A History of the United States* (New York: Random House, 2021).

4. See, for example, F. Cooper, *Citizenship between Empire and Nation: Remaking France and French Africa 1945–1960* (Princeton, NJ: Princeton University Press, 2014); C. Hall, N. Draper, K. McClelland, K. Donington, and R. Lang, *Legacies of British Slave-Ownership: Colonial Slavery and the Formation of Victorian Britain* (Cambridge:

work is also inspired by the renewal of research on people's history and the history of popular struggles.[5]

In addition, this brief history could not have been written without the progress made in understanding the historical distribution of wealth among social classes. This domain of research itself has a long history. All societies have produced knowledge and analyses of real, supposed, or desirable differences in wealth between the poor and the rich, at least since *The Republic* and *The Laws* (in which Plato recommends that these differences not exceed a ratio of one to four). In the eighteenth century, Jean-Jacques Rousseau explained that the invention of private property and its immoderate accumulation are the origin of inequality and discord among people. However, not until the arrival of the Industrial Revolution did genuine inquiries into workers' salaries and living conditions develop, along with new sources dealing with income, profits, and properties. In the nineteenth century, Karl Marx tried to make best use of the British financial and inheritance data of his time, even if the means and the material at his disposal were limited.[6]

Cambridge University Press, 2014); O. Rosenboim, *The Emergence of Globalism: Visions of World Order in Britain and the United States 1939–1950* (Princeton, NJ: Princeton University Press, 2017); E. Saada, *Les Enfants de la colonie. Les métis de l'empire français, entre sujétion et citoyenneté* (Paris: La Découverte, 2007); P. Singaravélou and S. Venayre, eds., *Histoire du monde au xixe siècle* (Paris: Fayard, 2017); S. Subrahmanyam, *Empires between Islam and Christianity, 1500–1800* (Albany, NY: SUNY Press, 2019); A. Stanziani, *Les Métamorphoses du travail contraint. Une histoire globale, xviiie–xixe siècles* (Paris: Presses de Sciences Po, 2020).

5. H. Zinn, *A People's History of the United States* (1980; New York: Harper, 2009); M. Zancarini-Fournel, *Les Luttes et les Rêves. Une histoire populaire de la France de 1685 à nos jours* (Paris: La Découverte, 2016); G. Noiriel, *Une histoire populaire de la France de la guerre de Cent Ans à nos jours* (Marseille: Agone, 2018); D. Tartakowsky, *Le pouvoir est dans la rue. Crises politiques et manifestations en France, xixe–xxe siècles* (Paris: Aubier, 1998); B. Pavard, F. Rochefort, and M. Zancarini-Fournel, *Ne nous libérez pas, on s'en charge! Une histoire des féminismes de 1789 à nos jours* (Paris: La Découverte, 2020).

6. T. Piketty, *Capital in the Twenty-First Century* (Cambridge, MA: Belknap Press of Harvard University Press, 2014), 3–11, 229–230.

In the course of the twentieth century, research on these questions took a more systematic turn. Researchers began to collect on a large scale data regarding prices and salaries, land income and profits, inheritances and plots of land. In 1933, Ernest Labrousse published his *Esquisse du mouvement des prix et des revenus en France au xviiie siècle* (Sketch of the movement of prices and income in France during the eighteenth century), a monumental study in which he shows how in the course of the decades preceding the French Revolution, agricultural wages fell behind relative to the price of wheat and to land income, all in the context of strong demographic pressure. Without claiming it was the sole cause of the Revolution, it seems clear that this development could only increase the growing unpopularity of the aristocracy and of the established political regime.[7] In 1965, on the first page of their study *Le Mouvement du profit en France au xixe siècle* (The movement of profit in France in the nineteenth century), Jean Bouvier and his coauthors described the research program with which they identified: "So long as the incomes of contemporary social classes remain beyond the scope of scientific inquiry, it will be pointless to try to write a valid economic and social history."[8]

Often associated with the Annales school, which was particularly influential in French historical research between 1930 and 1980, this new economic and social history did not neglect the study of property systems. In 1931, Marc Bloch published his classic study on the typology of medieval and modern agrarian systems.[9] In 1973, Adeline Daumard presented the results of a vast investigation carried out

---

7. E. Labrousse, *Esquisse du mouvement des prix et des revenus en France au xviiie siècle* (Paris: Dalloz, 1933). Compare A. Chabert, *Essai sur les mouvements des prix et des revenus en France de 1798 à 1820* (Paris: Librairie de Medicis, 1949), which documents an increase in wages during the Revolution and the Empire.

8. J. Bouvier, F. Furet, and M. Gilet, *Le Mouvement du profit en France au xixe siècle. Matériaux et études* (Paris: Mouton, 1965).

9. M. Bloch, *Les Caractères originaux de l'histoire rurale française* (Paris: Armand Colin, 1931).

in nineteenth-century French inheritance archives.[10] Since the 1980s, the movement has slowed a bit, but it has left a lasting mark on the practices of research in the social sciences. In the course of the twentieth century, numerous historical studies on wages and prices, income and wealth, and tithes and properties have been published by a multitude of historians, sociologists, and economists, from François Simiand to Christian Baudelot and from Emmanuel Le Roy Ladurie to Gilles Postel-Vinay.[11]

In parallel, US and British historians and economists also paved the way for a history of the distribution of wealth. In 1953, Simon Kuznets combined the first national accounts, which he had helped establish following the trauma of the Depression, with data from the federal income tax (created in 1913, after a long political and constitutional battle) in order to estimate the share of high incomes in national income.[12] The study concerned only a single country (the United States) and a relatively short period (1913–1948), but it was the first study of this kind, and it caused a great stir. Robert Lampman did the same in 1962 with data from the federal tax on inheritance.[13] In 1978, Tony Atkinson pushed the analysis further, using British sources on inheritance.[14] Alice Hanson Jones went even further back in time,

---

10. A. Daumard, *Les Fortunes françaises au XIXe siècle. Enquête sur la répartition et la composition des capitaux privés à Paris, Lyon, Lille, Bordeaux et Toulouse d'après l'enregistrement des déclarations de successions* (Paris: Mouton, 1973).

11. In addition to the works already cited, see F. Simiand, *Le Salaire, l'Évolution sociale et la Monnaie* (Paris: Alcan, 1932); C. Baudelot and A. Lebeaupin, *Les Salaires de 1950 à 1975* (Paris: INSEE, 1979); J. Goy and E. Le Roy Ladurie, *Les Fluctuations du produit de la dîme. Conjoncture décimale et domaniale de la fin du Moyen Âge au XVIIIe siècle* (Paris: Mouton, 1972); G. Postel-Vinay, *La Terre et l'Argent. L'agriculture et le crédit en France du XVIIIe siècle au début du XXe siècle* (Paris: Albin Michel, 1998); J. Bourdieu, L. Kesztenbaum, and G. Postel-Vinay, *L'Enquête TRA.* vol. 1: *1793–1902: histoire d'un outil, outil pour l'histoire* (Paris: Institut national d'études démographiques, 2013).

12. S. Kuznets, *Shares of Upper Income Groups in Income and Savings* (Cambridge MA: National Bureau of Economic Research, 1953).

13. R. J. Lampman, *The Share of Top Wealth-Holders in National Wealth, 1922–56* (Princeton NJ: Princeton University Press, 1962).

14. A. B. Atkinson and A. J. Harrison, *Distribution of Personal Wealth in Britain* (Cambridge: Cambridge University Press, 1978).

publishing in 1977 the results of a vast inquiry into the property inventories of Americans in the colonial period.[15]

Drawing on all the earlier studies, a new program of historical research on income and wealth was established in the early 2000s, a program in which I had the good fortune to participate with the decisive support of numerous colleagues, including Facundo Alvaredo, Tony Atkinson, Lucas Chancel, Emmanuel Saez, and Gabriel Zucman.[16] In comparison to earlier works, this new wave had the advantage of advanced technical means. Between 1930 to 1980, Labrousse, Daumard, and Kuznets carried out their research almost exclusively by hand, on file cards. Every collection of data and every table of results required a substantial technical investment, sometimes leaving the researcher with little energy for the work of historical interpretation, mobilization of other resources, and critical analysis of the categories, an obligation that no doubt helped weaken a history sometimes seen as too narrowly "serial" (that is, too centered on the production of historical series comparable in time and space, an exercise that may be seen as necessary, but not in any way sufficient, for making progress in the social sciences). In addition, the sources collected during this first wave of studies left few traces, which limited the possible reutilizations and the establishment of a genuine cumulative process.

Conversely, the progress of computerization since 2000 has made it possible to extend the analysis to longer periods and to a greater number of countries. Proceeding from this research program, in 2021 the World Inequality Database (WID.world) brought together the combined efforts of almost a hundred researchers concerning eighty countries on every continent, with data on the distribution of income

---

15. A. H. Jones, *American Colonial Wealth: Documents and Methods* (New York: Arno Press, 1977).

16. T. Piketty, *Les Hauts Revenus en France au xxe siècle* (Paris: Grasset, 2001); and then A. B. Atkinson and T. Piketty, *Top Incomes over the 20th Century* (Oxford: Oxford University Press, 2007); and A. B. Atkinson and T. Piketty, *Top Incomes: A Global Perspective* (Oxford: Oxford University Press, 2010).

and wealth going back, in some cases, to the eighteenth and nine-teenth centuries, and going forward as far as the first decades of the twenty-first century.[17] This broader temporal and comparative perspective has made it possible to multiply comparisons and achieve important advances in the social, economic, and political interpreta-tion of the developments observed. This collective work led me to publish in 2013 and 2019 two studies proposing the first interpretive syntheses on the historical evolution of the distribution of wealth, studies that have helped inform public debates on these questions.[18] New research conducted with Amory Gethin and Clara Martínez-Toledano has re-cently set out to study the transformations of the structure of social inequalities and political cleavages, in line with the studies launched in the 1960s by the political scientists Seymour Lipset and Stein Rokkan.[19] While these various research programs have made certain advances possible, we must nevertheless emphasize that much remains to be done to combine diverse methodologies, sources, and research skills to provide a satisfactory analysis of the representations and in-stitutions, the mobilizations and struggles, the strategies and actors involved in the transformations brought to light.

   A Brief History of Equality has also been made possible by a new generation of researchers, and interdisciplinary studies that have renewed reflection on the sociohistorical dynamics of equality and inequality at the frontier of history, economics, sociology, law, anthro-

---

17. The World Inequality Database was initially created in 2011 under the name "World Top Incomes Database," before taking its current name with the publication in French and then in English of F. Alvaredo, L. Chancel, T. Piketty, E. Saez, and G. Zucman, *World Inequality Report 2018* (Cambridge, MA: Belknap Press of Harvard University Press, 2018).

18. Piketty, *Capital in the Twenty-First Century*; T. Piketty, *Capital and Ideology* (Cambridge, MA: Belknap Press of Harvard University Press, 2020).

19. A. Gethin, C. Martínez-Toledano, and T. Piketty, eds., *Political Cleavages and So-cial Inequalities: A Study of Fifty Democracies, 1948–2020* (Cambridge, MA: Harvard University Press, 2021). Compare S. Lipset and S. Rokkan, "Cleavage Structures, Party Systems and Voter Alignments: An Introduction," in *Party Systems and Voter Align-ments: Cross-national Perspectives,* ed. Lipset and Rokkan (New York: Free Press, 1967).

pology, and political science. I refer to the research of Nicolas Barreyre, Erik Bengtsson, Asma Benhenda, Marlène Benquet, Céline Bessière, Tithi Bhattacharya, Rafe Blaufarb, Julia Cagé, Denis Cogneau, Nicolas Delalande, Isabelle Ferreras, Nancy Fraser, Sibylle Gollac, Yajna Govind, David Graeber, Julien Grenet, Stéphanie Hennette, Camille Herlin-Giret, Élise Huillery, Alexandra Killewald, Stephanie Kelton, Claire Lemercier, Noam Maggor, Ewan McGaughey, Dominique Meda, Eric Monnet, Pap Ndiaye, Martin O'Neill, Hélène Périvier, Fabian Pfeffer, Katharina Pistor, Patrick Simon, Alexis Spire, Pavlina Tcherneva, Samuel Weeks, Madeline Woker, Shoshana Zuboff, and many others whom I cannot cite here, but whose names and work will appear throughout the book.[20]

The Revolts against Injustice and Learning about Equitable Institutions

What are the main lessons that can be drawn from this new economic and social history? The most obvious is no doubt the following: inequality is first of all a social, historical, and political construction. In other words, for the same level of economic or technological development, there are always many different ways of organizing a property system or a border system, a social and political system or a fiscal and educational system. These options are political in nature. They depend on the state of power relationships between the various social groups and the worldviews involved, and they lead to inegalitarian levels and structures that are extremely variable, depending on societies and periods. All creations of wealth in history have issued from a collective process: they depend on the international division of labor, the use of worldwide natural resources, and the accumulation of knowledge since the beginnings of humanity. Human societies constantly invent rules and institutions in order to structure

---

20. The complete references will be given as they are used.

themselves and to divide up wealth and power, but always on the basis of reversible political choices.

The second lesson is that since the end of the eighteenth century there has been a long-term movement toward equality. This is the consequence of conflicts and revolts against injustice that have made it possible to transform power relationships and overthrow institutions supported by the dominant classes, which seek to structure social inequality in a way that benefits them, and to replace them with new institutions and new social, economic, and political rules that are more equitable and emancipatory for the majority. Generally speaking, the most fundamental transformations seen in the history of inegalitarian regimes involve social conflicts and large-scale political crises. It was the peasant revolts of 1788–1789 and the events of the French Revolution that led to the abolition of the nobility's privileges. Similarly, it was not muted discussions in Paris salons but the slave revolt in Saint-Domingue in 1791 that led to the beginning of the end of the Atlantic slavery system. In the course of the twentieth century, social and trade-union mobilizations played a major role in the establishment of new power relationships between capital and labor and in the reduction of inequalities. The two world wars can also be analyzed as the consequence of social tensions and contradictions connected with the intolerable inequality that prevailed before 1914, both domestically and internationally. In the United States, it took a devastating civil war to put an end to the slavery system in 1865. A century later, in 1965, the Civil Rights movement succeeded in abolishing the system of legal racial discrimination (without, however, putting an end to discrimination that was illegal and nonetheless still very real). Examples are many: in the 1950s and 1960s the wars of independence played a central role in ending European colonialism; it took decades of riots and mobilizations to do away with South African apartheid in 1994, and so on.

In addition to revolutions, wars, and revolts, economic and financial crises often serve as turning points where social conflicts are crystallized and power relationships are redefined. The crisis of the 1930s played a central part in the long-lasting delegitimation of economic liberalism and the justification of new forms of state intervention. More recently, the financial crisis of 2008 and the worldwide Covid-19 pandemic in 2020–2021 have already begun to overturn various certainties that shortly before had been considered irrefutable, certainties concerning, for example, the acceptable level of public debt or the role of central banks. On a more local but still significant scale, the revolt of the *gilets jaunes* ("yellow vests") in France in 2018 ended with the government's abandonment of its plan to increase the carbon tax, which is particularly inegalitarian. At the beginning of the 2020s, the Black Lives Matter, #MeToo, and Fridays for Future movements are showing an impressive ability to mobilize people around racial, gender, and climatic inequalities, across national borders and generations. Taking into account the social and environmental contradictions of the current economic system, it is likely that such revolts, conflicts, and crises will continue to play a central role in the future, under circumstances that it is impossible to predict with precision. The end of history will not come tomorrow. The movement toward equality still has a long way to go, especially in a world in which the poorest, and particularly the poorest in the poorest countries, are preparing to be subjected, with increasing violence, to climatic and environmental damage caused by the richest people's way of life.

It is also important to highlight another lesson issuing from history, namely that struggles and power relationships are not sufficient as such. They are a necessary condition for overturning inegalitarian institutions and established powers, but unfortunately they do not in any way guarantee that the new institutions and the new powers that will replace them will always be as egalitarian and emancipatory as we might have hoped.

The reason for this is simple. Although it is easy to denounce the inegalitarian or oppressive nature of established institutions and governments, it is much harder to agree on the alternative institutions that will make it possible to make real progress toward social, economic, and political equality, while at the same time respecting individual rights, including the right to be different. The task is not at all impossible, but it requires us to accept deliberation, the confrontation of differing points of view, compromises, and experimentation. Above all, it requires us to accept the fact that we can learn from the historical trajectories and experiences of others, and especially that the exact content of just institutions is not known *a priori* and is worth debating as such. Concretely, we will see that since the end of the eighteenth century, the march toward equality has been based on the development of a number of specific institutional arrangements that have to be studied as such: equality before the law; universal suffrage and parliamentary democracy; free and obligatory education; universal health insurance; progressive taxes on income, inheritance, and property; joint management and labor law; freedom of the press; international law; and so on.

However, each of these arrangements, far from having reached a complete and consensual form, is connected with a precarious, unstable, and temporary compromise, in perpetual redefinition and emerging from specific social conflicts and mobilizations, interrupted bifurcations, and particular historical moments. They all suffer from multiple insufficiencies and must be constantly rethought, supplemented, and replaced by others. As it currently exists almost everywhere, formal equality before the law does not exclude profound discriminations based on origins or gender; representative democracy is only one of the imperfect forms of participation in politics; inequalities of access to education and health care remain extremely intractable; progressive taxes and redistribution of wealth must be completely reconceived on the domestic and international scale; power-sharing in business enterprises is still in its infancy; control of almost all the media by a few oligarchs can hardly be considered the most complete form of a free press; the international legal system, founded on the uncontrolled circulation of capital without any social or climatic objective, is usually related to a kind of neocolonialism that benefits the wealthiest people, and so on.

To continue to shake up and redefine established institutions, crises and power relations are necessary, as was the case in the past, but we will also need processes of learning and collective engagement, as well as mobilization around new political programs and proposals for new institutions. This requires multiple frameworks for the discussion, elaboration, and diffusion of knowledge and experiences: political parties and labor unions, schools and books, travel and meetings, newspapers and electronic media. The social sciences naturally have a role to play in this, a significant role, but one that must not be exaggerated: the processes of social adaptation are the most important. Above all, this adaptation also involves collective organizations, whose forms themselves remain to be reinvented.

Power Relationships and Their Limits

In sum, two symmetrical pitfalls must be avoided: one consists in neglecting the role of struggles and power relationships in the history of equality. The other consists, on the contrary, in sanctifying and neglecting the importance of political and institutional outcomes along with the role of ideas and ideologies in their elaboration. Resistance by elites is an ineluctable reality today, in a world in which transnational billionaires are richer than states, much as in the French Revolution. Such resistance can be overcome only by powerful collective mobilizations during moments of crisis and tension. Nonetheless, the idea that there is a spontaneous consensus regarding equitable and emancipatory institutions, and that breaking elites' resistance would be sufficient to put these institutions in place, is a dangerous illusion. Questions regarding the organization of the welfare state, the recasting of the progressive income tax and international treaties, postcolonial reparations, or the struggle against discrimination are both complex and technical and can be overcome only through a recourse to history, the diffusion of knowledge, deliberation, and confrontation among differing points of view. Social class, no matter how important, does not suffice to forge a theory of a just society, a theory of property, a theory of borders, of taxation, of education, of wages and salaries, or of democracy. For any particular social experience, there will always be a form of ideological indetermination, on the one hand because class is itself plural and multidimensional (status, property, income, diplomas, gender, origin, and so on), and on the other because the complexity of the questions asked does not allow us to suppose that purely material antagonisms could lead to a single conclusion regarding equitable institutions.

The experiment of Soviet communism (1917–1991), a major event that runs through and to a certain extent defines the twentieth century, perfectly illustrates these two pitfalls. On the one hand, it was in fact power relationships and intense social struggles that allowed the Bolshevik revolutionaries to replace the czarist regime with the first "proletarian state" in history, a state that initially achieved considerable advances in education, public health, and industry, while at the same time making a major contribution to the victory over Nazism. Without the pressure of the Soviet Union and the international communist movement, it is not at all certain that the Western property-owning classes would have accepted Social Security and progressive income taxes, decolonization and civil rights. On the other hand, the sanctification of power relationships and the Bolsheviks' certainty that they knew the ultimate truth concerning equitable institutions led to the totalitarian disaster we witnessed. The institutional arrangements put in place (a single political party, bureaucratic centralization, hegemonic state property, and a rejection of cooperative property, elections, labor unions, and so on) claimed to be more emancipatory than bourgeois or social-democratic institutions. They led to levels of oppression and imprisonment that completely discredited this regime and ultimately caused its fall, while at the same time contributing to the emergence of a new form of hypercapitalism. That is how, after being in the twentieth century the country that had entirely abolished private property, Russia became at the beginning of the twenty-first century the world capital of the oligarchs, financial opacity, and tax havens. For all these reasons, we have to examine closely the genesis of these different institutional arrangements, just as we have to study the institutions set up by Chinese communism, which might prove more durable, though no less oppressive.

I have sought to avoid these two pitfalls: power relationships must be neither ignored nor sanctified. Struggles play a central role in the history of equality, but we must also take seriously the question of equitable institutions and egalitarian deliberation about them. It is not always easy to find a balanced position between these two points: if we overemphasize power relationships and struggles, we can be accused of yielding to Manichaeism and neglecting the question of ideas and content; conversely, by focusing attention on the ideological and programmatic weaknesses of the egalitarian coalition, we can be suspected of further weakening it, and underestimating the dominant classes' ability to resist and their short-sighted egoism (which is, however, often patent). I have done my best to escape these two pitfalls, but I am not sure I have always succeeded, and I beg my readers' indulgence in advance. Above all, I hope the historical and comparative materials presented in this book will be useful in clarifying the nature of a just society and the institutions that compose it.

1

THE MOVEMENT TOWARD EQUALITY

The First Milestones

Let's start at the heart of the matter. Human progress exists: the movement toward equality is a battle that can be won, but it is a battle whose outcome is uncertain, a fragile social and political process that is always ongoing and in question. I shall begin by recalling the historical progress that has been achieved in terms of education and health care before examining the highly political questions raised by the choice of socioeconomic indicators. Then, in the following chapter, we will examine a few basic elements and orders of magnitude concerning the slow deconcentration of power, property, and income.

Human Progress: Education and Health Care for All

Human progress exists: to be convinced of this, it suffices to observe the development of health care and education in the world since 1820 (see Figure 1). The available data are incomplete, but there is no doubt about the tendency. On average, life expectancy at birth has risen worldwide, from about twenty-six years in 1820 to seventy-two years in 2020. At the beginning of the nineteenth century, about 20 percent of newborns on the planet died in the course of their first year, as compared with less than 1 percent today. If we concentrate on people who reached age one, life expectancy at birth has risen from about thirty-

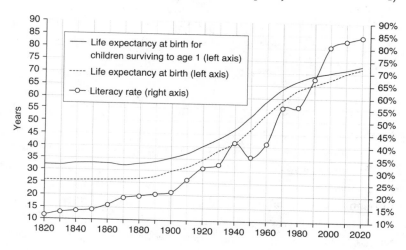

FIGURE 1. Health Care and Education in the World, 1820–2020
Worldwide life expectancy at birth (all births taken together) has risen from about twenty-six years on average in 1820 to seventy-two years in 2020. Life expectancy at birth among persons reaching the age of one has risen from thirty-two years to seventy-three years (infant mortality before the age of one has decreased from about 20 percent in 1820 to less than 1 percent in 2020). The literacy rate in the world population aged fifteen or more has risen from 12 percent to 85 percent. *Sources and series:* piketty.pse.ens.fr/equality

two years in 1820 to seventy-three years in 2020. Two centuries ago, only a small minority of the population could hope to live to be fifty or sixty years old; today, that privilege has become the norm.

At present, humanity is in better health than it has ever been; it also has more access to education and culture than ever before. Information collected in many inquiries and censuses allows us to estimate that at the beginning of the nineteenth century, hardly 10 percent of the world population over the age of fifteen could read and write, whereas today more than 85 percent is literate. There again, more refined indicators confirm the diagnosis. The average number of years of education has risen from hardly one year two centuries ago to more than eight years worldwide today, and more than twelve years in the most advanced countries. In 1820, less than 10 percent of the world population attended primary school; in 2020, more than half of the young generation in wealthy countries attended a university: what had always been a class privilege is gradually becoming open to the majority.

To be sure, this great leap forward merely shifted inequalities to another level. Disparities in access to education and basic health care between global North and South remain very deep, and they are still considerable nearly everywhere at more advanced levels of the health care or educational systems—for example, in higher education. We shall see that this is a major issue for the future. At this point, let us say simply that it always works this way: the march toward equality passes through successive stages. As access to certain fundamental rights and goods (such as literacy or elementary health care) is gradually extended to the whole population, new inequalities appear at higher levels and require new responses. Like the quest for ideal democracy, which is nothing other than the march toward political equality, the march toward equality in all its forms (social, economic, educational, cultural, political) is an ongoing process that will never be completed.

We can already observe that in terms of life expectancy and literacy, the most important progress was achieved in the twentieth century, a period when the welfare state was greatly expanded, and social security and progressive income taxes were instituted after intense political battles. We will return to this topic at length. In the nineteenth century, social welfare budgets remained parsimonious, taxes were regressive, and the progress made by these indicators was extremely slow, not to say insignificant. Human progress never evolves "naturally": it is subject to historical processes and specific social battles.

World Population and Average Income: The Limits of Growth

To become aware of the scope of the historical transformations involved, we must also remember that human population and average income have both multiplied more than tenfold since the eighteenth

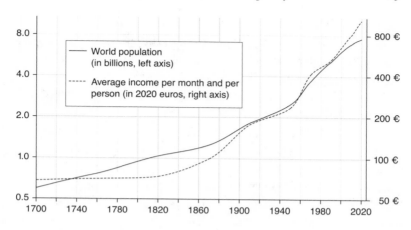

FIGURE 2. Population and Average Income in the World, 1700–2020

The world population and the average income per person increased more than tenfold between 1700 and 2020: the former rose from about 600 million in 1700 to more than 7 billion in 2020; the latter, expressed in 2020 euros and in purchasing power parity, rose from scarcely 80 euros per month per person in 1700 to about 1,000 euros per month in 2020. That corresponds in both cases to an average growth of about 0.8 percent per year, accumulated over 320 years. *Sources and series:* piketty. pse.ens.fr/equality

century. The former has risen from about 600 million in 1700 to more than 7.5 billion in 2020 while the latter, so far as we can measure it on the basis of the imperfect historical data available to us regarding salaries and wages, production, and prices, has risen from an average purchasing power (expressed in 2020 euros) of less that 100 euros per month per inhabitant of the planet in the eighteenth century to about 1,000 euros per month per inhabitant at the beginning of the twenty-first century (see Figure 2). It will be noted that the historical progress of the average income becomes truly significant only starting in the last third of the nineteenth century, and especially in the course of the twentieth century. According to the available sources, it would seem that the development of purchasing power in the eighteenth century and during most of the nineteenth century was insignificant, or even occasionally negative (as is indicated, for example, by the agricultural wages studied by Labrousse in the case of pre-revolutionary France). For the world population, growth has been more regular over the past three centuries, but it also accelerated in the twentieth century.

Can these tenfold increases be described as human progress? The interpretation of these transformations is in reality far more complex than it is for health care and education. The spectacular growth of the world population reflects, of course, real improvement in the conditions of individuals' lives, particularly thanks to advances in agriculture and food supply that have made it possible to escape from cycles of overpopulation and shortages. It also derives from the fall in infant mortality and from the fact that an increasing number of parents have been able to grow old with living children, which is not insignificant. Unfortunately, on the collective level, everything indicates that over the long term, such an exponential growth of the population is unsustainable for the planet. If the demographic expansion of the past three centuries were to continue in the future, there would be more than 70 billion of us by 2300, and 7,000 billion by the year 3000, which seems neither plausible nor desirable. It will also be noted that this multiplication by ten of the world population between 1700 and 2020 corresponds to an average population growth of scarcely 0.8 percent per annum, though accumulated over more than three hundred years.[1] This reminds us that there is something totally insane about the very idea of perpetual and unidimensional growth, prolonged indefinitely over thousands and millions of years, and in any event it cannot constitute a reasonable objective for human progress. In this case, taking into account the observed decline in the birth rate, it would seem that demographic growth is destined to decrease sharply in the course of the twenty-first century. Moreover, if we believe the central scenario of projections from the United Nations (UN), which is at this point very uncertain, the world population may

---

1. More precisely: $1.008^{300} = 10.9$.

stabilize at around 11 billion humans between now and the end of the century.

The Choice of Socioeconomic Indicators: A Political Question

The spectacular increase in average income raises problems of interpretation that are different, but in part come down to the same thing. In absolute terms, the fact that the average income has risen so much may certainly be considered a positive development, and one that is, moreover, inseparable from progress in ensuring the food supply and increasing life expectancy (processes which reinforced one another). However, several points need to be made. In general, the choice of socioeconomic indicators is an eminently political one: no indicator should be regarded as sacred, and the nature of the indicators chosen must be at the heart of public debate and democratic confrontation.

Concerning indicators such as income, it is first of all essential to move beyond averages and aggregates, and to examine the real distribution of wealth among social classes, within countries as well as at the global level. For example, according to the available data, the global average income did reach approximately 1,000 euros per month per inhabitant at the beginning of the 2020s, but it is scarcely 100 to 200 euros a month in the poorest countries, whereas it rises above 3,000 to 4,000 euros a month in the richest countries. Within countries, whether rich or poor, inequalities remain considerable. We will return at length to these questions all through this book. We shall see, for instance, that although the inequalities between countries have decreased since the colonial period, they remain extremely high, reflecting in part the fact that the organization of the global economic system is still very hierarchical and inequitable.[2]

We must also put into perspective the idea of a purchasing power multiplied by ten since the eighteenth century (and in reality, since

---

2. See in particular Chapter 9.

the end of the nineteenth century). The order of magnitude is expressive and powerfully conveys the idea of a massive quantitative increase, which is incontestable, but in truth the precise figure is not very significant. It may make sense to compare incomes in order to evaluate inequalities within a given society (insofar as the different social groups interact and maintain relations with one another through monetary exchanges) or between countries in a given period (also insofar as these societies maintain such contacts with each other, which has become more and more frequently the case at the global level since the eighteenth century), or to study the evolution of purchasing power on the scale of a few years or a few decades. On the other hand, the exercise loses its meaning as soon as we consider temporal advances as gigantic as the one in question here.

To grasp such radical transformations of ways of life, no unidimensional indicator can be sufficient. It is better to resort to a multidimensional approach in order to gauge the evolution of access to concrete goods such as education, health care, food, clothing, housing, transportation, culture, and so on. In this case, depending on the kind of good (that is, from a technical point of view, depending on the composition of the basket of goods used to calculate the price index), we could just as well conclude that average purchasing power has been multiplied by two or three or fifteen or twenty (and not by ten) between 1860 and 2020.[3]

---

3. For concrete examples of the rise in purchasing power of the average income expressed in terms of kilograms of carrots or meat, in newspapers, hairdressers, bicycles, or apartment rents in France over the course of the twentieth century, see T. Piketty, *Top Incomes in France in the Twentieth Century* (Cambridge, MA: Harvard University Press, 2018), 71–82; and T. Piketty, *Capital in the Twenty-First Century* (Cambridge, MA: Belknap Press of Harvard University Press, 2014), 87–90. In sum: purchasing power expressed in manufactured goods has increased more than average, while purchasing power expressed in terms of services has increased much less than average increase (or even not at all, in the case of certain services). Purchasing power expressed in terms of food is near average.

For a Plurality of Social and Environmental Indicators

Moreover, it is crucial to account for the fact that the general increase in population, production, and incomes since the eighteenth century took place at the price of overexploiting the planet's natural resources, and to examine the sustainability of such a process and the institutional mechanisms that would make its radical reorientation possible. Here again, this requires setting up a whole series of indicators permitting social actors to define a multidimensional, balanced conception of economic, social, and environmental progress. To begin with macroeconomic indicators, it is greatly preferable to use the notion of *national income* rather than that of *gross domestic product* (GDP). There are two essential differences: national income is equal to the GDP (the sum of goods and services produced in a country in the course of one year) minus the depreciation of capital (that is, wear and tear on tools, machines, and furniture used in production, including, in principle, natural capital), plus or minus the net income from capital and labor collected from or paid out to the rest of the world (this set can be either positive or negative, depending on each country's situation, but by definition these cancel each other out at the global level).

Let's take an example. A country that extracts 100 billion euros' worth of petroleum from its land generates a supplementary GDP of 100 billion euros. On the other hand, the corresponding national income is nil, because the stock of natural capital has been reduced by the same amount. If in addition we attribute a corresponding negative value to the social cost of carbon emissions produced by burning the petroleum in question—which, though we ought, we do not always do, for we now know that these emissions will contribute to global warming and make life on Earth infernal—then we obtain a strongly negative national income.[4] The importance of the choice of

---

4. For example, if we applied a minimal value of 100 euros per ton to the approximately 50 billion tons of annual emissions of carbon equivalents (on average, about 6.2

the indicator is clear: the same economic operation can lead to a positive GDP or a negative national income. This can radically change the collective evaluation of this or that investment at the level of a country or an enterprise.

Although it is preferable to focus on the national income (after taking into account the consumption of natural capital and the corresponding social cost) and on the inequality of its distribution, rather than confining ourselves to the GDP and to averages, that is nonetheless not sufficient. In fact, no matter what monetary value is assigned to the social cost of carbon emissions or other *externalities* (a generic term used by economists to designate the undesirable effects of economic activities such as warming, air pollution, or traffic jams), this unidimensional type of monetary accounting does not make it possible to correctly take into account either the damage done or the stakes involved. In some cases, this approach can even help maintain the illusion that we can always counterbalance damage with money, provided that we find the right "relative price" to valorize the environment, which is a false and dangerous idea.[5] To escape this kind of intellectual and political dead end, it is also and especially essential to choose genuinely environmental indicators, such as explicit temperature limits that must not be exceeded, binding indicators bearing on biodiversity, and objectives formulated in terms of carbon emissions.

Just as for incomes, we must take an interest in the unequal distribution of carbon emissions, both from the point of view of the persons responsible for them and from that of those who will suffer the

---

tons per inhabitant of the planet), we would end up with an annual social cost of 5 trillion euros, or about 5 percent of the world GDP. If we assigned a value of several hundred euros per ton, which is probably indispensable for envisaging an ambitious climate policy, then that would have a massive impact on the calculation of the global income and the contribution of the various countries to collective well-being.

5. Technically, no one can predict a century in advance what the "relative value" of the environment will be. Markets and their waves of speculation predict even less well than the world as a whole.

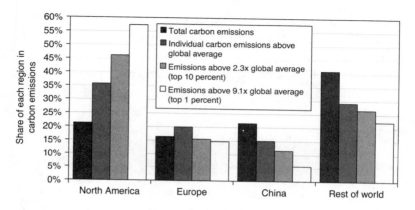

FIGURE 3. Worldwide Distribution of Carbon Emissions, 2010–2018

North America's share (United States and Canada) in total carbon emissions (direct and indirect) was 21 percent on average in 2010–2018; it rose to 36 percent of individual emissions above the global average (6.2 tons of CO_2 per year), 46 percent of the emissions above 2.3 times the global average (or the top 10 percent of individual emissions worldwide, responsible for 45 percent of total emissions, versus 13 percent for the least-emitting 50 percent), and 57 percent of the emissions above 9.1 times the average (or the top 1 percent of individual emissions worldwide, responsible for 14 percent of emissions). *Sources and series:* piketty.pse.ens.fr/equality

consequences. For instance, for the period 2010–2018, we find that of the 1 percent of the planet's inhabitants who emit the most carbon, almost 60 percent reside in North America (see Figure 3), and that their total emissions are higher than the combined emissions of the 50 percent of the planet's inhabitants who emit the least.[6] It happens that most of the latter live in Sub-Saharan Africa and in South Asia, and will be the first affected by global warming. In the future, this kind of indicator could play a growing role in assessing the extent to which countries respect their commitments and in defining compensation mechanisms, as well as in developing a system of individual

6. L. Chancel and T. Piketty, "Carbon and Inequality: From Kyoto to Paris," 2015, WID.world. Compare L. Chancel, "Global Carbon Inequality in the Long Run," 2021, WID.world.

carbon cards, which will certainly be part of the indispensable institutional tools for meeting the climatic challenge. More generally, it is difficult to rethink the organization of the economic system on both the global and the national levels if we do not have an objective basis for evaluation using this type of indicator.

No Sustainable Development without a Measure of Inequality

We must be wary: the solution cannot be found only among purely environmental indicators, to the exclusion of socioeconomic indicators, including incomes. The reason for this is simple: human beings need to live in harmony with nature, but they also need housing, food, clothing, and access to culture. Above all, they need justice. Unless we are capable of measuring incomes, the inequality of their distribution, and their development over time, it is hard to see how we could develop norms of justice that would allow us to concentrate our efforts on the wealthiest people and rethink the organization of the global economic system in a way acceptable to the humblest. Without resolute action seeking to drastically compress socioeconomic inequalities, there is no solution to the environmental and climatic crisis.[7] To make progress in this direction, we must combine different indicators—environmental and economic, for example—and independently set targets for carbon emissions or biodiversity while at the same time formulating objectives that include the reduction of inequalities in income and the distribution of fiscal and social deductions and public expenditures. In this way we may compare different sets of public policies that make it possible to achieve our environmental objectives.

---

7. L. Chancel, *Unsustainable Inequalities: Social Justice and the Environment* (Cambridge, MA: Harvard University Press, 2020). Compare E. Laurent, *Sortir de la croissance: mode d'emploi* (Paris: Les liens qui libèrent, 2019).

In addition, though it is generally preferable to concern ourselves with the distribution of income among social classes and not only with the average income, in certain contexts it is indispensable to resort to macroeconomic aggregates such as the national income (or if necessary, the GDP), for example to express the weight of the different categories of taxes or the size of the budgets allocated for education, health care, or the environment as a percentage of the national income (or of the GDP). This is the least bad method we have for comparing in an intelligible way the evolution of these sums over time and from one country to the next. I shall demonstrate this in the following chapters, when we study, for example, the increasing power and the fiscal and military capacity of European states in the eighteenth and nineteenth centuries, or the development of the welfare state in the twentieth century. At first, thinking in terms of a "percentage of national income," or reducing all the sums mentioned to the average income or average salary of each period (which amounts to the same thing), may seem abstract and irksome to many. But if we do not overcome this technical obstacle, then we are almost inevitably vulnerable to manipulations of the data.

For example, established governments (as well as their opposition) regularly announce investment plans expressed in millions or billions of euros (or dollars or yuan). Upon examination, it often turns out that these plans extend over ten or twenty years, not a single year. The annual amount, correctly recalculated, represents in reality only a minuscule fraction of the national income, or else the increase envisaged is less than the predicted rate of inflation or of growth over the same period (so that the fabulous investment announced, instead of increasing, actually diminishes as a proportion of the national income). Ideally, the media would systematically convert these sums into intelligible scales. But at present, we are far from this ideal and must do the work ourselves and demand that the media do it also. The choice of socioeconomic indicators is eminently political: it concerns each of us and cannot be left to others. If we do not act, we must not be surprised if the indicators selected reflect priorities other than the ones we care about.

Let us restate the point clearly: socioeconomic indicators, like the historical series presented in this work and all statistics in general, are nothing more than imperfect, temporary, and fragile constructions. They do not claim to establish "the" truth of figures or the certainty of "facts." There are always several legitimate ways of combining the materials available to confer a specific social, economic, and historical intelligibility on the given information. The indicators seek above all to develop a language enabling us to establish orders of magnitude, and especially to compare in the most sensible way possible situations, historical moments, epochs, and societies that often consider themselves to be very distant from one another, but which it may nonetheless be useful to correlate in spite of their irreducible specificity and uniqueness. We cannot be content to say that each statistic is a social construction: that is, of course, always true, but it is insufficient because it amounts to abandoning the field. Used properly, moderately, and critically, the language of socioeconomic indicators is an indispensable complement to the natural language for fighting intellectual nationalism, escaping the manipulations of economic elites, and building a new egalitarian horizon.

Finally, it will be noted that rather than using a multiplicity of indicators, one alternative solution might consist in synthesizing them in a single indicator. For example, the Human Development Index (HDI) worked out by the United Nations aggregates data regarding health care, education, and national income to arrive at a worldwide classification of countries. The ecologist and economist Tim Jackson has developed a Global Progress Indicator (GPI) combining, notably, environmental data with data concerning the national income and the latter's distribution.[8] These studies have the immense merit of

---

8. T. Jackson, *Prosperity without Growth: Foundations for the Economy of Tomorrow*, 2nd ed. (Abingdon, UK: Routledge, 2017). Compare J. Hickel, *Less Is More: How Degrowth Will Save the World* (Portsmouth, NH: Heinemann, 2020).

showing how little meaning the obsession with the GDP has: to make deep changes in the classification of countries and developments over time, it suffices to adopt a more balanced indicator. However, I do not think the best solution is to replace the GDP by another single indicator (even if it is more balanced). By definition, indicators that seek to sum up a multidimensional reality in a unidimensional index do so at the cost of a certain opacity. As a general rule, it seems to me preferable to resort to a multiplicity of indicators bearing explicitly and transparently on carbon emissions and their distribution, inequalities in income, health care, education, and so on. For the same reasons of transparency, I advise against the use of synthetic indices that are supposed to sum up the level of inequality in a society (like Gini's and Theil's coefficients, which are relatively abstract to interpret). In my view it is more appropriate to use more intuitive notions such as the proportion of incomes going to the poorest 50 percent or to the richest 10 percent, the proportion of the emissions caused by the heaviest 1 percent of emitters, and so on, which everyone can easily understand.[9]

---

9. Gini's coefficients are also available on WID.world, but I suggest using instead the series broken down by deciles or centiles, on which I will focus in this work.

2

THE SLOW DECONCENTRATION

OF POWER AND PROPERTY

We now come to another socioeconomic indicator that will play an important role in our inquiry: property and its distribution. Unlike income, which represents what one earns over a given period of time, property refers to everything one owns at a certain point in time. Like income, property is a social relationship, in the sense that it acquires its full meaning only within a particular society that is characterized by a set of rules and specific power relations between social groups. Property is a historically situated notion: it depends on the way each society defines the legitimate forms of ownership (land, houses, factories, machines, seas, mountains, monuments, financial assets, knowledge, slaves, and so on), as well as the legal procedures and practices that structure and delimit property relations and power relations among the social groups concerned.

The Evolution of the Concentration of Property since the Eighteenth Century

Let us begin by examining the evolution of the concentration of property in France since the end of the eighteenth century, first by comparing the share of the richest 1 percent with that of the poorest

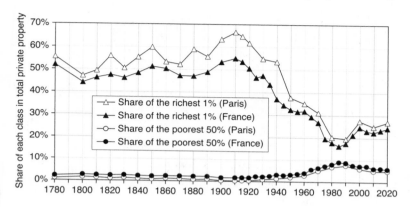

FIGURE 4. A Limited, Impeded March toward Equality: The Concentration of Property in France, 1780–2020

After a slight diminution during the Revolution, the concentration of property (real, occupational, and financial assets, net of debt) increased in France in the nineteenth century and until World War I before declining steeply following the world wars and until the 1980s. In all, the share held by the richest 1 percent fell from 55 percent in 1910 to 24 percent in 2020, but this did not much benefit the poorest 50 percent, whose share rose from 2 percent in 1910 to 6 percent in 2020. *Sources and series:* piketty.pse.ens.fr/equality

50 percent (see Figure 4).[1] The case of France is particularly interesting because the French Revolution, having failed to establish a perfectly egalitarian society (far from it!), has bequeathed to us an incomparable vantage point for monitoring wealth, in the form of its inheritance archives and its sophisticated system for registering property and the transmission of it.[2] As we shall see, in the case of France

1. By definition, the missing share is held by the 49 percent of the population that falls between the poorest 50 percent and the richest 1 percent. See Figure 6 for a complete breakdown.

2. The results presented here are based on a major project of data collection in the inheritance archives in Paris and the departments. See in particular T. Piketty, G. Postel-Vinay, and J.-L. Rosenthal, "Wealth Concentration in a Developing Economy: Paris and France, 1807–1994," *American Economic Review* 96, no. 1 (2006): 236–256; and T. Piketty, G. Postel-Vinay, and J.-L. Rosenthal, "Inherited vs. Self-Made Wealth:

the changes observed over the long term are, moreover, representative of those seen in other European societies for which we have comparable (though less systematic) sources, such as, for example, the United Kingdom and Sweden.

We note first of all that the richest 1 percent's share of the total of private property (that is, of total wealth of land, buildings, business assets, and industrial and financial wealth of all kinds, net of debt) has decreased only very slightly since the Revolution, and that it remained astronomically high throughout the nineteenth century and as late as the beginning of the twentieth century. Thus, the wealthiest 1 percent held around 45 percent of total property in France in 1810, and about 55 percent of the total in 1910. In Paris, where considerable financial and industrial fortunes had accumulated by the end of the nineteenth century and during the Belle Époque, the richest 1 percent's share even exceeded 65 percent on the eve of the First World War. Then, in the course of the twentieth century, we observe a very strong deconcentration of fortunes: in the whole of France, the richest 1 percent's share fell from 55 percent in 1914 to less than 20 percent at the beginning of the 1980s, before beginning a slow increase; in 2020, that share was nearly 25 percent.

The results reproduced in Figure 4 illustrate the general thesis presented in this book: on the one hand, there is a long-term movement toward equality, and in this case, toward a lower concentration of property and thus of social and economic power; on the other hand, inequality nevertheless continues to be very high, even intolerable, and it is very difficult to be satisfied with such a situation or to claim that it would be in the interest of the majority.[3] Concretely, the richest

---

Theory and Evidence from a Rentier Society (Paris 1872–1927)," *Explorations in Economic History* 51 (2014): 21–40.

3. This is a classical justification of inequality, which is found not only in "The Declaration of the Rights of Man and of the Citizen," (1789), Article 1: "Social distinctions may be based only on considerations of the common good" (https://www.elysee.fr/en/french-presidency/the-declaration-of-the-rights-of-man-and-of-the-citizen), but also in John Rawls, *A Theory of Justice* (Cambridge, MA: Belknap Press of Harvard Univer-

1 percent's share of total private property is currently two times smaller than it was a century ago, but it still remains on the order of five times larger than the share held by the poorest 50 percent, who today own scarcely more than 5 percent of the total (despite the fact that they are by definition fifty times more numerous than the richest 1 percent). To be sure, in the nineteenth century and at the beginning of the twentieth century, the share of the poorest 50 percent was barely 2 percent: thus a certain progress was made in a century, but it was infinitesimal. In reality, the deconcentration of property was made almost exclusively to the benefit of social groups situated between the richest 1 percent and the poorest 50 percent, but it was of very little benefit to the latter, who virtually never owned anything.

Property and Power: A Bundle of Rights

Before going further, several points must be clarified. First, it is necessary to emphasize the fact that this way of quantifying the evolution of the monetary concentration of property, as useful and revealing as it may be, allows us to analyze only part of the profound transformations involved. In reality, it is the very conditions of the exercise of the right to property that have been redefined since the end of the eighteenth century. But the varying monetary valuations of the different goods, such as real estate and stock prices, used to evaluate wealth and its distribution provide only an imperfect measure of property in terms of power and opportunity, and more generally the social value of goods for the multiple social actors concerned. Generally speaking, property should be conceived not as an absolute, atemporal right, but rather as a set of rights peculiar to each sociohistorical context, a kind of "bundle of rights" making it possible to characterize the scope of the powers and capacities at the disposal of

---

sity Press, 1971). It is potentially acceptable, provided it is based on a specific historical analysis and not used randomly to justify any level of inequality, without even trying to put it in perspective or to evaluate the extent to which it is truly based on considerations of the common good.

the various actors and stakeholders involved in this relation, whether they own property or not, collect a salary or not, or are members of local collectives or family groups.[4]

On the eve of the French Revolution, the aristocratic class, which at that time represented less than 1 percent of the population but more than 50 percent of the large private property owners, also had substantial fiscal, political, and jurisdictional privileges, so that its power (compared with bourgeois property owners) was not limited to the monetary value of its goods. The Revolution established equality before the law for all property owners, while at the same time radicalizing their right to dominate people who did not own property (without any social duty or counterpart), and in particular the right of the white male property owner. The French Civil Code of 1804 adopted an absolutist definition of property that is still in force in France.[5] Considered as a whole, however, the legal system has changed since then. A married woman, whose legal status was long inferior to that of her husband—for example, when she wanted to open a bank account, sell property, or sign a labor contract—has had equivalent formal rights since the 1960s and 1970s. Salaried employees and renters, whether men or women, now have rights incommensurate with those of the past. In the nineteenth century, an employer could dismiss an employee or change his working conditions or remuneration at will, or almost, just as a landlord could evict his renter or double his rent without mercy or prior notice. Things are different in these

---

4. This approach to property in terms of a "bundle of rights" has been developed notably by Elinor Ostrom with regard to different ways of managing "the commons" (exhaustible natural resources such as pastures, forests, rivers, ponds, game, and fish) throughout history, but we will see that the principle is more generally applicable.

5. "Ownership is the right to enjoy and dispose of things in the most absolute manner, provided they are not used in a way prohibited by statutes or regulations," Code civil, art 544, D. Gruning, A. R. Levasseur, J. R. Trahan, and E. Roy, "Traduction du Code Civil Français en Anglais," version bilingue, 2015, https://halshs.archives -ouvertes.fr/halshs-01385107/document. On the problems raised by this definition and the alternatives adopted elsewhere, see below, Chapter 5.

early decades of the twenty-first century; the multiple rules and regulations are far from being purely theoretical, even if the rights of employees, like those of renters, remain limited and could be made far more extensive and emancipatory.

Examples illustrating the transformations of property law are many. Until 1848, when slavery was abolished in the French islands where it still existed, property recorded in inheritance archives included plantations and the monetary value of the enslaved people who labored there. Until the early 1960s, the wealth studied included assets held in the colonies, assets that had been accumulated in the framework of profoundly asymmetrical juridical relationships and relations of extreme political and military domination. We will return to these various developments all through this book, and we shall see that the march toward equality over the past two centuries has taken the form of a profound re-equilibration of the law in favor of those who are not property owners. This transformation of property law, chiefly in the course of the second half of the nineteenth century and all through the twentieth century, has been a central stake in social and political struggles. It has contributed not only to greater socioeconomic equality, but also to greater prosperity, thanks to everyone's increased participation in social and economic life. I will also defend the idea that this historical movement might very well continue in the twenty-first century—if new struggles and historical ruptures allow us to advance in that direction. At this stage, let us simply note that property owners' rights were on the whole far more absolute at the beginning of the nineteenth century than they are today. From that point of view, we can say that the deconcentration of property and of the power conferred by property has been even greater than what the strictly monetary view expressed in Figure 4 seems to indicate. To put it in another way, the poorest 50 percent are perhaps still as poor, in the sense that their share of total property has scarcely risen since the nineteenth century, but they are a little less at the mercy of property owners (employers or landlords, husbands or colonists) than they used to be.

Owning the Means of Production, Housing, the State, and the Rest of the World

To analyze the power relations at stake in property relations, and also to better understand the evolution of the monetary distribution of property, it is indispensable to distinguish the different categories of goods that can be owned. If we set aside the ownership of other human beings through slavery, to which we shall return, we can distinguish four main categories of possession: the ownership of the means of production, housing, the state, and the rest of the world. The means of production include agricultural land and equipment, factories and machinery, offices and computers, shops and restaurants, salary advances and working capital, and more generally all the goods necessary to produce other goods and services. These means of production can be held directly by the farmer or business owner, or through stocks, bonds, shares in corporations or other financial securities. Or they can be held indirectly through deposits and bank accounts (in which case it is the banks or financial intermediaries that exercise power over the enterprises in which they decide to invest on the basis of savers' deposits and the legal regulations in force).

In the traditional Marxist approach, only ownership of the means of production truly pertains to capitalist property: it is what leads to the extraction of a profit by exploiting the labor force, and it is this profit that feeds in turn the accumulation of capital. Without seeking to deny the specificity of the exceedingly hierarchized social relations that are formed in this framework, it seems important to emphasize the fact that all property relations imply specific power relations that must be analyzed as such, no matter what the forms of ownership in question may be.[6] In particular, the ownership of housing involves

---

6. An exception, perhaps, can be made for the possession of works of art and precious objects, but these represent only a tiny fraction of total private property (between 1 percent and 2 percent, depending on the period and the country). See T. Piketty, *Capital in the Twenty-First Century* (Cambridge, MA: Belknap Press of Harvard University Press, 2014), 179–180.

strategies of extraction and relations of power between landlords and renters that are occasionally extremely violent and intrusive, even if they have been tamed and restricted (in part) over time. The question of access to housing and of the right to have a home involves what is most private in each of us. This is the sphere of family life and "social reproduction," in the sense used by authors of feminist critiques. These authors rightly stress the fact that this sphere, which is essential for the overall functioning of the economic system (including, of course, the reproduction of the labor force and the accumulation of capital) and the deep inequalities and relations of domination that are at play in it, has often been neglected by classical Marxist analyses, to the benefit of the so-called "productive" sphere alone.[7] In reality, it is indispensable to look into both the ownership of the means of production and the ownership of housing if we want to have an overarching view of the socioeconomic system and the power relations implied by property relations. At the same time, when a finer-grained analysis of the multiple institutional mechanisms and social processes involved is undertaken, we must of course distinguish the different ways of holding property.

On the whole, in terms of monetary value, housing generally represents a considerable share of private property, often about half, whereas the means of production (as measured by the monetary value of enterprises) represents approximately the other half. For example, in France in the early 2020s, total private property amounts to about 220,000 euros per adult (or the equivalent of six years of average income), including about 110,000 euros in the form of housing (net of debt) and 110,000 euros in that of business and financial assets.[8] However, it must be emphasized that this average conceals immense

---

7. See, for example, T. Bhattacharya, *Social Reproduction Theory: Remapping Class, Recentering Oppression* (London: Pluto Press, 2017). See also C. Arruza, T. Bhattacharya, and N. Fraser, *Feminism for the 99%: A Manifesto* (London: Verso, 2019).

8. At the beginning of 2020, on the eve of the Covid-19 pandemic, the national income in France was about 2,000 billion euros (a level that according to INSEE was expected to be reached again in 2022), or around 37,000 euros (3,100 euros per month) on

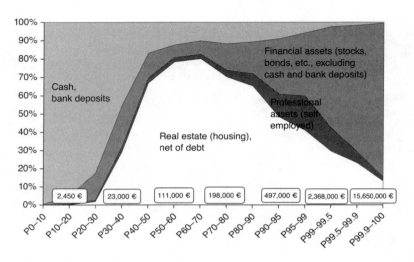

FIGURE 5. The Composition of Property in France, 2020

In France in 2020 (as in all countries for which such data are available), small fortunes are composed principally of cash and bank deposits, middle-sized fortunes of real estate, and large fortunes of financial assets (especially stocks).

Note: The distribution indicated here is that of wealth per adult. The wealth of couples is divided by two. *Sources and series:* piketty.pse.ens.fr/equality

disparities, in terms of both the amount and the composition of wealth (see Figure 5).

For the poorest 20 or 30 percent, the very notion of property is relatively abstract: some have only debts, whereas others have at best a few thousand euros—one or two months of salary—in liquid assets in a bank or savings account. Then the amounts gradually rise but remain very modest: the average fortune held by the poorest 50 percent is scarcely 20,000 euros (about one-tenth of the average wealth of the whole of the population, amounting to 5 percent of total wealth). The median fortune, that is, wealth above which half the population is situated, is about 100,000 euros, or around half the average. If we

average for each of some 53 million adults, whereas total private wealth (net of debt) was approaching 12,000 billion euros, or approximately 220,000 euros per adult.

examine the next 40 percent, that is, the people falling between the poorest 50 percent and the richest 10 percent, whose fortunes range approximately from 100,000 to 400,000 euros, we see that their wealth is held mainly in housing. Among the richest 10 percent, beyond 400,000 euros, property becomes increasingly diversified: business and especially financial assets (notably stocks) play a growing role in the hierarchy of fortunes. These assets become preponderant among the richest 1 percent (more than 1.8 million euros). It will be noted that the latter own, on average, about 5 million euros, or around twenty-five times the average fortune, which explains why their share is nearly 25 percent of total wealth. That also shows us what a society would look like, quantitatively, if the richest 1 percent owned 50 or 70 percent of total property, as was the case in the past.

Several points must be clarified. We can define the *disadvantaged classes* as the poorest 50 percent, the *middle classes* as the next 40 percent, and the *upper classes* as the richest 10 percent. Within the latter, which are very heterogeneous, we can distinguish the *wealthy* classes (the least rich 9 percent) and the *dominant* classes (the richest 1 percent). In sum, the disadvantaged classes have very little in savings; the assets of the middle class are centered on housing; the wealthy classes distribute their assets between housing, business assets, and financial assets; the dominant classes concentrate on ownership of the means of production (business assets and especially stocks and financial securities). Terms based on classes are meaningful if they are not reified or rigidified. In practice, class identities are always flexible and multidimensional. They can never be reduced to the crossing of some sort of monetary threshold. Social class depends not only on the ownership of the means of production and housing, and on the extent of that ownership, but also on level of income, education, occupation, the sector of activity, age and gender, regional or foreign origin, and sometimes on ethno-religious identity, in accord with modalities that are flexible and changeable, depending on sociohistorical contexts.

We must add that financial assets, even if they correspond mainly to the ownership of enterprises and the means of production, through stocks, bonds, corporate shares, and other financial securities, also represent in part the ownership of state securities, domestic and foreign. The possession of public bonds is certainly not equivalent to "owning the state," in the sense in which one might own an enterprise. Moreover, in history there are many other, more direct ways to own the state, or at least to participate in and control it, and to co-produce it more closely than ordinary citizens do, whether through the poll tax, which was implemented in the nineteenth century and up to the beginning of the twentieth century in many countries, or through the intermediary of systems of private financing for political parties, the media, and think tanks that operated almost everywhere in the early twenty-first century. In every period the ownership of the public debt represents an additional way of owning the state, in the sense, for example, that the state can end up selling what it owns (buildings, roads, airports, or public enterprises) in order to repay its debts. The state can also be reduced to transforming its historical monuments into advertising spaces or semiprivate properties (sometimes to the benefit of actors who have succeeded in convincing the state that they should not be made to pay taxes), or more generally to becoming dependent on its creditors and financial markets, or subjecting itself to the influence of policies and other approved "reforms." Property is always a relationship of power, and not only when it is a question of owning the means of production. In the eighteenth century, the question of the public debt—the power it confers and the different modalities of its accumulation, its repayment, or its cancellation—played a major role in triggering the French Revolution, as well as in the movement toward equality and the desacralization of property in the twentieth century. It will surely continue to play a central role in the twenty-first century. We will return to this subject at length.

After the means of production, housing, and the state, the other major form of property is the ownership of the rest of the world, that is, assets held in foreign countries. These may include the Suez Canal, rubber plantations in Southeast Asia, and Russian or Argentine debt securities. In practice, everything in the rest of the world can be owned: the means of production, the state, and sometimes housing.

This form of transnational ownership nonetheless puts into play institutional mechanisms and specific relations of domination on the juridical-political and sometimes military levels that are worth examining in themselves. In the case of France in 2020, the assets held in the rest of the world by French proprietors happen to be almost exactly equal to the assets held in France by property owners in the rest of the world, so that the "net foreign assets" are virtually nil (which does not mean, however, that these enormous transborder ownerships on both sides are without importance—on the contrary). Conversely, in the colonial period, net foreign assets were substantial and occupied a central place in the overall structure of property and inequalities between social classes, on national and international levels. Here, too, in subsequent chapters we will return at length to the crucial role played by foreign and colonial assets, both their disappearance in the movement toward equality in the course of the twentieth century and the role such transnational possessions may play in the future.

The Difficult Emergence of a Patrimonial Middle Class

Let us return to the evolution of the distribution of property since the end of the eighteenth century. We have already noted that the share held by the richest 1 percent was divided by more than two at the beginnings of the twentieth and the twenty-first centuries, even though it remained on the order of five times higher than the share held by the poorest 50 percent (see Figure 4). If we now examine the development of the distribution as a whole, we see that the reduction of inequalities took place mainly to the benefit of what may be called the *patrimonial middle class,* that is, the 40 percent between the poorest 50 percent and the richest 10 percent (see Figure 6).

Concretely, we observe first that the share of the richest 10 percent in total private property was about 85 percent at the beginning of the twentieth century and on the eve of World War I, before gradually

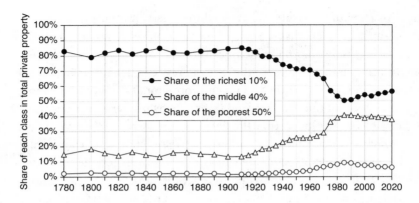

FIGURE 6. The Distribution of Property in France, 1780–2020: The Difficult Emergence of a Patrimonial Middle Class

The share of the richest 10 percent in total private property (real, occupational, and financial assets net of debt) was between 80 and 90 percent in France between 1780 and 1910. The deconcentration of wealth began following World War I and ceased in the early 1980s. It benefited primarily the patrimonial middle classes (the middle 40 percent), defined here as the group between the disadvantaged classes (the poorest 50 percent) and the well-to-do (the richest 10 percent). *Sources and series:* piketty.pse.ens.fr/equality

declining until it was barely 50 percent at the beginning of the 1980s, and then climbing back to a little over 55 percent in 2020. It will be noted that these variations correspond almost exactly to those observed at the level of the richest 1 percent's share (see Figure 4). In other words, it was the dominant classes (the richest 1 percent) who saw their relative position collapse, whereas the share of the wealthy classes (the next 9 percent) remained almost stable throughout the twentieth century (around 30 percent of total wealth). Conversely, the share of the 40 percent between the poorest 50 percent and the richest 10 percent underwent spectacular growth: at the beginning of the twentieth century, this share was barely 13 percent of total wealth, which then tripled between 1914 and 1980, reaching almost 40 percent in the early 1980s and subsequently stabilizing at that level (though with a slight decline).

Let us repeat clearly: the concentration of property remains extremely high, and the scope of this march toward equality must not be overestimated. At the beginning of the 2020s, the richest 10 percent owned more than 55 percent of everything that can be owned in France (and the richest 1 percent own almost 25 percent), whereas the poorest 50 percent own next to nothing (hardly 5 percent of the total). If we focus on the ownership of the means of production, which determines the distribution of economic power and the structure of hierarchical relations in workplaces, the concentration is still higher (in particular at the level of the 0.1 percent or of the 0.01 percent of the largest fortunes, a tiny group that has experienced a very clear upturn over recent decades).[9] We also note that the share of total wealth held by the poorest 50 percent, which has always been minuscule, has in addition declined substantially since the 1980s (a clearer decline than that of the next 40 percent). Finally, we must emphasize that this extreme concentration of property is not a bias connected with the profile of wealth by age: it is found in every age group, from young to old.[10]

It nonetheless remains that the emergence of a patrimonial middle class constitutes a major transformation on the social, economic, and

---

9. The richest 1 percent includes around 500,000 persons (out of about 50 million adults). According to the magazine *Challenges,* the 500 largest fortunes in France alone (approximately 0.001 percent of the population) increased from 200 billion euros in 2010 (10 percent of the GDP) to 710 billion in 2020 (30 percent of the GDP), that is, from approximately 2 percent to 6 percent of total wealth.

10. The concentration is especially strong among those between twenty and thirty-nine years old, with 62 percent of total wealth held by the richest 10 percent within that age class in 2018 (taking into account the size of the inheritance among the rare property owners of that age), as compared with 54 percent among those between forty and fifty-nine years old, 51 percent among those sixty years and older, and 55 percent on average for the whole of the population. Within each age group, the poorest 50 percent own next to nothing (scarcely 5–10 percent of total wealth in every case). See T. Piketty, *Capital and Ideology* (Cambridge, MA: Belknap Press of Harvard University Press, 2020), 554–557, fig. S11.18. For detailed results concerning the profiles and composition by age, see B. Garbinti, J. Goupille-Lebret, and T. Piketty, "Accounting for Wealth Inequality Dynamics: Methods and Estimates," 2018, WID.world.

political levels. Simplifying, we can say that until the beginning of the twentieth century, there was no genuine middle class, in the sense that the middle 40 percent were almost as poor (in terms of their share in total property ownership) as the poorest 50 percent. Conversely, at the end of the twentieth century and the beginning of the twenty-first century, the patrimonial middle class was made up of persons who were certainly not immensely rich on the individual level but were far from being completely poor (they owned, roughly speaking, between 100,000 and 400,000 euros per adult). Collectively, they owned a nonnegligible share of total wealth: around 40 percent,[11] or almost twice that of the richest 1 percent (24 percent of the total), whereas on the eve of World War I they held between three and four times less (13 percent as compared with 55 percent). In sum, the middle classes today are collectively twice as rich as the dominant classes, whereas a century ago they were three times poorer. The concentration of property never ceased to be extreme, but within this general framework we nonetheless see a clear inflection. These two assertions may seem contradictory, but they are both true. This complexity of the world is part of our historical heritage.

The reduction of inequalities is partly the consequence of wars and economic crises, but it also derives, especially, from new social and fiscal policies implemented since the end of the nineteenth century and in the course of the twentieth century: the increased power of the welfare state, the establishment of a certain equality of access to fundamental goods such as education and health care, and the development of a strongly progressive tax on high income and wealth. Along with the profound changes in the legal system and property rights already mentioned, it was, above all, these radical institutional transformations, borne by intense social and political struggles, that have made greater equality possible. Is it desirable to continue in this

---

11. The fact that this social group, constituting 40 percent of the population, owned about 40 percent of total wealth corresponds to the fact that average wealth within this group is approximately equal to the average wealth of the population as a whole (about 220,000 euros per adult in 2020).

direction, and if so, how should we proceed? I shall defend the idea that this (limited) march toward equality has been beneficial from every point of view, including, of course, productive efficiency and collective prosperity, because it has allowed all citizens to participate more fully in social and economic life. The ability of the dominant classes to spend and invest has certainly been severely reduced since the nineteenth century, since their share of total wealth has collapsed, but that has been more than compensated for by the rise in the power of the middle classes and, to a lesser extent, that of the disadvantaged classes. The idea that we have to be satisfied with current levels of inequality, or that it would be healthy for the poorest 50 percent to own hardly 5 percent of the total wealth, is not founded on any solid empirical basis. It is both desirable and possible to further the prospects of a welfare state and progressive taxes.

The Long March toward a Greater Equality of Income

To complete this initial survey, it is also useful to familiarize ourselves with the orders of magnitude that characterize the long-term evolution of the distribution of income. Generally speaking, the inequality of income is always smaller than the inequality of property. Let us recall that income includes income from work (wages and salary, other income from work, retirement pensions, unemployment benefits) and income from capital (profits, dividends, interest, capital gains, and so on). Income from capital usually represents between a quarter and a third of total income, sometimes almost half, depending on power relations between employees and employers and on the legal and social system in force (rent control, corporate law, labor law, and so on), and notably the role given to labor unions and the latter's negotiating power.[12] By construction, the concentration of income from capital is

---

12. In the United Kingdom, as in France, the share of income from capital reached 40–45 percent of national income in the nineteenth century before diminishing at the end of the century and oscillating between 25 and 35 percent over the course of the

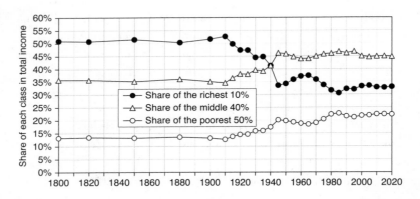

FIGURE 7. The Distribution of Income in France, 1800–2020: The Beginning of a Long-Term Movement toward Equality?

The share of the richest 10 percent in total income, including income from unsalaried activity, retirement pensions, and unemployment insurance, and income from capital, including profits, dividends, interest, rents, capital gains, and so on, was about 50 percent in France between 1800 and 1910. The deconcentration of income began following the two world wars and benefited both the disadvantaged classes (the poorest 50 percent) and the middle classes (the middle 40 percent), to the detriment of the well-to-do (the richest 10 percent). *Sources and series:* piketty.pse.ens.fr/equality

just as extreme as the concentration of the ownership of capital.[13] The inequality of income from work, though considerable, is in comparison clearly less pronounced, with important variations depending,

---

twentieth century. See Piketty, *Capital in the Twenty-First Century,* 200–201, figs. 6.1 and 6.2. Currently, the share of capital may reach 40–50 percent of national income (or even more than 50 percent) in some poor and emerging countries where the negotiating power of employees and informal workers vis-à-vis international investors and owners of capital is particularly weak. See WID.world; and "The Global Labour Income Share and Distribution," International Labour Organization, July 2019.

13. Or even more extreme, because in practice profit from capital increases strongly with the amount held: small bank deposits yield at best a few interest payments that are not comparable with income from large stock portfolios. Over the long term these bring in more than the middle classes' profit from real estate. Again, this depends on multiple institutions and specific power relationships. See Piketty, *Capital and Ideology,* 427, fig. 10.6.

once again, on the parties' negotiating power and on numerous legal and social rules: the existence of a minimum wage; salary scales; mechanisms favoring equal access to training, qualifications, and occupations; and the struggle against sexism and discrimination. The total inequality of income falls between income from capital and income from work, and is generally closer to the latter, given the preponderant weight of income from labor.[14]

Concretely, if we examine the share of total income going to the richest 10 percent of the income distribution, we see that in France at the beginning of the twentieth century it was situated around 50–55 percent before declining to less than 35 percent between 1914 and 1945, and it has oscillated between 30 and 38 percent since that date (see Figure 7). The share of total income going to those in the category of the lowest 50 percent of income was about 12 to 13 percent at the beginning of the twentieth century, before reaching 20 percent in 1945 and then oscillating between 18 and 23 percent since. After 1945, the share going to the middle 40 percent has even risen above that going to the richest 10 percent. That is not extraordinary in itself, given that the first group is numerically four times more numerous than the second. In fact, inequality of income remains very strong in France at the beginning of the twenty-first century: the differences from the average income range from one to eight between the poorest 50 percent and the richest 10 percent, from one to twenty between the poorest 50 percent and the richest 1 percent, and from one to seventy between the poorest 50 percent and the richest 0.1 percent. Nonetheless, these orders of magnitude characterizing the inequality of income are considerably smaller than those observed for inequality of property. Above all, the general movement toward equality is more impressive in the first case than in the second (see Figure 6). These developments in France can be found in most European countries and to a lesser degree in the United States. There, however, the rise in inequality since 1980 has been much clearer.

---

14. Piketty, *Capital and Ideology,* 427–428, figs. 10.6, 10.7.

3

THE HERITAGE OF SLAVERY

AND COLONIALISM

How did Europe and the United States attain such a dominant position on the global level, at least until recently? Although no single explanation exists, we shall see that slavery and colonialism played a central role in the Western world's acquisition of wealth. Today, the distribution of wealth among countries, as well as within them, is still deeply marked by this heritage. Therefore, it is particularly important to examine these historical episodes closely.

The Industrial Revolution, Colonialism, and Ecology

All the research at our disposal demonstrates that the development of Western industrial capitalism is closely linked to the international division of labor, the unrestrained exploitation of natural resources, and the military and colonial domination that developed gradually between the European powers and the rest of the planet starting in the fifteenth and sixteenth centuries and accelerating during the eighteenth and nineteenth centuries. More generally, it is impossible to write a history of equality and inequality at the global level without first assessing the importance of this colonial heritage. European expansion began around 1450–1500, with the first Portuguese trading posts on the coast of Africa, Vasco da Gama's voyage to India, and Columbus's expedition to America. It ended in the 1960s, if we include brutal wars of independence (such as in Indochina or Algeria), even in the 1990s if we include the case of South African apartheid. Over the long term, the reality is that we have just emerged from the colonial experiment. It would be naïve to imagine that its effects can be erased in a few decades. Those who are born today are not individually responsible for this burdensome heritage, but we are all responsible for the way in which we choose or fail to take it into account in analyzing the world economic system, its injustices, and the need for change.

Ken Pomeranz's work on the "great divergence" between Europe and Asia, published in 2000, has emphasized the fact that without the establishment of a system of supply and of the mobilization of the labor force on the planetary scale, Western industrial development would soon have collided with a huge ecological constraint.[1] In particular, he shows the extent to which the Industrial Revolution, beginning in the United Kingdom at the end of the eighteenth century and spreading throughout Europe over the course of the nineteenth century, was fueled by the large-scale extraction of raw materials (especially cotton) and of energy sources (particularly wood) from the rest of the world, all within the framework of a coercive and colonialist organizational scheme.

For Pomeranz, the central fact is that around 1750–1800, the most advanced regions of China and Japan were in a state of development comparable to the corresponding regions of Western Europe. In particular, we observe in these different cases quite similar kinds of socioeconomic structures founded not only on sustained demographic and agricultural growth (made possible by improved farming techniques and a substantial increase in cultivated land, achieved by clearing and deforestation), but also on comparable processes of proto-industrialization and the accumulation of capital, especially in the key sector of the textile industry. In Pomeranz's analysis,

---

1. K. Pomeranz, *The Great Divergence: China, Europe and the Making of the Modern World Economy* (Princeton, NJ: Princeton University Press, 2000).

two essential elements led to diverging trajectories starting in the second half of the eighteenth century. First of all, the most striking constraint connected with European deforestation—lack of wood—combined with the presence of ideally situated deposits of coal, particularly in England, rapidly led to the use of forms of energy other than wood, and to the early development of the corresponding technologies. Second, and especially, the fiscal and military abilities of the European states, emerging from their past rivalries largely strengthened by the technological and financial innovations proceeding from competition among states, allowed them to organize an international division of labor and supply that was particularly profitable.

Concerning deforestation, Pomeranz stresses the fact that by the end of the eighteenth century, Europe had spent nearly all its available resources. In the United Kingdom as in France, in Denmark as in Prussia, in Italy as in Spain, forests had disappeared at a rapid rate in the course of the preceding centuries, decreasing from around 30 to 40 percent of the surface area around the year 1500 to scarcely more than 10 percent in 1800 (16 percent in France, 4 percent in Denmark). Initially, trading in wood with regions of eastern and northern Europe that were still forested made it possible to compensate in part for these losses, but very soon that was no longer sufficient. We also see a gradual deforestation in China between 1500 and 1800, but it is less marked, in part because of a greater political and commercial integration between the most advanced regions and the wooded regions of the interior.

In the case of Europe, the "discovery" of America, the triangular trade with Africa, and the exchanges with Asia overcame the constraints. The exploitation of land in North America, the West Indies, and South America, to which the labor force from Africa had been transported, made it possible to produce raw materials (in the form of wood, cotton, and sugar) that were used to supply profits for the colonists and for the textile factories that were in full development between 1750 and 1800. Military control of the most distant sea lanes also made it possible to develop large-scale complementarities. Thus, food for the slaves of the West Indies and the southern United States was financed by British exports of textiles and manufactured goods to North America, which were themselves made possible by the wood and cotton coming from the plantations. Let us add that in the eighteenth century, a third of the textiles used to clothe slaves came from India, and that these imports from Asia (textiles, silks, tea, porcelain, and so on) were paid for in large part by the money that had been coming from America since the sixteenth century. Around 1830, imports of wood, cotton, and sugar received by England from the plantations corresponded, according to Pomeranz's calculations, to the exploitation of more than 10 million hectares of arable land, or between one-and-a-half and two times the total arable land in the United Kingdom.[2] Had their colonies not allowed European countries to transcend their territorial limits, it would have been necessary to find these sources of supply elsewhere. It is difficult but not impossible to imagine historical and technological scenarios in which an autarkic Europe would have achieved the same industrial prosperity: for example, fertile cotton plantations maintained by English peasants from Lancashire, or trees growing to the skies near Manchester. In any case, that would be a truly different story, the story of another world with little relation to ours.

---

2. Pomeranz, *The Great Divergence,* 211–230, 264–297, 307–312. These imports of wood continued to play an outsized role much later than is sometimes thought. Contrary to what the optimistic notion of an "energy transition" tends to suggest, in history we witness an increase in sources of energy (wood, coal, petroleum) and not a substitution. Around 1900, France imported the equivalent of half of its national production of wood (which the country burned on top of its own production), and the United Kingdom burned the equivalent of more than two years of the French production (its own production being long since largely exhausted). The imports came from northern Europe (Russia, Sweden, Finland) and North America, and also from Africa, Latin America, and Asia. See J.-B. Fressoz, "Pour une histoire des symbioses énergétiques et matérielles," *Responsabilité et environnement, Annales des Mines,* 101, no. 1 (2021): 7–11. On the intensity of deforestation in Europe and North America in the eighteenth and nineteenth centuries, compare L. Chancel, "Global Carbon Inequality in the Long-Run," 2021, WID.world.

At the Origins of the Great Divergence:
European Military Domination

As Pomeranz shows, it is striking to note the extent to which the military institutions and strategies that led Europe to success in the eighteenth and nineteenth centuries had little to do with the virtuous institutions recommended by Adam Smith's *Wealth of Nations* (1776). In this book, a foundational text for economic liberalism, Smith advised governments to adopt low taxes and balanced budgets (with little or no public debt), to show absolute respect for property rights, and to develop markets for labor and goods that were as unified and competitive as possible. But from all these points of view, the institutions in force in China in the eighteenth century were much more in accord with Smith's ideas than those applied in the United Kingdom. In particular, the markets were more strongly unified in China. The grain market in China operated over a larger geographical area, and labor was considerably more mobile there. Feudal institutions still held Europe in a powerful grip, at least until the French Revolution. Serfdom persisted in Eastern Europe until the nineteenth century (whereas in China it had almost completely disappeared by the beginning of the sixteenth century), and in the eighteenth century mobility was still restricted in Western Europe, especially in the United Kingdom and in France, due to the Poor Laws. Elites and local seigneurial courts enjoyed considerable autonomy in imposing coercive rules on the working classes. Ecclesiastical properties that were partially frozen on the exchanges were also larger in Europe.

Finally, and above all, taxes were much lower in China, as they were in the Ottoman Empire. The Qing dynasty had practiced strict budget orthodoxy; taxes always financed expenditures, without deficits. Conversely, the European states, beginning with the kingdom of France and the United Kingdom, were almost continually at war between 1500 and 1800, and they accumulated substantial public debts despite high taxes because fiscal receipts never sufficed to cover the exceptional expenses connected with the conflicts. Expenses were also swollen by interest payments linked to preceding debts. But it was precisely this fiscal, financial, and military capacity that was to prove decisive for the rise of Europe's power. Concretely, whereas the Chinese or Ottoman states were militarily neck and neck with the European states in the sixteenth century and for most of the seventeenth (the Ottomans' last siege of Vienna dates from 1683), the continual competition among European states helped them develop a state capacity that resulted in their acquisition of an absolute military domination starting in the late eighteenth century and continuing throughout the nineteenth. Around 1550, the Ottoman infantry and navy consisted of 140,000 men, as many as the French and English forces taken together. By 1780, the Ottoman forces had hardly changed at all (150,000 men), while French and British land and sea forces had reached a total of 450,000 men, together with a clearly superior naval fleet and greater firepower. In addition, at that time we must also count 250,000 men for Austria and 180,000 for Prussia (whereas these two states were militarily nonexistent in 1550).[3]

As imperfect as they may be, the sources at our disposal, namely tax receipts, confirm the existence of a major divergence between European states and non-European states between 1500 and 1800 (see Figure 8). Receipts are very low almost everywhere until 1600–1650. Then an increasingly clear divergence appears in 1700–1750 as the European states are consolidated. At the end of the eighteenth century and the beginning of the nineteenth, Chinese and Ottoman tax receipts in urban areas still amounted to between two and four days' salary per inhabitant (about 1 to 2 percent of the national income), whereas in the main European states they represented between fifteen

---

3. K. Karaman and S. Pamuk, "Ottoman State Finances in European Perspective," *Journal of Economic History* 70, no. 3 (2010): 593–629; and T. Piketty, *Capital and Ideology* (Cambridge, MA: Belknap Press of Harvard University Press, 2020), 369–371.

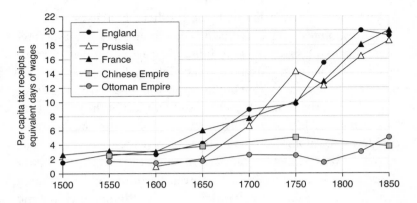

FIGURE 8. At the Origins of the Great Divergence: The Rise of European States' Fiscal and Military Capabilities, 1500–1850

Around 1500–1600, the per capita tax receipts in Europe were equivalent to two to four days' wages for unskilled urban workers; between 1750 and 1850 they were between ten and twenty days' wages. In comparison, the tax receipts remained stable at around two to five days' wages in the Ottoman and Chinese Empires. With a national income of around 250 days of urban wages, that means that receipts stagnated at around 1 to 2 percent of national income in the Chinese and Ottoman Empires, whereas they rose from 1–2 percent to 6–8 percent of the national income in Europe. *Sources and series:* piketty.pse.ens.fr/equality

and twenty days' salary (about 6 to 8 percent of the national income).[4] However imprecise the sources may be, there is no doubt about the divergence, and it corresponds to a major transformation. In concrete terms, a state that levies taxes amounting to only 1 percent of the national income has very little power and capacity to mobilize society. Roughly speaking, it can put 1 percent of the population in its service

4. Taking into account the uncertainties connected with the estimation of national income, it is preferable to make use of measures expressed in terms of days of urban salary, which are magnitudes less poorly known over the long term, in particular in the construction sector. We find the same massive divergence between European states and the Ottoman and Chinese states in the eighteenth century if we express fiscal receipts in terms of tons of silver. See Piketty, *Capital and Ideology,* 364–365, fig. 9.1.

to perform functions that it considers useful.[5] Such states are often barely able to guarantee the security of goods and persons on their territory, and must rely for that on multiple local elites. Conversely, a state that can put in its service the equivalent of 6 to 8 percent of its population has far greater abilities, especially in terms of maintaining order and military reach abroad. As long as all the states on the planet were equally weak, a certain balance prevailed. But from the moment that several European states developed a significantly greater fiscal, administrative, and military capacity, a new dynamic emerged.

The Cotton Empire: Taking Control of the Global Textile Industry

Recent research has largely confirmed Pomeranz's conclusions regarding the origins of the "great divergence" and the central role played by military and colonial domination, and by the technological and financial innovations that resulted from it. Studies have stressed the fact that the political fragmentation of Europe allowed European states to gain the upper hand over China and the world between 1750 and 1900, thanks to the innovations arising from military rivalries.[6]

---

5. This assumes that the people employed by the state (such as police officers, soldiers, and administrators) are paid at the average rate in the society in question, and that the equipment and supplies they need to perform their jobs cost an average amount. If they cost two or three times more than the average, the ability to hire is reduced by the same amount.

6. It must be emphasized that the key roles played by slaveholding and colonial extraction in the development of industrial capitalism have already been analyzed by many nineteenth-century observers (beginning with Karl Marx), as well as by Eric Williams, a historian, economist, and also the first minister of Trinidad and Tobago from 1956 to 1981. E. E. Williams, *Capitalism and Slavery* (New York: Capricorn Books, 1944). In comparison, Max Weber focused on cultural and religious factors, whereas Fernand Braudel brought out in particular the role of high finance that proceeded from both Catholic and Protestant Europe. M. Weber, *Die protestantische Ethik und der Geist des Kapitalismus* (Tübingen: J. C. B. Mohr, 1905), first translated into English as Weber, *The Protestant Ethic and the Spirit of Capitalism*, trans. T. Parsons (London: G. Allen and Unwin, 1930); F. Braudel, *Civilisation matérielle, économie et capitalisme: xve–xviiie*

This political fragmentation has had effects that can be considered negative over the long term, as is illustrated by the cycle of nationalist and genocidal self-destruction into which the European colonial powers plunged between 1914 and 1945; or, in a less extreme way, by the persistent difficulties the European Union has encountered in trying to organize and unite itself politically in the early 2020s.

Sven Beckert's research on the "cotton empire" has also shown the crucial importance of slave labor in the extraction of cotton when the British and Europeans seized control over worldwide textile production between 1750 and 1860.[7] Until about 1780 to 1790, the West Indies and especially Saint-Domingue were the primary cotton producers. After the collapse of the plantations on Saint-Domingue following the slave revolt of 1791, the US South took up the torch and pushed the acquisition of slaves and the capacity for cotton production to unprecedented levels. The ban on a black slave trade took effect in 1808, but in reality, clandestine trading continued for a few decades (particularly to Brazil). Above all, the plantation owners realized that encouraging or forcing slaves to reproduce was a far faster and more efficient way to increase their labor force. Between 1800 and 1860, the number of slaves grew fourfold in the American South, rising from one to four million (see Figure 9). The production of cotton increased tenfold, taking into account the improvement of techniques and the intensification of production. On the eve of the Civil War, 75 percent of the cotton imported to European textile factories came from the southern United States, which reflects quite clearly the crucial role of the slave system.

---

siècle, 3 vols. (Paris: A. Colin, 1979), first translated into English as Braudel, *Civilization and Capitalism, 15th–18th Centuries,* 3 vols., trans. Siân Reynold (New York: Harper and Row, 1982–1984). The recent works by Pomeranz, Parthasarathi, and Beckert, which are much less Eurocentric, represent a kind of return to Marx and Williams, but use tools and the richer sources associated with connected world history. P. Parthasarathi, *Why Europe Grew Rich and Asia Did Not: Global Economic Divergence 1600–1850* (Cambridge: Cambridge University Press, 2011); S. Beckert, *Empire of Cotton: A Global History* (New York: Alfred A. Knopf, 2014); Pomeranz, *The Great Divergence.*

7. Beckert, *Empire of Cotton.*

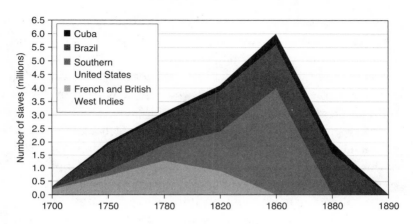

FIGURE 9. The Rise and Fall of Euro-American Slavery, 1700–1890

The total number of slaves on Euro-American plantations in the Atlantic sphere reached 6 million in 1860 (including 4 million in the southern United States, 1.6 million in Brazil, and 0.4 million in Cuba). Slavery in the French and British West Indies (to which I have added Mauritius, La Réunion, and the Cape Colony) reached its apogee around 1780–1790 (1.3 million), then declined following the revolt in Saint-Domingue (Haiti) and the abolitions of 1833 and 1848. *Sources and series:* piketty.pse.ens.fr/equality

Prasannan Parthasarathi's works have made it possible to emphasize the key role of anti-Indian protectionist policies in the emergence of the British textile industry.[8] In the seventeenth and eighteenth centuries, exports of manufactured products (textiles of all kinds, silks, porcelain) came chiefly from China and India, and they were largely financed by imports of silver and gold coming from Europe and America, as well as from Japan. Indian textiles, and especially printed fabrics and blue calicos, were madly popular in Europe and throughout the world. At the beginning of the eighteenth century, 80 percent of the textiles traded by British merchants for slaves in West Africa were made in India, and this proportion still reached 60 percent at the end of the century. Maritime registers indicate that in the 1770s Indian tex-

---

8. Parthasarathi, *Why Europe Grew Rich and Asia Did Not.*

tiles by themselves represented a third of the cargos loaded in Rouen on ships engaged in the slave trade. Ottoman reports attest that Indian textile exports to the Middle East were still at that time larger than those sent to West Africa. This does not seem to have been a problem for the Turkish authorities, who were more concerned with the interests of the local consumer than with those of the producers.

In Europe, merchants very quickly saw the interest they might have in encouraging protests against Indian textiles, and in appropriating part of this know-how to develop their own trans-continental projects. In 1685, the British Parliament introduced tariffs of 20 percent, raised them to 30 percent in 1690, and finally imposed a complete ban on the importation of printed or colored textiles in 1700. From that time on, only undyed fabric was imported from India, which allowed British producers to innovate, dyeing and printing their own. Similar measures were adopted in France, and they were strengthened in the United Kingdom throughout the eighteenth century, notably with the institution in 1787 of a duty of 100 percent on all Indian textiles. The pressure exercised by slave traders in Liverpool, who had a vital need for quality textiles to develop their commerce on the coast of Africa without spending all their coin, played a decisive role, especially between 1765 and 1785, a period during which British production rapidly improved. It was only after having acquired an incontestable comparative advantage in the textile industry, in particular thanks to the use of coal, that the United Kingdom began, starting in the middle of the nineteenth century, to adopt a more assertive free-trade discourse. The British also made use of protectionist measures in the naval industry, which had flourished in India in the seventeenth and eighteenth centuries, by instituting in 1715 a special tax of 15 percent on all goods imported on ships made in India, and then by decreeing that only British vessels could import to the United Kingdom merchandise coming from east of the Cape of Good Hope. Even if it is difficult to propose an overall estimate, it seems clear that the whole of these protectionist measures, imposed on the rest of the world by the threat of an attack by British gunboats, played a significant role in British and European industrial domination. According to available estimates, China's and India's share in worldwide manufacturing, which was still 53 percent in 1800, was no more than 5 percent in 1900.[9]

Protectionism, Center-Periphery Relations, and World-Systems

Let us add that protectionism played a central role not only in Europe's rise to power, but also in almost all the successful experiments in economic development. Japan since the end of the nineteenth century, South Korea or Taiwan since the middle of the twentieth century, and China since the end of the twentieth century and at the beginning of the twenty-first century have all practiced in one way or another a targeted protectionism that allowed them to develop a specialty and knowledge in sectors considered priorities. At the same time, these countries have drastically limited any opportunity for foreign investors to seize control of the production units being formed in these priority sectors. It is only after having established their supremacy over certain products that the countries that have become dominant begin to lapse into the free-trade discourse, which in practice often ends up making other, less advanced countries permanently dependent on them. Wallerstein's research on world-systems and center-periphery relations has abundantly illustrated this reality in the long-term history of capitalism.[10] Other studies have analyzed the

---

9. See Parthasarathi, *Why Europe Grew Rich,* 97–131, 234–235. Compare P. Singara-vélou and S. Venayre, *Histoire du monde au xixe siècle* (Paris: Fayard, 2017), 90–92.

10. I. Wallerstein, *The Modern World-System* 4 vols. (New York: Academic Press, 1974–1989); G. Arrighi, *The Long Twentieth Century: Money, Power and the Origins of Our Time* (London: Verso, 1994). Compare D. Harvey, *Spaces of Capital: Towards a Critical Geography* (Edinburgh: Edinburgh University Press, 2001).

central role played by national industrial strategies in more recent periods.[11]

Concerning the rise of Europe's power in the eighteenth and nineteenth centuries, the only genuine specificity is the immoderate and uninhibited use of military force at the global level, in the absence of any true internal or external counterweight. The first European commercial companies, such as the British East India Company or the Dutch East Indies Company, were like genuine enterprises of transnational militarized robbery, with private armies subjugating whole populations under their ruthless control.[12] The history of the opium wars is a good example. Recognizing that the silver from the Americas that had allowed them up to that point to balance their books with China and India was almost exhausted, Europeans at the beginning of the eighteenth century worried about no longer having anything to trade in exchange for their imports of silks, textiles, porcelain, spices, and tea coming from the two future Asian giants. The British then intensified their opium-growing efforts in India in order to export the drug to China. That is how opium trafficking expanded considerably in the course of the eighteenth century, and in 1773 the British East India Company established its monopoly over the production and exportation of opium from Bengal.

Confronted by an enormous increase in the volume of opium traded, the Qing Empire finally took action. It had been trying since 1729, without success, to enforce its interdiction on opium consumption, for obvious reasons of public health. In 1839, the emperor ordered his envoy in Canton to put a stop to the traffic and to burn the stock of opium immediately. A violent anti-Chinese press campaign financed by the opium merchants was then set up in the United

---

11. For example, H. J. Chang, *Kicking Away the Ladder: Development Strategy in Historical Perspective* (London: Anthem, 2002); M. Mazzucato, *Entrepreneurial State: Debunking Public vs. Private Sector Myths* (London: Anthem, 2013).

12. W. Dalrymple, *The Anarchy: The Relentless Rise of the East India Company* (New York: Bloomsbury, 2019).

Kingdom, in order to denounce the intolerable violation of the right to property and the unacceptable challenge to the principles of free trade. The Qing emperor had clearly underestimated the United Kingdom's increasing fiscal and military power, and the first Opium War (1839–1842) ended with a quick rout of the Chinese. The British sent a fleet that bombarded Canton and Shanghai, which allowed them to obtain a signature in 1842 on the first of the "unequal treaties" (an expression popularized by Sun Yat-sen in 1924). The Chinese paid financial compensation for the opium destroyed and for the costs of the war. At the same time they granted legal and fiscal privileges to British merchants and ceded to them the island of Hong Kong.

However, the Qing government still refused to legalize the opium trade. The Second Opium War (1856–1860) and the sack of the Summer Palace by French and British troops in Beijing in 1860 finally led the emperor to capitulate. In 1860–1862, the Chinese state had to grant the Europeans a series of commercial trading posts and territorial concessions, as well as heavy war reparations. In the name of religious freedom, it also had to allow Christian missionaries to roam freely about the country (without considering that Buddhists, Muslims, or Hindus could be granted the same right in Europe). An irony of history: it was following this military tribute imposed by the French and British that the Chinese state had to abandon its Smithian budgetary orthodoxy and resort, for the first time, to a major public debt. This debt snowballed and forced the Qing Empire to raise taxes to reimburse the Europeans, and then cede to them a growing share of the country's fiscal sovereignty, in accord with a classic colonial scenario of coercion through debt that we find in many other countries (such as Morocco).[13]

---

13. A. Barbe, *Dette publique et impérialisme au Maroc (1856–1956)* (Casablanca: La Croisée des chemins, 2020). Compare N. Barreyre and N. Delalande, *A World of Public Debts: A Political History* (London: Palgrave, 2020); P. Penet and J. Zendejas, *Sovereign Debt Diplomacies: Rethinking Sovereign Debt from Colonial Empires to Hegemony* (Oxford: Oxford University Press, 2021).

This internal public debt was contracted by European states to finance their internal wars throughout the seventeenth and eighteenth centuries, but it also played a central role in the process of securitization and financial innovation. Some of these experiments ended with resounding bankruptcies, beginning with John Law's famous bankruptcy of the French Banque Générale in 1718–1720, which arose from the efforts made by the French and British states to rid themselves of their respective debts by offering shares in more or less crazy colonial companies—such as the Mississippi Company, whose failure triggered the collapse of the financial bubble. At the time, most of these projects for joint-stock companies were based on the exploitation of commercial or fiscal monopolies of the colonial type, and had little to do with entrepreneurs who actually produced things. By developing financial and commercial techniques on the global level, Europeans helped establish the infrastructures and comparative advantages that were to prove decisive in the age of globalized industrial and financial capitalism at the end of the nineteenth century and the beginning of the twentieth.[14]

Provincializing Europe and Rethinking the West's Specificity

In short, colonialism and military domination permitted Western countries to organize the world-economy to their benefit and relegated the rest of the planet to an enduring peripheral position. Let us repeat:

---

14. In their recent synthesis on the history of capitalism, Pierre François and Claire Lemercier distinguish the age of commerce (1680–1880), the age of the factory (1880–1980), and the age of finance (since 1980). During the age of commerce, Western countries took control of the planet and its maritime networks: they imposed their military and commercial preeminence on the rest of the world, which allowed them to accumulate capital that would later play a central role in the transition to the age of the factory. See P. François and C. Lemercier, *Sociologie historique du capitalisme* (Paris: La Découverte, 2021).

there is nothing specifically European about this strategy. Japan experimented with it, at the expense of part of Asia, during the first half of the twentieth century, and it was only after the end of Japanese colonialism that South Korea and Taiwan were able to establish an autonomous development strategy. Once it escaped colonial control by both the West and Japan, China was able to work out its own development strategy in the early 1980s, after a few decades of hesitation. This strategy has already led China to make numerous poorer and less well-positioned Asian and African economies dependent on it. Europe's claim to originality consists in having been the first to try out this strategy and the first to extend it to the global scale and over several centuries, supported by a military domination that long remained uncontested and by the persistent absence of any sufficiently organized internal or external opposition.

However, the fact that colonialism played a central role in the emergence of Western capitalism does not settle all the questions, far from it. Next, we have to explain the reasons for the fiscal and military superiority developed in Europe. This is usually done by stressing the particular forms adopted by interstate competition and European territorial structures between 1500 and 1800, though these explanations are not exhaustive. For example, interstate competition was also very strong in the Indian subcontinent, but their system of borders was much less stable than Europe's. Some authors defend the thesis that specifically capitalist social relations of production (not found elsewhere in the world) developed in the English countryside in the sixteenth and seventeenth centuries, long before colonial expansion played a decisive role, in connection with an early process of state centralization.[15] Although these studies are thought-provoking, when

---

15. R. Brenner, "Agrarian Class Structure and Economic Development in Pre-Industrial Europe," *Past and Present* 70, no. 1 (1976): 30–75; E. Meiksins Wood, *The Origin of Capitalism: A Longer View,* new ed. (London: Verso, 2002); A. Bihr, *Le Premier Âge du capitalisme,* vol. 1: *L'Expansion européenne (1415–1763)* (Paris: Syllepse, 2018).

examined carefully, we find that the supporting source material seems thus far too fragile (and too Eurocentric) to establish such a conclusion on a firm basis. At this stage, the most convincing thesis seems to be the one developed by Pomeranz and Parthasarathi, according to which the socioeconomic structures in force in the most advanced regions of Europe, China, Japan, and India remained almost the same until the middle of the eighteenth century and began to diverge only in the context of colonial and military domination.

It is, however, completely possible that new research or previously unknown sources will make it possible to further develop this conclusion, now fragile and provisional. Many other factors might explain an earlier proto-capitalist divergence. For example, the medievalist Giacomo Todeschini proposes that the Catholic Church developed a particularly sophisticated system of financial, commercial, and property law in Europe in order to ensure its permanence as a simultaneously religious, political, and property-owning organization, even though the clergy's celibacy forbade it to exist as a class.[16] Before him, the anthropologist Jack Goody proposed the hypothesis that several factors specific to Europeans, in particular family structure (the prohibition of marriage between cousins, adoptions, and the remarriage of widows, which were all against Catholic regulations), are connected with the Christian church's firm desire to receive goods and assert itself as a property-owning organization rivaling families.[17]

Many studies, such as those of Sanjay Subrahmanyam, have emphasized geopolitical and religious motivations that may have even more decisively influenced European expansionism. The intent was to encircle the eternal Muslim enemy: the Portuguese set out to round the Cape of Good Hope in search of a hypothetical Christian realm in East Africa that would have allowed them to attack Islam from behind. After a fruitless quest on the eastern coast of Africa, they

---

16. G. Todeschini, *Les Marchands et le Temple. La société chrétienne et le cercle vertueux de la richesse du Moyen Âge à l'Époque moderne* (Paris: Albin Michel, 2017).

17. J. Goody, *The European Family* (Malden, MA: Blackwell, 2000).

ended up reaching the coast of India. It then took them several years to realize that the sovereigns encountered near Calcutta and Kochi by Vasco da Gama, who himself belonged to the military orders active during the Reconquista, were Hindus and not Christians.[18] The motivating role of the rivalry with Islam was also stressed by Edward Saïd, who showed how the discourse seeking to stigmatize the Orient and Muslims, who were considered to be vicious by nature and incapable of governing themselves, has been used to justify the colonial project.[19]

On a completely different level, Claude Lévi-Strauss emphasized the deep anthropological connections that he claims unite the Far West and the Far East. These ends of the world benefited from natural frontiers that favored the formation of the state—notably the case for the British Isles and Japan, but also to a lesser degree for France—but since the age of the Neolithic migrations the Far West and the Far East had also been receptacles for mythologies, ideologies, and knowledge about the world.[20] Research on the formation of the first states in the Neolithic age also shows the importance of ritual constructions and

18. S. Subrahmanyam, *The Career and Legend of Vasco da Gama* (Cambridge: Cambridge University Press, 1997).

19. In 1833, Lamartine published his famous *Voyage en Orient,* in which he theorizes the European right to sovereignty over the Orient at a time when France was waging a brutal war of conquest in Algeria. Shortly before, in *Le Génie du christianisme* and then in his *Itinéraire de Paris à Jérusalem,* Chateaubriand had written very harsh pages justifying the civilizing role of the Crusades and condemning Islam without reservations: "Some have censured the knights for going in quest of the infidels even into their own countries; but such are not aware that, after all, this was but making just reprisals upon nations who had been the first aggressors: the Moors exterminated by Charles Martel justify the Crusades. Did the disciples of the Coran remain quiet in the deserts of Arabia? Have they not on the contrary extended their doctrines and their ravages to the walls of Delhi and the ramparts of Vienna? It would perhaps have been better to wait till the haunts of these ferocious beasts were again replenished." François-René vicomte de Chateaubriand, *The Beauties of Christianity,* tr. F. Shoberl (London: Henry Colburn, 1813), 166–167. See E. Saïd, *Orientalism* (New York: Vintage Books, 1978), 171–174. Compare Piketty, *Capital and Ideology,* 325–330.

20. C. Levi-Strauss, *The Other Face of the Moon* (Cambridge, MA: Belknap Press of Harvard University Press, 2013).

the extreme fragility of state structures, with the exception, however, of places that are restricted territorially (islands, seaboards).[21]

The Role of Economic and Social History in the Construction of the State

All these religious, ideological, and anthropological factors have undoubtedly had a great influence on the history of Europe, as they have in other parts of the world, and it would be illusory and puerile to claim to be able to ferret out, among all these elements, a single root cause of historical events as they unfolded. At this point, it seems to me more useful to note that the development of Western and world capitalism was based on the international division of labor and the unrestrained exploitation of the planet's natural and human resources, and that the power relationships between states have played an absolutely central role in that history. The important point is that the construction of the state does not simply involve the development of a fiscal and military capability. It is inseparable from the worldviews, ideologies, identities, institutions, languages, and "imaginary communities" connecting millions of persons who have never met and never will, but who nonetheless agree, willingly or unwillingly, to obey the rules of a common state authority.[22] For centuries, these state constructions have generally been controlled by the dominant classes, which are sometimes themselves in discord, intent as they have been on developing their own projects of political, colonial, religious, or commercial domination in the rest of the world. Subaltern classes nevertheless play a growing role in revolts and social struggles at the end

---

21. J.-P. Demoule, "Naissances des inégalités et prémisses de l'État," in *La Révolution néolithique dans le monde,* ed. Demoule (Paris: CNRS Editions, 2010).

22. On the construction of the imaginary communities at the origin of modern nation-states in connection with the spread of printing, see the classic book by B. R. Anderson, *Imagined Communities: Reflections on the Origin and Spread of Nationalism,* rev. ed. (London: Verso, 2006).

of the eighteenth century and after, and thus help determine the type of state power that develops and what political project it has in view. In itself, the state is neither egalitarian nor inegalitarian: everything depends on who controls it and for what purpose. To a certain extent, we find the same ambivalence in the first states,[23] or during certain periods before the eighteenth century, even if the sources needed to study them in a satisfactory way are lacking.[24]

---

23. See A. Testart, *L'Institution de l'esclavage. Une approche mondiale* (Paris: Gallimard, 2018). Testart defends the idea that the formation of the state usually leads to abolishing internal slavery and regulating relations of extreme dependency between possessors and possessed (not because they like equality, but because they want to avoid fracturing the community into scattered sovereignties—in other words, in order to establish a unified state sovereignty). Conversely, several authors stress the fact that the first states were based on oppression and forced labor, and propose to rehabilitate alternative decentralized political forms. See P. Clastres, *La Société contre l'État* (Paris: Minuit, 1974); J. Scott, *Against the Grain: A Deep History of the Earliest States* (New Haven CT: Yale University Press, 2017); D. Graeber and D. Wengrow, "How to Change the Course of Human History," *Eurozine*, March 2, 2018; D. Graeber and D. Wengrow, *The Dawn of Everything: A New History of Humanity* (London: Allen Lane, 2021).

24. However, see the works of G. Alfani, "Economic Inequality in Preindustrial Times," *Journal of Economic Literature* 59, no. 1 (2021): 3–44; and G. Alfani and M. Di Tullio, *The Lion's Share: Inequality and the Rise of the Fiscal State in Preindustrial Europe* (Cambridge: Cambridge University Press, 2019), which highlight, on the basis of local urban sources in Italy and the Netherlands, a tendency for property to become more concentrated between 1500 and 1800, and explain this development by the regressiveness of the fiscal and state systems. Taking into account the fact that the poor rural and urban population is less well registered at the beginning of this period, it is nonetheless not completely certain that this evolution is significant. Compare B. Van Bavel, *The Invisible Hand? How Market Economies Have Emerged and Declined since AD 500* (Oxford: Oxford University Press, 2016).

4

THE QUESTION OF REPARATIONS

The exit from slavery and colonialism, a major step in the long march toward equality studied in this book, involves conflicts and struggles, liberations and injustices—for example, the financial compensation paid to slaveholders (and not to former slaves). This episode, which should be better known, raises the question of modern-day reparations. No matter how complex this question is, it cannot be evaded forever: it is time to act, unless we want deep and lasting injustice to continue. More generally, a colonial heritage of slaveholding forces us to rethink the connection between reparatory justice and universalist justice all over the world.

The End of Slavery: Financial Compensation for Slaveholders

In the eighteenth and nineteenth centuries, slavery increased in scope within the Atlantic sphere. In the US South, the number of slaves quadrupled between 1800 and 1860. The plantation system, which reached a size never before seen in history, played a central role in the Western textile industry. A few decades earlier, up to the end of the eighteenth century, the heart of the plantation economy was French and British. In the 1780s, the French slaveholding islands held the largest concentration of slaves in the Euro-American world—about 700,000—compared with 600,000 in the British possessions, and 500,000 on the plantations in the southern United States.

In the French West Indies, the main concentrations of slaves were in Martinique, Guadeloupe, and especially Saint-Domingue. Renamed Haiti in the Declaration of Independence of 1804, Saint-Domingue was the jewel of the French colonies at the end of the eighteenth century, the most prosperous and most profitable of all French possessions owing to its production of sugar, coffee, and cotton. Santo Domingo, as the colony was previously known, came under French control in 1626 and encompassed the western part of the island of Hispaniola, where Columbus had landed in 1492. The eastern part of the island was a Spanish colony that later became the Dominican Republic. The neighboring island of Cuba also remained under Spanish control, and slavery continued there until 1886–1887, as it did in Brazil. In the Indian Ocean, the two French slaveholding islands were Île de France and Île Bourbon. In the eighteenth century, Île de France was the more important of the two, but it was occupied by British soldiers in 1810 and became a British possession, renamed Mauritius, in 1815. Île Bourbon, however, remained French and was renamed Île de la Réunion. In all, around 1780 there were almost 100,000 slaves on the plantations of these two islands and 600,000 in the French West Indies, almost 450,000 of them in Saint-Domingue.

We must also emphasize that these were truly slave islands, in the sense that the proportion of slaves rose as high as 90 percent of the total population of Saint-Domingue in the 1780s (or even 95 percent if we include free Blacks and *métis,* those of mixed-race descent). In the course of the period 1780–1830, we find comparable levels in the rest of the British and French West Indies: 84 percent in Jamaica, 80 percent in Barbados, 85 percent in Martinique, 86 percent in Guadeloupe. These are the highest levels ever observed in the history of Atlantic slaveholding societies, and more generally in the world history of slaveholding societies (see Figure 10). In comparison, during the same period slaves represented between 30 and 50 percent of the population of the southern United States and Brazil, and the available sources suggest comparable proportions in Athens and in Rome in antiquity. The British and French West Indies of the eighteenth and

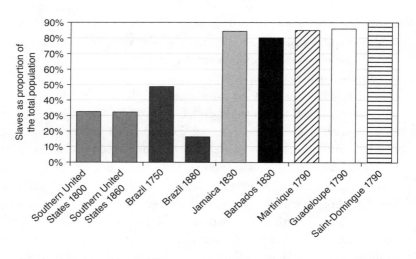

FIGURE 10. Atlantic Slaveholding Societies, Eighteenth and Nineteenth Centuries
The slaves represented approximately one-third of the population in the southern
United States from 1800 to 1860. In Brazil, this proportion declined from almost
50 percent to less than 20 percent between 1750 and 1880. It exceeded 80 percent in
the slaveholding islands of the British and French West Indies in 1780–1830, and
even reached 90 percent in Saint-Domingue (Haiti) in 1790. *Sources and series:*
piketty.pse.ens.fr/equality

early nineteenth centuries offer the best-documented historical examples of societies in which nearly the entire population consisted
of slaves.

It is obvious that when the proportion of slaves reaches 80 or
90 percent, the risk of rebellion becomes very high, no matter how
ferocious the repressive apparatus might be. The case of Haiti was particularly extreme in that the slave population grew very rapidly, and
the number of slaves was significantly greater than on the other islands. Around 1700, the total population of the island was about
30,000 inhabitants, of which barely half were slaves. At the beginning
of the 1750s, Haiti had 120,000 slaves (77 percent of the total population), 25,000 Whites (19 percent), and 5,000 *métis* and free Blacks
(4 percent). At the end of the 1780s, the colony had more than 470,000

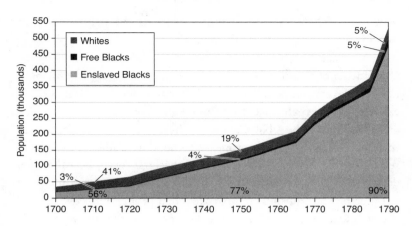

FIGURE 11. A Slaveholding Island in Expansion: Saint-Domingue, 1700–1790

The total population of Saint-Domingue (Haiti) rose from barely 50,000 persons in 1700–1710 (including 56 percent slaves, 3 percent free Blacks and *métis*, and 41 percent Whites) to more than 500,000 persons in 1790 (including 90 percent slaves, 5 percent free Blacks and *métis*, and 5 percent Whites). *Sources and series:* piketty.pse.ens.fr/equality

slaves (90 percent of the population), 28,000 Whites (5 percent), and 25,000 *métis* and free Blacks (5 percent) (see Figure 11).

On the eve of 1789, about 40,000 Africans had been forcibly transported every year in Port-au-Prince and Cap-Français to replace deceased slaves and replenish the slave trade, which was then growing at an extremely fast pace. The system was in a phase of accelerated expansion when the French Revolution broke out. In 1789–1790, free Blacks claimed the right to vote and to participate in assemblies. This seemed to them logical, given the resounding proclamations regarding equal rights that were being made in Paris, but they were refused that right. The slave uprising began in August 1791, after a meeting at Bois-Caïman on the Northern Plain, in which thousands of maroons took part, those who had over the decades escaped slavery and taken refuge in the mountains. Despite military reinforcements sent from France, the insurgents rapidly gained ground and took control of the plantations, whereupon the planters fled the country. The new commissioners sent from Paris decreed the emancipation of slaves in August 1793, a decision that was extended to all the colonies by the Convention of February 1794, which by declaring the general abolition of slavery marked itself as different from proclamations of earlier and later regimes (even if this decision was, in reality, imposed on the regime by the rebels). There was hardly any time to implement this decision. In 1802, the property owners persuaded Napoleon to reestablish slavery in all the slaveholding islands except Haiti, which declared its independence in 1804, after having once again driven out the French troops sent to take back their property. It was not until 1825 that Charles X recognized Haiti's independence, and it was only in 1848 that a new law of abolition was adopted and implemented in the other territories, in particular Martinique, Guadeloupe, and La Réunion.

Should the French State Reimburse the Debt Paid by Haiti?

The case of Haiti is emblematic, not only because it was the first abolition of slavery in the modern age after a victorious slave revolt, and the first independence from a European power won by a Black population, but also because this episode ended with a gigantic public debt that undermined Haiti's development over the following two centuries. Although in 1825 France finally agreed to accept the country's independence and to put an end to its threats to send troops to invade the island, that was only because Charles X had obtained from the Haitian government a commitment to repay to France a debt of 150 million gold francs to indemnify the slaveholders for the loss of their property. The Port-au-Prince government did not really have a choice, given France's clear military superiority, the embargo imposed by the French fleet, and the genuine risk that the island would be occupied. This veritable tribute represented more than 300 percent of Haiti's national income in 1825—more than three years of production—a huge sum that it was materially impossible to repay in a short time. In this case, the treaty stipulated a rapid payment of the whole amount to the Caisse des dépôts et consignation (a banking institution that was created by the Revolution and still exists today), with the Haitian government being responsible for refinancing itself and paying interest to French private banks in order to spread out the repayment. The Haitian debt was the object of multiple, chaotic negotiations, but it was largely repaid (capital and interest), with an average payment of about 5 percent of the Haitian national income per annum between 1840 and 1915, even if the French banks regularly complained about late payments.[1] With the support of the French government, the banks finally decided to cede the rest of their receivables to the United States, which occupied Haiti from 1915 to 1934 to reestablish order and safeguard its own financial interests.

The 1825 debt, transferred from one creditor to another, was officially extinguished and definitively repaid by the beginning of the 1950s. For more than a century, from 1825 to 1950, the price that France tried to make Haiti pay for its freedom had one main consequence: the island's development was overdetermined by the question of the indemnity, which was sometimes violently denounced and sometimes accepted with resignation, according to the ebb and flow of endless political cycles.[2]

---

1. T. Piketty, *Capital and Ideology* (Cambridge, MA: Belknap Press of Harvard University Press, 2020), 217–220. Compare S. Henochsberg, "Public Debt and Slavery: The Case of Haiti (1760–1915)," unpublished manuscript, Paris School of Economics, December 2016.

2. These devastating cycles began in 1804, when Jean-Jacques Dessalines took power. After the capitulation in 1803 of the French expeditionary force (a force whose assignment had been to exterminate all the insurgents) and the arrest, in 1802, of Toussaint Louverture, who defended tooth and nail the maintenance of a White presence, along with the possibility of a peaceful association with France and Haiti's integration into the international economy, Dessalines established a hyper-authoritarian, monarchical regime that was anti-White and isolationist. The later history of the island is marked by similar cycles of denunciation and resignation.

Suppose the French state finally decides to reimburse the debt paid by Haiti, as the Haitian state has been asking it to do for decades. What should the amount of this reparation be? There is no single answer to this question, and it deserves to be the subject of a democratic debate. But it cannot be evaded. A simple, transparent solution might consist in setting the amount at 300 percent of the Haitian national income in 2020, or about 30 billion euros. This proposal is far from being maximalist, in the sense in which it includes the interest due only very partially.[3] Other modes of calculation could be used that would lead to similar or higher amounts.[4] For France, these 30 billion euros would represent the equivalent of a little more than 1 percent of the current public debt, a negligible amount. For Haiti, on the other hand, they would make an enormous difference in terms of investments and infrastructures. It would really be a new start, making it possible to liquidate a major historical injustice.

The counterargument regularly used by French authorities, that this history is too distant to be indemnified, is not very convincing. There are many processes of compensation that continue to take place today for expropriations and injustices that took place in the first half of the twentieth century. For example, consider the spoliation of Jewish property perpetrated by Nazi authorities during World War II, for which restitution procedures are ongoing, in particular since the creation of the Mattéoli Mission in France in 1997. The heirs of the Hohenzollern (the Prussian royal family, which fell from power in 1918) are currently suing the German state for residences and works of art for which they claim they were insufficiently indemnified. We could also mention the Civil Liberties Act of 1988 in the United States,

---

3. Considering a constant proportion of the national income over time amounts to indexing the initial sum to the nominal growth of the economy, which leads to intermediary results between an indexation solely at the level of prices and an indexation to the nominal interest rate.

4. For example, the 150 billion gold francs represented 2 percent of the French national income in 1825. Applying the same proportion of the French national income in 2020, we arrive at 40 billion euros.

according \$20,000 to each of the Japanese Americans interned during World War II.[5] By rejecting any discussion of a debt that Haiti had to pay to France for ending slavery, even though the payments made from 1825 to 1950 are well documented and are not contested by anyone, we risk giving the impression that some injustices are more important than others. This kind of attitude helps create conflict between persons of different origins, whereas we should do all we can to reconcile them on the basis of principles of justice that are as neutral and universal as possible. Let us hope that the French state, under pressure from its citizens, will be able to find a solution before Haiti's next centennial.[6]

The British and French Approaches: 1833 and 1848

In addition to the case of Haiti, we must also recall that substantial financial compensation was paid to slaveholders after the British and French abolished slavery in 1833 and 1848, respectively. Following the

5. The indemnification was reserved for individuals still alive in 1988, contrary to what is done in the case of spoliation of property, which is generally transmitted to the heirs. There is obviously nothing particularly "natural" about this difference in treatment; it is the result of a political choice. It seems to me that it is for democratic deliberation to set the right level of indemnification and transmission in time, taking its inspiration, for example, from the tax scales that are applied to inheritance and property (see Chapter 7, Table 2).

6. In 1904, when the first centennial of the island's independence was being celebrated, the authorities of the Third Republic refused to send an official delegation to Haiti. The French government was not satisfied with the pace of the repayment of the debt, and it was out of the question to show clemency to such a bad payer, especially in a context in which the colonial empire frequently relied on coercion by debt. In 2004, the authorities of the Fifth Republic came to the same conclusion, but for different reasons. The French president refused to attend the commemoration ceremonies because it was feared that the Haitian president would seize the opportunity to demand that France reimburse the odious debt that Haiti had paid off, a subject that the French government did not want to be brought up under any pretext. In 2015, the French president, who was visiting Haiti after a major earthquake, reiterated this position. France did have a kind of "moral" debt to Haiti, he said, but an agreement to talk about monetary reparations was out of the question. Fortunately, the French state has eighty years to redefine its attitude for the tricentennial in 2104.

successful rebellion in Saint-Domingue in 1791, slaveholders were on alert. The great revolt of Guadeloupe in 1802 ended with the execution or deportation of some 10,000 slaves, that is, 10 percent of the population. This was to lead French authorities to authorize slave trading temporarily, from 1810 to 1820, in order to repopulate the island and restart the sugar plantations. A further revolt took place in British Guiana in 1815, which was also put down by bloody repression. The most decisive event was undoubtedly the great revolt in Jamaica at Christmas 1831, a revolt whose gory echoes in the British press made a strong impression on British public opinion and gave a boost to the abolitionists in the debates of 1832–1833. These events helped to convince property owners that it was wiser to accept a generous financial compensation than to risk further confrontations.

In practice, the law of abolition passed by the British Parliament in 1833 put in place full compensation for property owners. Relatively sophisticated scales were drawn up on the basis of the slaves' age, gender, and productivity, so that the compensation might be as fair and as exact as possible. In this way, some 20 million pounds sterling, or about 5 percent of the United Kingdom's national income at the time, was paid to 4,000 slaveholders. Today, if a government decided to devote to such a policy the same proportion of the British national income, it would have to pay approximately 120 billion euros, or about 39 million euros, on average, for each of the 4,000 property owners. Here we are talking about owners with very large holdings, often several hundred slaves, and sometimes several thousand. All this was financed by a corresponding increase in the public debt, which was itself repaid by all British taxpayers, but in practice mainly by modest, middle-level households, given the great regressiveness of the fiscal system, which was based principally on indirect taxes.[7]

---

7. To determine the orders of magnitude, we can also note that in the United Kingdom of the nineteenth century, total expenditures earmarked for education (at all levels) never exceeded 0.5 percent of the national income each year (see Chapter 6). Thus, the equivalent in public funds of ten years of investment in education was distributed to compensate slaveholders.

The parliamentary archives describing these operations have recently been systematically explored. At the time these operations appeared perfectly reasonable and justified, at least in the eyes of the minority of those citizens who were property owners and held political power. This reexamination has led to the publication of several books, and the complete database, including the names of the slaveholders compensated, is available on the Internet.[8] It has thus been found, for example, that among the descendants of the slaveholders generously compensated in the 1830s is a cousin of the Conservative prime minister David Cameron. Demands were made that the sums in question be returned to the Public Treasury. It was pointed out that these sums were the origin of the Cameron family fortune, including the financial and real estate portfolio it still held at the beginning of the twenty-first century, and that the same could be said about many other British family fortunes. Nothing came of the protest, however, and the situation remains unchanged.

A similar compensation was paid to slaveholders after the French abolition of 1848, and the corresponding archives have also been studied and put online.[9] For most of the "liberal" elites of the period, the principle behind this kind of compensation was obvious and incontestable. For example, during the French debates of the 1840s Alexis de Tocqueville won fame for proposals he considered both generous (to slaveholders) and ingenious. Part of the cost would be borne by the Treasury, and another part would be borne by the slaves themselves, who would work for low wages for ten or twenty years to reimburse the difference. Victor Schoelcher, who is still remembered

---

8. N. Draper, *The Price of Emancipation: Slave-Ownership, Compensation and British Society at the End of Slavery* (Cambridge: Cambridge University Press, 2010); C. Hall, N. Draper, K. McClelland, K. Donington, and R. Lang, *Legacies of British Slave-Ownership: Colonial Slavery and the Formation of Victorian Britain* (Cambridge: Cambridge University Press, 2014). The database LBS (Legacies of British Slave-Ownership) is available at http://www.ucl.ac.uk/lbs/.

9. The website *Esclavages et indemnités* (http://esclavage-indemnites.fr), created in 2021 by Myriam Cottias and her team, includes the complete database of the indemnities paid to slaveholders after the agreement with Haiti in 1825 and the abolition of 1848.

as a great abolitionist, said he was embarrassed by the compensations, but that it was impossible to proceed otherwise once slavery had been enshrined in a legal framework.[10] In other words, if slaveholders had been despoiled of their property without compensation, then what could be done with those who had sold their slaves a few years earlier, and now had a portfolio of financial securities, a château near Bordeaux, or an apartment building in Paris? Wasn't one going to end up putting in question the whole social order and the system of private property? In fact, retrospectively, it would have been possible to believe a just abolition would have implied compensation for slaves (and not for their masters) on the basis of their decades of mistreatment and unpaid labor. This compensation would have been financed by everyone who had been enriched by slavery, directly or indirectly—that is, by all the wealthy property owners of the period. Indeed, during the Revolution some actors, like the marquis de Condorcet or Thomas Paine, had defended (without success) the idea of an abolition with compensation for slaves, in the form of a pension paid by the former masters or of a piece of land. But that was not at all the view defended by the dominant elites, who in considering slaves as property swore only by absolute respect for property rights and preferred not to open that dangerous Pandora's box.

In addition to indemnification of property owners, the decrees of abolition promulgated on 27 April 1848 include articles "punishing vagabondage and begging while calling for disciplinary workshops in the colonies" that were intended to ensure cheap labor for the planters. In other words, not only were compensation of slaves and access to

---

10. Lamartine, who was also an abolitionist, made this point forcefully before the Chamber of Deputies: "We have to accord an indemnity to the colonists for the portion of their legal property that was taken from them in the form of their slaves: we will never see this differently. Only revolutions dispossess without compensation. Legislators do not act in that way: they change, they transform, they never ruin; whatever the origin might be, they take established rights seriously." Chamber of Deputies, sessions of April 22, 1835 and May 25, 1836. Piketty, *Capital and Ideology*, 220–226, quotation on 225. On these debates, see C. Oudin-Bastide and P. Steiner, *Calcul et morale. Coûts de l'esclavage et valeur de l'émancipation (XVIIIe–XIXe siècles)* (Paris: Albin Michel, 2015).

parcels of land not considered, but Schoelcher's emancipation was accompanied by a system of quasi-forced labor, making it possible to keep the ex-slaves under the control of the planters and the state authorities for additional decades. On La Réunion, the prefect immediately explained how the decrees of abolition would be implemented: the former slaves had to present a long-term labor contract, either as a worker on the plantations or as a domestic employee; if they had neither, they would be arrested for vagabondage and sent to the disciplinary workshops provided for in the decrees.

In 2020, some observers in the United Kingdom and France were astonished when statues of slave traders or of people like Schoelcher, who had indemnified slaveholders, were pulled down as a consequence of the Black Lives Matter movement. Remembering the historical injustices that took place during each country's abolition may help us to understand this anger better, and also to reflect on solutions. During the debates preceding the vote on the French law of 2001 enshrining Slave Remembrance Day and recognizing the slave trade and slavery as "crimes against humanity," the deputy from French Guiana, Christiane Taubira, proposed in vain to the majority that they accept the principle of a reparation and create a committee entrusted with examining how it might be implemented.[11] Today, beyond the financial reparation owed to Haiti, the principal question remains that of agrarian reform in La Réunion, Martinique, Guadeloupe, and French Guiana, so as to finally allow those descended from slaves to gain access to parcels of land when, at present, ownership of land and financial assets remains largely the prerogative of Whites, some of whom are descended from families of planters who benefited from the indemnities of 1848. No matter how complex, it seems to me that this question must be answered.

---

11. The proposed article 5 of Act 2001-434 in France, Taubira's Law, provided that: "There be established a committee of qualified persons entrusted with determining the damage suffered and examining the conditions of reparation due in consideration of this crime. The jurisdictions and missions of this committee are to be set by decree in the State Council."

The United States: The Long March of a
Slaveholding Republic

We come now to the case of the United States, where the debate on reparations is particularly intense. Slavery has played a central role in the development of the United States, which at its creation resembled a genuine slaveholding republic. Of the fifteen presidents who preceded Lincoln, no less than eleven owned slaves, including Washington and Jefferson, both of whom were natives of Virginia, the pulsing heart of the young federation. The slave system developed rapidly between 1800 and 1860. But the Northeast and especially the Midwest (from which Lincoln came) developed even more rapidly. These two areas were based on a different economic model, whose foundation was the colonization by free workers of the lands in the West through displacement of Indigenous peoples, and thus these regions tried to block the expansion of slavery to the new territories.

After his victory in 1860, the Republican Lincoln was ready to negotiate with the South a peaceful and gradual end to slavery, with indemnification of slaveholders, as in the British and French abolitions of 1833 and 1848. Moreover, plans for ending slavery had been proposed in the 1820s by Jefferson and Madison: according to them, it would suffice to transfer most of the land in the West to the supporters of slavery, who would thus become large landowners in the new territories, while at the same time sending the slaves back to Africa, because they feared it would be difficult for slaves to live alongside their former masters. In reality, the size of the transfers envisaged made this option unrealistic.[12] The Southerners were aware of this, and like some of the White colonists in South Africa and Algeria in

---

12. Piketty, *Capital and Ideology*, 235–238. A total compensation would have required a transfer on the order of a year of US national income, or between three and four times more than the federal debt arising from the Civil War (which was, however, devastating). The magnitude of the phenomenon of slavery in the United States made a peaceful resolution with the owners infeasible. The project of transferring slaves to Africa ended with the troubled creation of Liberia.

the twentieth century, they preferred to play the secession card in the hope of saving their world. The Northerners refused to accept the South's departure from the Union, and the Civil War began in 1861. Four years later, with 600,000 dead (as many as the cumulative total of all the other conflicts in which the country has taken part, including the two world wars, Korea, Vietnam, and Iraq), the fighting ended with the Confederate surrender in April 1865. But some Northerners did not consider Black people ready to become citizens, and still less property owners. Whites in the South imposed a strict system of racial segregation that allowed them to remain in power for nearly another century, until the passage of the Civil Rights Act in 1964. In the meantime, the United States became the primary military power in the world, and was able to end destructive cycles of nationalism and genocide among European colonial powers between 1914 and 1945. Democrats, who had historically been the party of slavery in the United States, succeeded in becoming the party of the New Deal.[13] Driven by competition from communists and by the mobilization of Black people, they conceded civil rights.

After the damage done by secessionists during the Civil War, on the one hand it would have seemed incongruous to pay compensation to slaveholders, and unsurprisingly, all proposals of this kind were abandoned. On the other hand, in the last months of the war, in January 1865, the Northerners promised the emancipated slaves that after the war was won, they would each receive "forty acres and a mule." The idea was to motivate them to join the fight, to compensate them for decades of unpaid labor, and to permit them to turn toward a future as free workers. Had it been adopted, this program would have represented an agrarian redistribution of great scope, at the expense, especially, of major slaveholders. But as soon as the fighting

---

13. On the transformations of the structure of political conflict in the United States during the period of Reconstruction, see the fascinating book by N. Barreyre, *L'Or et la Liberté. Une histoire spatiale des États-Unis après la guerre de Sécession* (Paris: EHESS, 2014). Compare N. Maggor, *Brahmin Capitalism: Frontiers of Wealth and Populism in America's First Gilded Age* (Cambridge MA: Harvard University Press, 2017).

stopped, the promise was forgotten; no law providing for compensation was ever passed, and "forty acres and a mule" became a symbol of Northerners' deception and hypocrisy (to the point that the Black filmmaker Spike Lee ironically made it the name of his production company).

However, the question of reparations remains on the table. In 2021, the city of Evanston, Illinois, adopted a program of reparations to be paid to the Black population, with individual payments of as much as $25,000 in order to help purchase housing. That may seem modest, given the immense concentration of wealth in the United States, and in particular the size of racial inequalities in terms of assets and the magnitude of the damages suffered (during slavery and then segregation), but this may be a start.[14] Discussions are ongoing at the federal level, where the comparison is often made with the 1988 law indemnifying Japanese-Americans, which seemed inconceivable for decades before it was finally passed and implemented. The march toward equality and justice continues.

Postslavery Colonialism and the Question of Forced Labor

In addition to the question of reparations, colonial heritage in its entirety must be reexamined. Generally speaking, if we amass the available sources on the distribution of wealth, we see that slaveholding and colonial societies are among the most inegalitarian in history (see Figure 12). For the slaveholding islands such as Saint-Domingue, the historical apogee was reached on the eve of the French Revolution. According to the accounts of the plantations and the archives at our disposal, the slaveholders, colonists, *métis,* and free Blacks (10 percent of the population) were appropriating about 80 percent of production,

---

14. See, for example, the proposals made by W. A. Darity and A. K. Mullen, *From Here to Equality: Reparations for Black Americans in the Twenty-First Century* (Chapel Hill: University of North Carolina Press, 2020).

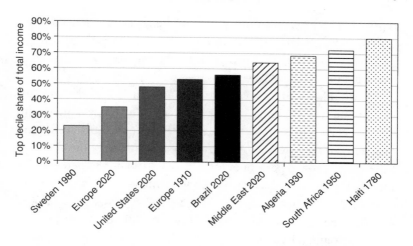

FIGURE 12. Extreme Inequality of Income in Historical Perspective: The Peak of Colonial and Slaveholding Societies

Over all of the societies observed, the share of total income going to the top decile (the highest 10 percent of income) varied from 23 percent in Sweden in 1980 to 81 percent in Saint-Domingue (Haiti) in 1780 (which included 90 percent slaves). Colonial societies like Algeria in 1930 or South Africa in 1950 had some of the highest levels of inequality observed in history, with about 70 percent of total income going to the top decile, which included the European population. *Sources and series:* piketty.pse.ens.fr/equality

while the food and clothing provided to the slaves (90 percent of the population) absorbed scarcely 20 percent.[15] In theory, it could be imagined that in the future, hyper-technological societies might succeed in establishing an even more extreme level of inequality: in principle, material abundance makes greater extraction possible, provided that the class of techno-billionaires in power in these hypothetical societies is able to develop adequate tools, in terms of both

---

15. Of the 80 percent of production appropriated by slaveholders, colonists, *métis,* and free Blacks, the equivalent of about 55 percent was exported to the benefit of the owners (less than 1 percent of the population), who used it to finance accumulations and consumption in metropolitan France and in the other colonies, and 25 percent was accumulated or consumed on site. See Piketty, *Capital and Ideology,* 218–220.

repression and persuasion. Up to now, however, this has not transpired, and the islands of enslaved people in the French West Indies between 1780 and 1790 continue to hold the prize for inequality in world history.[16]

We will also see that colonial societies such as French Algeria in 1930 or South Africa in 1950 are characterized by levels of inequality that are certainly more extreme than those found in slaveholding societies, but they are not totally unrelated (with part of the upper decile reaching 60–70 percent of total income, and not 80 percent). Put another way, in practice, there is a continuum between these different types of inegalitarian systems (see Figure 13).[17] In postslavery colonial societies, the mechanisms of inequality take different forms, in particular through a legal, social, fiscal, and educational system that is profoundly discriminatory. Research like that of Emmanuelle Saada on the French Empire has shown how until the middle of the twentieth century, the colonial powers developed specific legal systems in their empires allowing them to grant rights based on ethno-racial categories that they set about codifying with precision, even though with the abolition of slavery these categories were supposed to have been eliminated from metropolitan France.[18] In the case of the Dutch

---

16. Here we come back to the distinction between the redistribution of property and the redistribution of income (see Chapter 2). Property redistribution may be much more extreme, with one part going to the richest 10 percent, which often reaches 80–90 percent, as in France in 1914; income redistribution is more complicated (in part because of the constraint of subsistence) and requires a much harsher system of domination.

17. Studies have shown that the inequality of incomes in Réunion in 1960 was close to the level observed in French Algeria and in South Africa. See Piketty, *Capital and Ideology*, 263–264; Y. Govind, "Post-colonial Trends of Income Inequality: Evidence from the Overseas Departments of France," June 2020, WID.world; F. Alvaredo, D. Cogneau, and T. Piketty, "Inequality under Colonial Rule: Evidence from French Algeria, Cameroon, Tunisia, Vietnam and Comparison with British Colonies 1920–1960," July 2020, WID.world.

18. The decree of 1928 "defining the status of persons of mixed parentage (*métis*) born in Indochina whose legal parents are unknown," thus granted status as French to anyone who had at least one parent "presumed to be of the French race." This led courts to examine the physical and racial characteristics of the plaintiffs. See E. Saada, *Empire's Children: Race, Filiation, and Citizenship in the French Colonies*, trans. Art Goldhammer (Chicago: University of Chicago Press, 2012), 1.

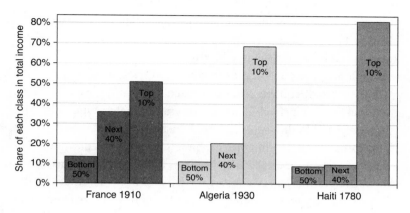

FIGURE 13. The Distribution of Income in Metropolitan France and in Its Colonies

In 1780, the share of the highest 10 percent of total income exceeded 80 percent in Saint-Domingue (Haiti), which was at that time composed of about 90 percent slaves and 10 percent European colonists, as contrasted with more than 65 percent in Algeria in 1930 (which was then composed of about 90 percent "Algerian Muslims" and 10 percent European colonists), and around 50 percent in metropolitan France in 1910. *Sources and series:* piketty.pse.ens.fr/equality

East Indies, Denys Lombard has shown the harmful role played by the colonial statute of 1854, which decided to strictly separate "natives" and "oriental foreigners" (a category in which various Chinese, Indian, and Arab minorities were placed).[19] In South Africa, discrimination took an extremely brutal form. With the Native Land Act of 1913, the Black population was *de facto* confined to reserves representing 7 percent of South Africa's territory. Black workers were forbidden to

---

19. This separation helped permanently establish identities and antagonisms, even though for more than a millennium, Insulindia had been characterized by a mixture of Hindu, Confucian, Buddhist, and Muslim cultures that was hardly in conformity with the martial view taken by the colonial powers. See D. Lombard, *Le Carrefour javanais. Essai d'histoire globale* (Paris: EHESS, 1990). On the antagonism between Buddhists and Muslims in Burma, see J. Lavialle-Prélois, "De la colonisation à la légitimation: l'autre 'terroriste' en Arakan," *Journal des anthropologues* 154–155, no. 3 (2018): 63–83. On the colonial rigidification of "ethnic" identities in Africa (Mali, Rwanda, Burundi, Congo), see J.-L. Amselle and E. M'Bokolo, *Au coeur de l'ethnie. Ethnies, tribalisme et État en Afrique* (Paris: La Découverte, 1985).

leave their zone of employment without a special pass. These measures were further radicalized with apartheid, which was officially instituted in 1948 and implemented until 1990. The legal systems in force were not always as extreme as in the South African case, but in the various colonial contexts, the colonized populations were *de facto* systematically deprived of access to employment, education, and property equal to that enjoyed by colonists.

We must also remember that in practice there is a continuum between pure slavery and the various forms of more or less forced labor. After the abolition of slavery, the British and French authorities developed new systems allowing them to bring in workers from more distant sources, in particular from India in the case of Réunion and Mauritius, by means of long-term contracts (in the French case they were called *"engagés,"* in the British case, "indentured workers"). For Indian workers, this "commitment" consisted in paying over a long period (for example, ten years) a large part of their wages to their employers to reimburse the latter for the cost of transporting them. In the event that an employee's performance was deemed insufficient or, worse yet, lacking in discipline, the repayment obligation could be prolonged by ten additional years or more. The legal archives have been preserved, and it is evident that in a context in which the juridical system is strongly biased in favor of the employers, it can lead to forms of exploitation and arbitrariness that are, to be sure, different from hard-core slavery, but not infinitely distant from it. The available sources also clearly show how employers and courts negotiate, so to speak, the transformation of the system of discipline at work. The property owners gradually agree to reduce the use of corporal punishment, which was common under slavery, but on the condition that the legal authorities help them impose financial sanctions that result in similar subjugation.[20]

---

20. A. Stanziani, *Les Métamorphoses du travail contraint. Une histoire globale, XVIIIe–XIXe siècles* (Paris: Presses de Sciences Po, 2020).

A revealing case is that of the forced labor practiced in a legal form (or at least in a form that tried to make itself look legal) in the French colonies from 1912 to 1946. At the end of the nineteenth century, when Europeans were beginning to penetrate into the interior of the African continent to exploit its natural resources, they resorted largely to forced labor, under conditions that were often very brutal. Controversies erupted over multiple reports of atrocities committed in the Belgian Congo, which since 1885 had been the personal property of King Leopold II. The rubber industry was based on particularly violent methods that sought to exploit and discipline the local labor force: villages were burned, hands were mutilated. Finally, the Europeans demanded the transfer of the territory to Belgium in 1908, in the hope that parliamentary oversight would make this regime less barbaric. Abuses committed in the French colonies were regularly denounced, and it was in this context that the Minister of the Colonies published texts that sought to define a legal framework for the "services" (more commonly called *corvées*) required of the inhabitants of French Africa.

The logic claimed to be unanswerable: the colonial administration was based on the payment of taxes by all, but some natives lacked sufficient resources to pay these taxes; consequently, they were also required to pay a supplementary tax-in-kind, in the form of unpaid labor for the local colonial authorities. In practice, these *corvées* were levied on top of very high taxes in cash and in kind (taken from the harvest) already paid by the colonized population. Also, the use of unpaid labor paved the way for all sorts of abuses, and was tantamount to legalizing them in advance. The decree of 1912 "regulating natives' services in the colonies and territories of French West Africa" established a few safeguards, but they were limited and poorly monitored.[21] Forced labor caused a scandal during the tragic construction of the Congo-Ocean Railway between 1921 and 1934. The administration of

---

21. M. van Waijenburg, "Financing the African Colonial State: The Revenue Imperative and Forced Labor," *Journal of Economic History* 78, no. 1 (2018): 40–80.

French Equatorial Africa had initially promised to provide about 8,000 local workers, which it thought it could "recruit" along a hundred-mile-long strip of territory adjoining the rail line. But the exceptionally high mortality on the job and the latter's proven dangers caused the recruits to flee, and the colonial authorities resorted to seeking "adult males" at the other end of the Middle Congo. Starting in 1925, they had to organize raids into Cameroon and Chad. Reports flowed in regarding the terrible expense of human lives denounced in André Gide's famous *Voyage au Congo* in 1927 and in Albert Londre's book *Terre d'ébène* in 1929.

International pressure on France grew, in particular on the part of the brand-new International Labour Organization (ILO), which was founded in 1919, at the same time as the League of Nations, and whose constitution began with the following preamble: "Whereas universal and lasting peace can be founded only if it is based upon social justice; And whereas conditions of labour exist involving such injustice, hardship, and privation to large numbers of people as to produce unrest so great that the peace and harmony of the world are imperiled; and an improvement of those conditions is urgently required . . . ; Whereas also the failure of any nation to adopt humane conditions of labour is an obstacle in the way of other nations which desire to improve the conditions in their own countries."

There follows a series of recommendations and reports regarding the length of the workday and its dangers, the setting of wages, and rights of workers and their representatives. However, the ILO lacked the means and power to impose sanctions to ensure that its recommendations were implemented. In the course of the 1920s, the ILO repeatedly called upon France to cease its practice of unpaid labor and forced transfer of workers from one site to another, which amounted, according to the international organization, to a kind of slave labor. But the French authorities rejected these accusations, emphasizing the fact that they had just extended to all "natives" (and not just the most "evolved"—the term used by the French colonial administration to designate the small minority of natives who had adopted a "European" way of life) the option of paying off their labor obligation with cash. Another of the French administration's favorite arguments was that many of the alleged offenses, particularly on the Congo-Ocean Railway, concerned not forced labor but rather military conscription, which was one of the few forms of unpaid labor authorized by the ILO, on the condition, however, that the military system not be misused to carry out civilian tasks. In this case, the ILO suspected France of doing just that. Outraged by such an infringement on what they considered to be their "national sovereignty," the French authorities refused to ratify the ILO's convention in 1930. That is why unpaid, forced labor, in the form of services and conscriptions, continued in the French colonies up to the eve of World War II, for example on the cocoa plantations in Ivory Coast. The decree of 1912 was finally revoked only in 1946, in response to explicit pressure exercised by Félix Houphouët-Boigny, the future president of Ivory Coast, at a time when France was suddenly ready to make any concession to avoid dismantling its empire.

France, a Colonial Republic That Doesn't Know It Is One

One of the most insidious and hypocritical forms of discrimination in colonial contexts, as in other inegalitarian systems, concerns access to education. In the southern United States, the prohibition on Black children attending the same schools as White children was one of the central pillars of the system of legal racial discrimination that was in force until 1964–1965. This discrimination was made illegal, but US society still bears the marks of these very profound racial and territorial inequalities, which have still not been completely erased. In Europe, and especially in France, it is sometimes imagined that this heavy legacy of legal racial discrimination in no way concerns continental Europe. In France, its "republican" heritage and "republican" values are ritually invoked, as if the fact that during the 1870s the various monarchical and imperial regimes were definitively replaced by a republic sufficed to guarantee respect for equal rights in general, and racial equality in particular.

In reality, the Third Republic did not hesitate to extract wealth from Haiti for decades, thereby prolonging until 1950 the tribute imposed by the monarchical state in 1825. It had no more qualms regarding the institution of a system of forced labor in 1912, in the form of "services" to be performed by the "natives" in the African colonies, a system that persisted until 1946. In Algeria, as in the rest of the French colonial empire, the republican state imposed a regime based explicitly on profound racial and ethno-religious discrimination until 1962. Concretely, up to the last day of the colonial empire, "Algerian Muslims" and other Indigenous populations never had the same rights as the colonists, whether political rights or social and economic rights.[22] In particular, the school system remained deeply segregated right up to the end, in the sense that the schools open to the colonists and the natives were usually strictly separated, in accord with modalities that, if not exactly the same as in the southern United States, were hardly more egalitarian. If the United States was a slaveholding republic, France was for a long time a colonial republic, or, if one prefers, a republic at the head of a colonial empire. The two republics organized the territories they controlled on an explicitly racial and discriminatory basis until the 1960s. If we want to escape this heritage someday, it would be better to start by trying to understand its importance.

Recent studies have enabled us to improve our comprehension of the structure of the colonial budgets used during French colonization and our recognition of these inequalities.[23] In Morocco, the primary

---

22. To be sure, between 1946 and 1962, the colonized populations had the right to seats in the National Assembly, but on a numerical basis that bore no relationship to their demographic weight. See Piketty, *Capital and Ideology*, 293–303; and the fascinating F. Cooper, *Citizenship between Empire and Nation: Remaking France and French Africa 1945–1960* (Princeton, NJ: Princeton University Press, 2014).

23. D. Cogneau, Y. Dupraz, and S. Mesplé-Somps, "Fiscal Capacity and Dualism in Colonial States: The French Empire 1830–1962," *Journal of Economic History* 81, no. 2 (2021): 441–480; E. Huillery, "The Black Man's Burden: The Costs of the Colonization of French West Africa," *Journal of Economic History* 74, no. 1 (2014): 1–38; M. Woker, "Em-

and secondary schools reserved for Europeans received 79 percent of the total expenditures for education in 1925 (even though Europeans constituted only 4 percent of the population). In the same year, less than 5 percent of native children in North Africa and Indochina were enrolled in school, and less than 2 percent in French West Africa. It is striking to note that this great inequality in expenditures seems not to have decreased after the end of colonization. In Algeria, budget documents show that the schools reserved for colonists received 78 percent of the total expenditures for education in 1925, a proportion that rose to 82 percent in 1955, when the fighting for independence had already begun. The colonial system was so inegalitarian in its functioning that reform seemed largely impossible. Let us add that the fiscal system used to finance these expenses was itself unfair and regressive, and that it bore essentially on the natives (taxes on consumption, indirect taxes, and so on). In short, the colonized populations paid heavy taxes in order to finance expenditures that benefited principally those who had come to dominate them politically and militarily.

The educational system implemented in continental France at the beginning of the twentieth century was, it is true, also extremely hierarchized and inegalitarian, and in large measure it has never ceased to be so. But it is important to realize that that is incommensurate with the level of inequality in educational means that characterized the colonial context (see Figure 14). In 1910, educational stratification was very great in France: the disadvantaged classes rarely went beyond the primary school certificate. If we gather together the available budgetary data, we find that the 10 percent of an age group benefiting from the largest educational investment (by reaching secondary school or, more rarely, higher education) received about 38 percent of the total expenditure, as compared with only 26 percent for the least educated 50 percent of the age group. This is a considerable inequality,

pire of Inequality: The Politics of Taxation in the French Colonial Empire, 1900–1950s" (PhD diss., Columbia University, 2020).

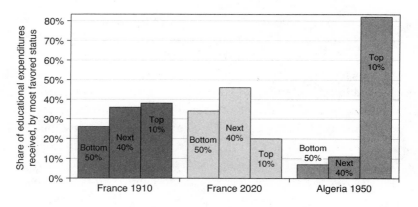

FIGURE 14. Colonies for Colonists: The Inequality of Educational Investment in Historical Perspective

In Algeria in 1950, the most favored 10 percent (the colonizers) benefited from 82 percent of the total expenditure for primary, secondary, and higher education. The comparable figure for France was 38 percent in 1910 and 20 percent in 2020, which is, nonetheless, twice as high as their share in the population. *Sources and series:* piketty.pse.ens.fr/equality

insofar as the second group is by construction five times more numerous than the first. In other terms, the most favored 10 percent of the children benefited from an individual educational investment almost eight times higher than the least favored 50 percent. Inequality in expenditure for education has decreased considerably between 1910 and 2020, even if the established system continues to invest almost three times more in public funds per student for the most favored 10 percent than it does for the least favored 50 percent, which is relatively astonishing for a system that is supposed to reduce *social reproduction,* the tendency for unequal classes to transfer their status from one generation to the next. We shall return to this point. At this stage, let us note simply that educational inequalities in colonial societies like French Algeria were of an incomparably greater magnitude: the ratio between the expenditure for the education of the colonists' children and the expenditure for the children of the colonized was forty to one.

The Question of Reparations: Rethinking Justice on a Transnational Scale

Let's sum up. The current distribution of wealth among the countries of the world and within countries bears the deep mark of the slave-holding, colonial past. Knowledge of this past is indispensable for improving our understanding of the origins and injustices of the present economic system, but in itself it does not suffice to formulate solutions and remedies. The question is complex and requires thorough, detailed examination. Sometimes, the solution involves explicit reparations, as it does in the case of the French debt to Haiti (where they seem inevitable), either agrarian reform and access to land in certain territories, or indemnities in the United States. Rejecting any discussion of reparations, even when other spoliations and injustices that are just as far in the past continue to be indemnified, considerably complicates the development of new norms of universal justice that are acceptable to all. It is time to understand that the logic of remedial justice and universalist justice are complementary and have to move forward in concert, the one supporting the other.

For all that, it is very clear that reparations alone will not allow us to settle all the problems. To repair the damage done by racism and colonialism, we also have to change the economic system on a systematic basis, by reducing inequalities and ensuring that everyone has the most egalitarian access possible to education, employment, and property, independently of his or her origins. To fight discrimination, we must also pursue policies that are as ambitious, coherent, and verifiable as possible, but without rigidifying identities, which are always plural and multidimensional. We shall see to what extent it is possible, on the basis of the experience accumulated thus far, to find a balance between social criteria and criteria related to origins. For similar reasons, we have to go beyond the opposition between redistribution at the national level and redistribution at the international level. In particular, each country, each citizen on the planet, should have some part of the tax revenues derived from multinational companies and the world's billionaires: first, because each human being should have a minimal equal right to health care, education, and development; and second, because the rich countries' prosperity would not exist without the poor countries. The growth of wealth in the Western world, like that in Japan or China, has long been based on the international division of labor and the feverish exploitation of natural and human resources worldwide. All these accumulations of wealth that have taken place on our planet depend on a global economic system, and it is at that level that the question of justice should be raised and the march toward equality pursued. Before going further in these various directions, we must nonetheless arrive at a better understanding of how the inequalities of status and class have been transformed since the eighteenth century, on the global scale and in particular within Western countries.

5

REVOLUTION, STATUS, AND CLASS

The slave revolt in Saint-Domingue in 1791 paved the way for the end of slavery and colonialism, but the battle for racial equality is still being fought. The same is true of inequalities in status in general: in 1789 the French Revolution took an essential step by abolishing the nobility's privileges, but it did not do away with the multiple privileges of money—far from it. We shall see that until the beginning of the twentieth century, electoral systems based on wealth qualifications were implemented in many countries, such as Sweden. Other forms of plutocratic systems, slightly toned down, still prevail in many forms today, whether in influencing elections or in concentrating power among stockholders, to the detriment of more competent persons involved in the process of production.

The End of Privileges and Unequal Status?

According to a rather widespread fairy tale, legal equality has been definitively established in Western countries since the Enlightenment and the "Atlantic revolutions." In this narrative, the French Revolution and the abolition of aristocratic privileges during the night of August 4, 1789, appear to be foundational events. The reality is obviously more complex. The republics of France and the United States were in essence slaveholding, colonial, and legally discriminatory until the 1960s. The same was true of the British and Dutch monarchies. Almost everywhere, the equality of rights proclaimed at the end of the eighteenth century is above all an equality of White men, and especially of property-owning White men.

Although the abandonment of privileges during the night of 4 August remains a seminal event, it must be seen as a long, unfinished battle for equality. There would have been no night of August 4 without the taking of the Bastille on July 14, and especially without the peasant revolts in the summer of 1789. During these revolts farmers and laborers attacked the lords and their châteaux, burning their titles to property. This convinced the deputies gathered in Paris that they had to act quickly to do away with the despised institutions of feudalism. These revolts followed decades of peasant rebellions that the divided government proved increasingly unable to control—the occupation of parcels of land and common goods, violence directed against landowners—particularly during the summer of 1788, when the question of the election of delegates to the Estates-General was finally clearly raised in a nearly insurrectional atmosphere.[1]

We must also emphasize that if the French nobility definitively lost its fiscal, political, and jurisdictional privileges in 1789, it retained for a long time afterward a privileged social position as a class of property owners. By studying family names in the Paris inheritance archives, we have found that while the nobility represented barely 1 percent of the population of Paris in the nineteenth century, between 1830 and 1840 it included no less than 40 to 45 percent of the wealthiest—just slightly less than it did on the eve of the Revolution. Not until the decades between 1880 and 1910 did the prominence of the nobility among the largest estates finally decrease (see Figure 15).

This persistence is explained by several factors. Exiled in the neighboring European monarchies between 1789 and 1815, the nobility

---

1. J. Nicolas, *La Rébellion française. Mouvements populaires et conscience sociale, 1661–1789* (Paris: Gallimard, 2002), which counts eighty-seven anti-seigneurial rebellions between 1730 and 1759 and 246 between 1760 and 1789. Compare G. Lemarchand, *Paysans et seigneurs en Europe. Une histoire comparée, xvie–xixe siècles* (Rennes: Presses universitaires de Rennes, 2011), which emphasizes the role of peasant revolts on the European scale, particularly in the years preceding the wave of revolutions in 1848.

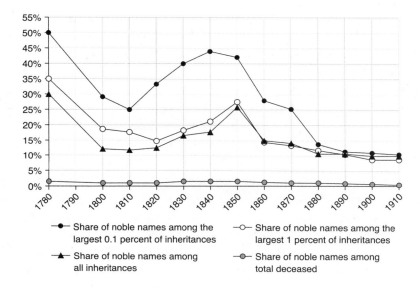

FIGURE 15. The Nobility in Parisian Inheritances, 1780–1910

The share of noble names among the 0.1 percent of the largest inheritances in Paris fell from 50 percent to 25 percent between 1780 and 1810, before climbing to about 40–45 percent during the period of the censitary monarchies (1815–1848), then declining to about 10 percent at the end of the nineteenth century and the beginning of the twentieth. In comparison, noble names still represented less than 2 percent of the total number of deaths between 1780 and 1910. *Sources and series:* piketty.pse. ens.fr/equality

returned en masse to France in 1815 and benefited from very favorable measures during the period of the monarchies, in which electors had to meet a certain tax threshold (1815–1848). We think especially of the emblematic law of the "billion for the emigrés" that transferred to these nobles considerable sums (almost 15 percent of the national income at the time, financed by taxes and public debt) to compensate them for the lands and rents lost under the Revolution. Debated during the first days of the Restoration, this law was adopted in 1825, under the government led by the Count de Villèle, who in that same year imposed on Haiti the indemnity in favor of the slaveowners (many of whom were aristocrats).

More generally, we must emphasize that the redistributions carried out under the Revolution were more limited than is sometimes imagined. Church properties, which represented almost 25 percent of the kingdom's total real estate (including the value of ecclesiastical tithes) were, of course, nationalized without compensation. But instead of being redistributed to the landless, they were auctioned off to benefit those who had the means to buy them. Abbé Siéyès, who had sided with the Third Estate in his famous pamphlet published in January 1789,[2] was scandalized by this operation, which would, according to him, only enrich property owners, noble or bourgeois, while at the same time drying up financing for the Church's charitable works, which included help for the poorest people, schools, and hospitals. In England, the dissolution of the monasteries, decreed by Henry VIII in 1536, had also strengthened the property-owning class. Meanwhile, the House of Lords was becoming an almost exclusively noble assembly, whereas the clergy had previously occupied half the seats. In France as in England, we thus move gradually from a trifunctional ideology to an ideology that can be described as "property-owning" or simply as "capitalist." In a trifunctional ideology, the position of the two dominant classes, the clergy and the nobility, is supposed to be justified by their service to the Third Estate and to society as a whole, through spiritual guidance and charitable works, in the case of the clergy, and order and protection, in the case of the nobility. According to the newer ideology, private property owners have as their sole mission to find the most profitable use for their goods and to enrich themselves, under the protection of the state, without making any contribution to the general welfare.

---

2. "Qu'est-ce que le tiers état? Tout. Qu'a-t-il été jusqu'à present dans l'ordre politique? Rien. Que demande-t-il? A devenir quelque chose." ("What is the Third Estate? Everything. What has it been hitherto in the political order? Nothing. What does it desire to be? Something.")

The Long Exit of Forced and Semiforced Labor

In the end, the French Revolution abolished the nobility's privileges while at the same time strengthening the rights of property owners. For those who owned nothing, the balance sheet is ambiguous. The fact that they were no longer subject to the lord's whims and that they benefited from a judicial system that was centralized at the national level and dealt with all citizens in the same way constituted, in theory, genuine progress. But the concentration of property in the hands of the richest 1 percent of the population, including both nobles and bourgeois, scarcely diminished between 1780 and 1800 before it started rising again between 1800 and 1910. For the poorest 50 percent, there was virtually no progress.[3]

We must also situate the Revolution in a long process of transforming the status of labor in French and other European societies. On the eve of 1789, servitude was supposed to have disappeared from the French countryside centuries earlier. An often-mentioned explanation is that the relative scarcity of labor, along with the collapse of institutions following the Black Death in the middle of the fourteenth century, favored the eviction and emancipation of the serfs. Many historians have emphasized the excessively mechanistic nature of this explanation. In reality, everything depended on the local power relationships, which is evident from the calcification of serfdom in Eastern Europe after the fourteenth century and its belated abolition in the nineteenth century.[4] For the most optimistic medievalists, it was the

---

3. See Chapter 2, Figure 4.

4. The calcification of serfdom in the East (and particularly around the Baltic) seems to be explained in part by the intensification of cereal exports to the West in the fourteenth and fifteenth centuries and the property owners' ability to impose a harsher system of labor. See T. Raster, "Serfs and the Market: Second Serfdom and the East-West Goods Exchange, 1579–1859," unpublished manuscript, Paris School of Economics, June 2, 2019. The abolition of serfdom in Prussia in 1807, in Austria-Hungary in 1848, and in Russia in 1861 was accompanied by compensations paid to property owners by the former serfs until the beginning of the twentieth century. See S. A. Eddie, *Freedom's*

trifunctional Christian ideology that made it possible to put a gradual end to servile labor and to unify workers within a single class of laborers who were free and celebrated as such in Western Europe, in accord with a process that was already well underway even before the Black Death.[5] That was perhaps partly the case, but in truth the available sources do not allow us to be very precise, so numerous are the local and regional variations.

What is certain is that pockets of serfdom still existed in France at the time of the Revolution, for example on the lands of the Abbey of St. Claude (a great ecclesiastical seigneury located in the Jura Mountains), and that restrictions on moving around to find work were not definitively and systematically lifted until the Revolution. The peasants generally had freedom of movement (a notion that was often merely theoretical when they had neither goods nor networks), but they owed days of unpaid work to their lord. Under the Revolution, these *corvées,* or labor obligations, would be the object of very lively debates. During the Revolution's most egalitarian and redistributive phase, in 1792–1794, the members of the Convention emphasized that the *corvées* betrayed by their very name their origins in serfdom and feudalism, and consequently they demanded that the *corvées* be abolished without compensation because they were aristocratic privileges, similar to those targeted on the night of August 4. But during most of the Revolution, in 1789 and then again starting in 1795, with the return of censitary suffrage,[6] a much more conservative notion was established, namely that *corvées* were ultimately only rent pay-

---

Price: *Serfdom, Subjection and Reform in Prussia, 1648–1848* (Oxford: Oxford University Press, 2013); T. Dennison, "The Institutional Framework of Serfdom in Russia: The View from 1861," in *Serfdom and Slavery in the European Economy, 11th–18th Centuries,* ed. S. Cavaciocchi (Florence: Florence University Press, 2014).

5. M. Arnoux, *Le Temps des laboureurs. Travail, ordre social et croissance en Europe (XIe–XIVe siècle)* (Paris: Albin Michel, 2012). Compare J. Le Goff, "Les trois fonctions indo-européennes, l'histoire et l'Europe féodale," *Annales histoire, sciences sociales* 34, no. 6 (1979): 1187–1215.

6. The Constitution of 1793 instituted universal male suffrage, but there was not time to implement it.

ments that should be simply renamed as such in the future, and that any other decision would risk damaging, by osmosis, the whole system of property. That is how the feudal *corvées* became capitalist rents, in most cases without further ado. One day's unpaid labor each week for example, could be converted to a rent equivalent to one-fifth or one-sixth of the agricultural product.[7]

We must also emphasize the harshness of the system of discipline at work and the tendency to strengthen property rights in the course of the eighteenth century and during a large part of the nineteenth century. In the United Kingdom, the Enclosure Acts, which were adopted beginning in 1604 and strengthened repeatedly, especially between 1773 and 1801, resulted in the erection of hedges around parcels of land and put an end to the poor's right to use common lands and pastures. They also helped fill the roads with unemployed workers who were easy to exploit, and whose labor fed British industrialization. The Black Act of 1723 also weakened the most deprived by instituting capital punishment for timber thieves and small game hunters, people who hunted or gathered at night, their faces blackened to avoid being recognized, on lands that were not their own, and that the property owners now wanted to reserve for their own exclusive use.[8] The

---

7. On these debates, see T. Piketty, *Capital and Ideology* (Cambridge, MA: Belknap Press of Harvard University Press, 2020), 102–109; and the fascinating R. Blaufarb, *The Great Demarcation: The French Revolution and the Invention of Modern Property* (Oxford: Oxford University Press, 2016). Eddie, in *Freedom's Price,* goes so far as to propose the idea that the abolition of serfdom in Prussia in 1807 (with compensations for property owners) ultimately did more for poor peasants than the French Revolution.

8. See the classic E. P. Thompson, *Whigs and Hunters: The Origin of the Black Act* (New York: Pantheon, 1975). This act targeted people who hunted stags, cut down trees, poached on fishponds, or pulled up copses. An alleged felon could be sentenced on the spot to be hanged. Initially intended to last three years, this law was extended and hardened over more than a century. We see a similar hardening of property law elsewhere in Europe, for example in Prussia in 1821, which had an impact on the young Karl Marx and helped convince him that property is a social relationship historically constructed and instituted under the aegis of the state and the propertied classes, and not a natural, atemporal reality. For its part, the French Revolution decreed that private lands and woods would be open to everyone for hunting, a measure that is still in force today.

new proletariat, reduced to poverty, was subject until 1875 to the aptly named Master and Servant Act, which gave employers full rights, including a rule that criminalized efforts to poach servants, making it possible to keep wages extremely low.[9]

In the colonies, the legal system was even less egalitarian: forced labor is clearly present until at least 1946 and even until independence was achieved. In French cities, labor union and worker mobilization, along with intense social struggles, were to make it possible to impose new norms more quickly. In France, laws on child labor were passed in 1841, on labor union freedom in 1884, on accidents at work in 1898, on collective conventions and the eight-hour workday in 1919, on paid vacations in 1936, and on Social Security in 1945. The establishment of regular salaries and a veritable "salaried society" marks a major advance in civilization that has appeared only gradually, in multiple forms, and over very long periods. For example, it was not until 1969–1977 that monthly salaries (guaranteeing a fixed income each month rather than each day or week) were to be found generally.[10] We also know that this evolution is partly reversible, depending on political and economic power relationships. Salarial status has thus diminished significantly of late, with the self-employed worker system introduced into the French 2008 law "modernizing" the economy. The keystone of that law is smaller social contributions and fewer legal

---

9. The best proof that living conditions were deteriorating at the end of the eighteenth century and the beginning of the nineteenth century is no doubt the diminution of the height of conscripts, in particular in urban and industrial centers. See S. Nicholas and R. H. Steckel, "Heights and Living Standards of English Workers during the Early Years of Industrialization," *Journal of Economic History* 51, no. 4 (1991): 937–957.

10. R. Castel, *Les Métamorphoses de la question sociale* (Paris: Folio, 1995) 594–595; R. Castel and C. Haroche, *Propriété privée, propriété sociale, propriété de soi* (Paris: Pluriel, 2001). Compare C. Didry, *L'Institution du travail. Droit et salariat dans l'histoire* (Paris: La Dispute, 2016); M. Margairaz and M. Pigenet, *Le Prix du travail. France et espaces coloniaux, xixe–xxie siècles* (Paris: Éditions de la Sorbonne, 2019). On the long process of the "socialization" of law through the case of labor law, see L. Duguit, *Les Transformations générales du droit privé depuis le Code Napoléon* (Paris: Alcan, 1912), which is situated in a framework close to the Solidarism and Durkheimian socialism of his time.

protections, a development whose harmful consequences for workers could be noted during the pandemic of 2020 and 2021. The development of digital platforms and gig workers paid by the task now constitutes as much a redoubtable threat to salarial status as to our liberties, and we will be able to fight it only if the public authority regains control of the sector and implements new laws.[11] We must also insist on the historical fact that the development of a more protective salarial status has occurred especially within the nation states of the North, sometimes at the price of reinforcing borders. Workers in the South have not been much involved in this movement; on the scale of the global economy, they are just as stuck in their territory of origin at the beginning of the twenty-first century as the serfs of the Abbey of St. Claude were in the eighteenth century. The march toward equality and dignity with regard to work is an ongoing battle that now requires a profound transformation of the world economic system. We will return to it.

Sweden in 1900: One Man, a Hundred Votes

Along with the battles for labor laws and workers' rights, the campaign for universal suffrage is the other great social and political struggle of the nineteenth and the beginning of the twentieth century. In 1815, Louis XVIII installed a political system like the one he had observed in England, with a Chamber of Peers reserved for the upper nobility (like the House of Lords) and a Chamber of Deputies elected by census suffrage (like the House of Commons, but in a still more limited way). Specifically, during the first Restoration, only the 1 percent of adult males who paid the most direct taxes had the right to vote. The

---

11. S. Zuboff, *The Age of Surveillance Capitalism* (New York: PublicAffairs, 2019); C. Durand, *Techno-féodalisme. Critique de l'économie numérique* (Paris: Zones, 2020); S. Abdelnour and D. Méda, *Les Nouveaux Travailleurs des applis* (Paris: PUF, 2020). The best solution is to define as a "systemic platform" all platforms used by a large fraction of the population and to treat them as a quasi-public service, with strict regulation of the algorithms and respect for fundamental rights.

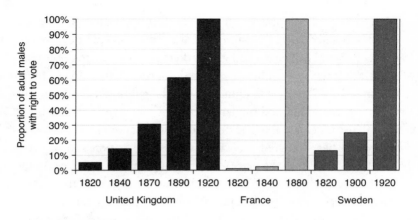

FIGURE 16. The Evolution of Male Suffrage in Europe, 1820–1920

In the United Kingdom, the percentage of adult males having the right to vote (taking into account the taxes owed and property held in order to have this right) rose from 5 percent in 1820 to 30 percent in 1870 and 100 percent in 1920. In France, it rose from 1 percent in 1820 to 100 percent in 1880. *Sources and series:* piketty.pse. ens.fr/equality

threshold that had to be met to be a candidate for office was even higher, and concerned only 0.2 percent of adult males.[12] Suffrage was slightly broadened after the Revolution of 1830: the number of electors under the July Monarchy rose to a little more than 2 percent of adult males, while the number of those eligible to be candidates for office was raised to about 0.4 percent of adult males. Universal suffrage for men was implemented briefly following the Revolution of 1848, and then definitively starting in 1871, before being finally extended to women in 1944. In the United Kingdom, the march toward universal male suffrage was much more gradual (see Figure 16). The proportion of adult males who had the right to vote was scarcely

---

12. The direct taxes involved were levied mainly on property (land and buildings) and on licenses (based on business assets: factories, equipment). To simplify, it concerned the largest property owners, just as in other censitary systems. In France the law of the "double vote" promulgated in 1820 introduced the possibility for the wealthiest censitary electors (roughly speaking, the ones eligible for office) to vote a second time to designate part of the deputies.

5 percent in 1820, then rose to 14 percent following the electoral reform of 1832, 30 percent after the reform of 1867, and especially
60 percent with the electoral law of 1884, which transformed the political situation and led to much more redistributive social and fiscal
legislation. Universal male suffrage was finally introduced in 1918, followed by universal female suffrage in 1928.

A particularly interesting but little-known case is that of Sweden.
From 1527 to 1865, the Swedish monarchy relied on a parliament, the
Riksdag, which included representatives of the four orders or estates
that then composed the kingdom: the nobility, the clergy, the urban
bourgeoisie, and the property-owning peasantry. In 1865, this system
was replaced by a censitary parliamentary system composed of two
chambers: an upper chamber elected by a small minority of large
property owners (scarcely 9,000 electors, or less than 1 percent of the
adult male population), and a lower chamber. The lower chamber was
also censitary, requiring property ownership, but considerably more
open. Suffrage was not expanded in Sweden until the reforms of 1909–
1911; property-owning conditions were completely abolished for men
only in 1919, and not until 1921 was universal suffrage extended to
include women. Around 1900, with a little more than 20 percent of
adult men having the right to vote, Sweden was one of the least advanced European nations.

Above all, the great peculiarity of the censitary system used in
Sweden between 1865 and 1911 is that the number of votes an elector
had depended on how much tax he paid and how much property and
income he had.[13] Within the 20 percent of men rich enough to be able
to vote, electors were divided into about forty groups, each associated
with a different electoral weight. Concretely, members of the least
wealthy group each had one vote, whereas those in the richest group
had as many as fifty-four votes each. The exact scale determining the

---

13. See the fascinating article by E. Bengtsson, "The Swedish Sonderweg in Question:
Democratization and Inequality in Comparative Perspective, c. 1750–1920," *Past and
Present* 244, no. 1 (2018): 123–161.

electoral weight (*fyrkar*) of each elector was set using a formula that depended on the amount of the taxes he paid, the properties he owned, and his income. A similar system was used for municipal elections, with the additional particularity that corporations also had the right to participate in these local elections, and they also had a number of votes depending on the amount of their taxes and the amount of their goods and profits. However, for urban municipalities, a single elector, whether a private person or an enterprise, could not have more than one hundred votes. For rural municipalities, on the other hand, there was no ceiling of this kind, to the point that during the municipal elections of 1871, there were fifty-four voting districts in Sweden in which a single elector cast more than 50 percent of the votes. The prime minister, Count Arvid Posse, was among these dictators enjoying impeccable democratic legitimacy. In the 1880s, Posse cast the majority of the votes in the district where he lived and where his family owned a vast estate. There were also 414 voting districts in which a single elector cast more than 25 percent of the votes.

Sweden's astonishing hypercensitary experiment is interesting in more than one way. In a few decades, Sweden moved from an extremely inegalitarian system based on property ownership to a relatively egalitarian society—at least more egalitarian than all other known societies. This change occurred when the Social Democrats came to power in the early 1920s, after an intense campaign by labor unions and workers, and then remained in power on a quasi-permanent basis from 1932 to 2006. On the eve of World War I, the concentration of property was just as extreme in Sweden as it was in France or the United Kingdom (see Figure 17), and Sweden was incontestably the European country that had gone furthest in the constitutional and electoral codification of its inequality.[14] Then, during the interwar

---

14. Another interesting case, though less extreme, is that of the Kingdom of Prussia, the chief component of the German Empire from 1871 to 1918. From 1848 to 1918 Prussia had an unusual electoral system involving three categories of citizens defined by the amount of taxes paid. More precisely, Prussian electors were divided into three classes

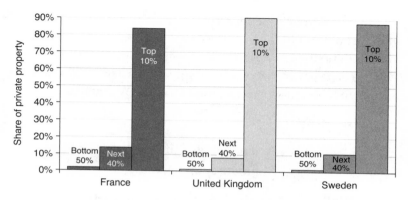

FIGURE 17. Extreme Patrimonial Inequality: European Property-Owner Societies in the Belle Époque (1880–1914)

The share of the highest 10 percent of wealth in total private property (real, occupational, and financial assets, net of debt) was on average 84 percent in France between 1880 and 1914 (as compared with 14 percent for the following 40 percent and 2 percent for the poorest 50 percent), 91 percent in the United Kingdom (as compared with 8 percent and 1 percent), and 88 percent in Sweden (as compared with 11 percent and 1 percent). *Sources and series:* piketty.pse.ens.fr/equality

period, the Social Democrats took control of the Swedish government and put their country's state power in the service of a completely different political project. Instead of using property registers and incomes to distribute the right to vote, they began to use them to make the richest people pay progressively heavier taxes, all in order to finance public services. These services allowed relatively egalitarian (here again, in comparison to other countries) access to health care and education for the whole of the population. This experiment shows how little anything is fixed. People sometimes imagine that there are cultures or civilizations that tend by nature toward equality or inequality: Sweden is supposed to have always been egalitarian, perhaps because of an ancient passion proceeding from the Vikings, whereas India and

---

defined in such a way that each class paid one-third of the total taxes and then elected a third of the Great Electors, who themselves elected the deputies.

its castes are eternally inegalitarian, no doubt for reasons just as mystical that proceed from the Aryans. In truth, everything depends on the institutions and rules that each human community gives itself, contingent on power relationships, mobilizations, and social struggles, within unstable trajectories that would merit close examination.

The Metamorphoses of Privileges: Democracy and Money

The path followed by Sweden also shows the boundless imagination that the property-owning classes can show in structuring institutions to their advantage. It would be a mistake to think that this ingenuity no longer exists: today's billionaires would not dare to openly demand rights to vote like the ones Sweden used to have, but they often resort to other methods to arrive at the same ends. In particular, we must emphasize that electoral democracies have never provided a truly satisfactory solution to the problem of financing political campaigns, far from it. Theoretically, we could imagine that an obvious corollary of universal suffrage would have been to set up an egalitarian system in which each citizen would have the same amount to contribute to parties and political movements of his choice, the keystone of the system being an absolute prohibition on larger donations and a strict limitation of electoral expenditures, so as to put all candidates and all voters on an equal footing. We could even imagine that this political equality might be constitutionally guaranteed, and that these arrangements would be protected with as much determination as universal suffrage itself.

However, not only is this not the case, but the opposite is true. Some countries have developed timid systems of public financing for campaigns and political parties—in Germany in the 1950s, in the United States and in Italy in the 1970s and 1980s, and also in France in the 1990s. But these systems are clearly insufficient, and they are usually completely overwhelmed by the flow of private money. This is particularly the case in the United States, where lobbyists have succeeded in convincing judges that no ceiling for political expenditures can be set (and that imposing any ceiling would be equivalent to violating the wealthiest people's freedom of expression).[15] But it is also the case in Europe, India, and Brazil. Almost everywhere, the tax deductions that are granted for political contributions, as well as for other kinds of donations, amount to subsidizing the wealthiest people's political or cultural preferences with the money of the poorest. In France, a wealthy voter giving 7,500 euros (the current ceiling) to his preferred political party has a right to a tax deduction of 5,000 euros, financed by the rest of the taxpayers. In comparison, the ordinary person has a right to a deduction of about 1 euro per voter in the form of public financing for political parties.[16] This example shows the extent to which censitary systems still exist: they have simply become a little less visible.

The question of how to finance the media, think tanks, and other organs that shape public opinion raises the same problems. Laws seeking to limit the concentration of the press or to reduce the power of stockholders relative to that of editors were set up in some countries, often shortly after World War II, but they are notoriously insufficient and have never been adapted to the digital age. In France, a handful of billionaires now owns more than half of the news media. This situation is found everywhere, in poor countries as well as in rich ones. The best solution would be to change the legal framework and

---

15. T. Kuhner, *Capitalism v. Democracy: Money in Politics and the Free Market Constitution* (Stanford CA: Stanford University Press, 2014); L. Bartels, *Unequal Democracy: The Political Economy of the New Gilded Age*, 2nd ed. (Princeton, NJ: Princeton University Press, 2016).

16. J. Cagé, *The Price of Democracy*, trans. P. Camiller (Cambridge, MA: Harvard University Press, 2020); J. Cagé, *Libres et égaux en voix* (Paris: Fayard, 2020). In all, tax deductions for political donations (benefiting mainly the wealthiest 1 percent of taxpayers, and especially the wealthiest 0.01 percent) cost the public treasury about the same amount as total official public financing (based particularly on the results of the last elections, and thus granting the same importance to all electors). The author proposes to replace this inegalitarian system with "democratic equality vouchers" of the same value for everyone, and to apply a similar system to philanthropy and to the media.

adopt a law that truly democratizes the media, guaranteeing employees and journalists half the seats in the governing organs, whatever their legal form might be, opening their doors to representatives from the reading public, and drastically limiting stockholders' power.[17]

The essential point is that this critique of contemporary democracy and of its capture by big money must be accompanied by proposals for precise institutional mechanisms making it possible to move toward greater equality. In the course of the twentieth century, the critique of "bourgeois" democracy has too often served as an excuse—by the leaders and bureaucratic classes holding power in the Soviet bloc, but also in some newly independent countries—for doing away with pluralist elections or taking control of the media. The refusal to hold elections is never justified. On the other hand, the establishment of a radically egalitarian way of financing political parties, electoral campaigns, and the media is not only justified but indispensable for being able to speak of a democracy that is truly based on a principle of equality. This must go hand-in-hand with a multiplicity of modes of political participation, notably in the form of citizen assemblies and deliberative referenda. But here as well, the question of how to finance campaigns and achieve equality in the production and diffusion of information must be dealt with rigorously.[18]

In practice, this protection of democracy and political equality does not exist. In most countries, the constitutions and the courts tend on the contrary to protect the established order, in the sense that they set up very strong legal constraints seeking to prevent a political majority from proceeding, for example, to undertake an ambitious revision of the property system (or even simply to limit the power of

---

17. J. Cagé and B. Huet, *L'information est un bien public. Refonder la propriété des médias* (Paris: Seuil, 2021).

18. The success of the referendum organized by Uber and Lyft to preserve their extremely precarious model in California in 2020 illustrates the limits of an idyllic vision of direct democracy, as well as the need to reconceive a salarial status that makes it possible to reconcile protection and autonomy.

stockholders). Redistribution of property is generally subjected to an obligation to indemnify, which in practice makes any genuine transfer impossible. If someone owns everything that can be owned in a country, and if it is necessary to fully indemnify him for any transfer of his properties to other persons or collectivities, that means it is impossible to change anything at all in the initial situation, at least within a legal framework. If we add that the rules governing constitutional amendments tend to make them very difficult (as in France, where the Senate, not a very democratic body, has the right to veto),[19] we can see that in some cases this can completely immobilize the situation. Unsurprisingly, each system often tries to prevent the principles it holds dear from being changed, and even attempts to make any effort to challenge them illegal.

The consequence is that these rules have been regularly broken in the course of history. The march toward equality is full of revolutionary moments when political institutions are redefined in order to make it possible to transform social and economic structures. When the Estates General met in 1789, no rule provided that a National Assembly could proclaim itself and give itself the right to abolish the nobility's privileges and decide to expropriate the clergy's property while at the same time trampling on the right of veto that the two privileged orders had enjoyed for centuries. We shall note, moreover, that none of the regime changes that have occurred in France since 1789 (there are about ten of them) took place in accord with the rules set forth by their predecessors.[20] In the United Kingdom, it was in a

---

19. In France, the Senate is elected by an electoral college that is structurally conservative because rural zones are overrepresented in it. In 1946, as a result of pressure exercised by socialists and communists, it lost its right to veto ordinary legislation (a right to veto that under the Third Republic had helped delay by several decades many essential fiscal and social reforms), but retained it for constitutional amendments, which must still be approved in identical terms by each of the two chambers by a simple majority vote before being submitted either to the two chambers in joint session, where they must be approved by a two-thirds supermajority, or to ratification by referendum.

20. Up until now, the most important constitutional revision made by the Fifth Republic, the one adopted in 1962 establishing the election of the president by universal

climate of extreme tension that the House of Lords, which clearly dominated British bicameralism until the end of the nineteenth century, was forced in 1909–1911 to renounce its right to veto and to yield power to the House of Commons forever, in the eruptive context of the vote on the "People's Budget" and the creation of a progressive tax on total income.[21] In the United States, Roosevelt had to threaten to "pack" the Supreme Court in 1937 so that it would lift the veto by which it was blocking his social legislation in the name of free enterprise, even though he had just been reelected with 61 percent of the vote.[22] It is probable that episodes of the same kind will occur in the future in times of crisis—times that it is impossible to foresee. Here, too, this observation must be used not as an excuse for trampling on all legal rules, but on the contrary, to propose new rules that are more profoundly egalitarian and democratic than the preceding ones, without losing sight of the fact that the law must be a tool for emancipation and not for the preservation of positions of power.

---

suffrage, was also made on the basis of General De Gaulle's blatant violation (for which the Constitutional Council he appointed had no difficulty pardoning him). Nothing, then or now, provided that such a revision can be decided by referendum without prior approval by the two chambers.

21. The Lords took the risk of vetoing this popular proposal. The Liberal prime minister, Lloyd George, feared his party might be replaced by Labour (which it ultimately was). He needed to give guarantees to the new electors coming from the disadvantaged classes, and thus decided to double down. He had the House of Commons adopt a constitutional law depriving the Lords of any legislative veto power, while at the same time calling fresh elections, which he won by a landslide. The Lords then found themselves caught in the trap of the Salisbury Doctrine, a verbal promise formulated in the 1880s according to which the Lords had to agree to ratify legislation for which the Commons had obtained explicit popular support. They were forced to approve the two texts and to sign their own death warrant after the king threatened to fill the House of Lords with several hundred new members if they dared to betray their promise to the country. See Piketty, *Capital and Ideology*, 176–181.

22. We may note in passing the archaic nature of the US Supreme Court, whose judges are named for life like the pope of the Catholic Church and the apostles of the Mormon church. However, a pontifical bull of 1970 denied cardinals over eighty years old the right to vote in papal elections, which proves that all institutions can be reformed, even the most venerable ones.

The Persistence of Censitary Voting: Economic Plutocracy

If there is a domain where censitary voting continues to reign, it is certainly that of economic power. In joint-stock companies, the stock-holders legally have all the power, with voting rights proportional to the number of stocks they hold. It might be said that this is the definition of capitalism, but in fact it is a specific institutional arrangement that is not particularly natural and has been established only gradually, in the context of specific circumstances and power relationships.[23] Theoretically, other rules are perfectly conceivable. For example, nothing guarantees that stockholders are more competent to manage an enterprise than a company's employees, or that they are more invested in its success over the long term. Often, the opposite is true: an investment fund can put capital into an enterprise and withdraw it again in a short period of time, whereas employees generally invest a major part of their lives, their energy, and their skills. In many respects, employees constitute the company's first long-term investors. If we look at the big picture, we can only be surprised by this persistence of plutocracy in economic matters.

More balanced systems have been tried since the middle of the twentieth century, even in nominally "capitalist" countries. In Germany, the system known as "comanagement" (sometimes still called

---

23. In the eighteenth century and the beginning of the nineteenth, the first joint-stock companies were established, often around a principle of equality among associates. They then gradually introduced systems with several classes of voting rights, so that the persons who contributed the most capital had more votes. However, they did not go so far as to institute a proportional voting system pure and simple, because it was feared that would lead to an excessive concentration of power in a small group of persons, and harm both the quality of the deliberation and relations among associates. In the United Kingdom, it was not until the enactment of the Company Law of 1906 that this principle of proportionality between the number of stocks owned and voting rights became by law the joint-stock companies' default mode of governance (the statutes may still depart from this principle, and distinguish several categories of stocks and all sorts of specific rules). See E. McGaughey, "Participation in Corporate Governance," unpublished ms., London School of Economics, November 4, 2014.

Mitbestimmung, or "codetermination") consists in dividing up the seats in a company's board of directors or supervisory board with one half being representatives of the employees and the other half representatives of the stockholders. This system was introduced in 1951 in the steel and coal industries, and then extended in 1952 to all large companies (all sectors taken together). The 1976 law established the system currently in force in Germany, with one-third of the seats for employees in companies with between 500 and 2,000 employees, and half the seats for those with more than 2,000 employees.[24] Comparable arrangements were adopted in Austria, Sweden, Denmark, and Norway, where the rules also apply to small and medium-sized enterprises.[25] On the other hand, comanagement is at this time not very widespread outside Germanic and Nordic Europe.[26]

In practice, the importance of this transformation must not be exaggerated: in the event of a tie vote, it is still the stockholders who make the decision. Nonetheless, it is a clear modification of the usual capitalist rules. It will be noted that 50 percent of the voting rights are attributed to employees as such, as "investors in labor," independently of any ownership of the capital. If in addition the employees own 10 or 20 percent of the capital, or if a public collectivity holds a 10 or 20 percent share, then a stockholder can find himself in the

---

24. E. McGaughey, "The Codetermination Bargains: The History of German Corporate and Labour Law," *Columbia Journal of European Law* 23, no. 1 (2017): 135–176. Compare S. J. Silvia, *Holding the Shop Together: German Industrial Relations in the Postwar Era* (Ithaca NY: Cornell University Press, 2013).

25. In Sweden, employees have only one-third of the seats, but the rule applies to all companies with more than twenty-five employees. The threshold is thirty-five employees in Denmark and fifty employees in Norway. In Austria, the rule is applied only beyond 300 employees, which in practice considerably limits its field of application (almost as much as in Germany).

26. Several proposed European directives seeking to impose minimal rules (between a third and half of the seats for employees) were debated in 1972, 1983, and 1988, but they met with fierce hostility from the conservative parties (and with the limited enthusiasm of the French socialists and the British Labour Party, who were at the time betting mainly on nationalizations).

minority, even if he owns 80 or 90 percent of the stock.[27] From the stockholders' point of view, this amounts to an unacceptable challenge to their natural rights. These measures in Germany were obtained after extremely tense social and political struggles, in a context in which the power relationships clearly favored labor, namely, after the trauma of the 1929 crisis and the compromising of the economic elites on account of their dealings with the Nazis. The German laws of 1951 and 1952 were passed by the Christian Democrats, but in response to intense pressure exerted by the Social Democrats and especially by labor unions, who at that point were making even more ambitious demands, such as their participation, on an equal footing, in regional and federal planning commissions.

We must also stress that these laws could be implemented only because the German constitution of 1949, the Basic Law for the Federal Republic of Germany, had previously adopted an innovative definition of property considered in terms of its social goal. In particular, the constitution asserts at the outset that the right to property is legitimate only insofar as it "shall . . . serve the public good" (Article 14). It explicitly mentions that the socialization of the means of production and the redefinition of the system of private property enter into the domain of the law, in terms that open the possibility of measures such as comanagement. This text is situated in the tradition begun by the German constitution of 1919, which was itself adopted in a quasi-insurrectional context, and which made possible redistributions of land and new social and syndical rights, rights that were suspended from 1933 to 1945.[28] Employers' groups repeatedly tried to contest comanagement in the courts, notably following the law of 1976 adopted by the Social Democrats, but their complaint was dismissed by the

---

27. For example, the German Land of Lower Saxony holds 13 percent of Volkswagen's capital, and the company's statutes guarantee it 20 percent of the voting rights, in addition to 50 percent of the votes going to employees.

28. "Land, natural resources, and means of production may . . . be transferred to public ownership or other forms of public enterprise by a law that determines the nature and extent of compensation" (Basic Law for the Federal Republic of Germany, Article 15).

Constitutional Court, on the basis of the constitution of 1949. Conversely, several countries, including France, have retained in their fundamental texts a definition of property seen as an absolute and natural right, a definition that comes from the end of the eighteenth century, so that the adoption of rules of comanagement in the German fashion without an amendment to the constitution would be very likely to be contested in court.[29]

Participatory Socialism and Power Sharing

In theory, a deepening of the rules of Germanic and Nordic comanagement is conceivable. All studies show that this system has made it possible to achieve a better involvement of employees in companies' long-term strategies and greater collective efficiency.[30] For example, we can imagine a system in which part of the employees' representatives would have 50 percent of the votes in all enterprises, including the smallest ones, and in which, on the other hand, the share of the voting rights held by an individual stockholder (within the 50 percent of voting rights reserved for stockholders) cannot exceed a certain threshold in sufficiently large companies. Thus an individual stock-

---

29. "The Declaration of the Rights of Man and of the Citizen" (1789) is still part of the constitutional corpus. Article 2 provides that: "The aim of every political association is the preservation of the natural and imprescriptible rights of Man. These rights are Liberty, Property, Safety, and Resistance to Oppression." The Constitution offers no explanation of the naturalist definition of property (like those provided by the German constitutions of 1919 and 1949), leaving judges free to interpret it as they understand it, and particularly in the conservative way most favorable to maintaining the already established rights of property owners. In 2013, a French law introduced for the first time a timid presence of employees on the governing boards of large companies (one seat out of twelve, a rule confirmed in 2019 with a slight extension of its field of application), but it is very possible that a law according half the seats to employees would be censured in the absence of a preceding constitutional amendment.

30. E. McGaughey, "A Twelve-Point Plan for Labour and a Manifesto for Labour Law," *Industrial Law Journal* 46, no. 1 (2017): 169–184; Silvia, *Holding the Shop Together*; S. Jäger, B. Schoefer, and J. Heining, "Labor in the Boardroom," *Quarterly Journal of Economics* 136, no. 2 (2021): 669–725; J. Harju, S. Jäger, and B. Schoefer, "Voice at Work," MIT, unpublished manuscript, June 2021.

holder might have a maximum of 90 percent of the stockholders' voting rights in small companies (fewer than ten employees), and this threshold would be lowered linearly to 10 percent of the stockholders' voting rights in larger companies (more than ninety employees).[31] In this way, a single stockholder who is also an employee of the company could have a majority of the votes in a very small company (in this case, as many as ten employees) but would have to rely increasingly on collective deliberation with other employees as soon as the company became significantly larger (see Figure 18). In a very small company, the maintenance of a strong connection between the amount of capital contributed and economic power can be justified: if all one's savings are invested in a life work (for example, opening an organic grocery store or a café-restaurant), there's nothing abnormal about that person having more votes than an employee hired the day before. These types of investors are more likely to reduce expenditures, for example, in order to develop the project.[32] On the other hand, if the project involves many employees and collective resources, such a concentration of power is no longer justified. A single stockholder who is not himself an employee would lose the majority of votes as soon as the first employee was hired in the system outlined here. If the employees themselves have contributed capital, even a minority stake, they would obtain a majority of the votes more rapidly. It goes without saying that all these parameters are given only as illustrations and would have to be the object of vast deliberation and experimentation.

The system of "participatory socialism" described here has only one objective: to illustrate the very great diversity of possible economic systems. On the basis of the historical experience at our disposal, it is

---

31. Piketty, *Capital and Ideology*, 972–975. This system generalizes the rules setting a ceiling on voting rights already proposed regarding media companies by J. Cagé, *Saving the Media* (Cambridge, MA: Belknap Press of Harvard University Press, 2016).

32. The form of the cooperative company based on a strict equality of voting rights among employees can be adapted for certain projects but imposing it systematically would be counterproductive.

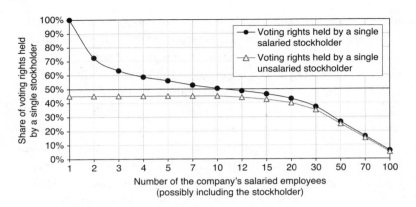

FIGURE 18. Participatory Socialism and Power Sharing

In the system of participatory socialism envisioned here, a single stockholder (owning 100 percent of the company's stock) has 73 percent of voting rights if the company has two salaried employees (including himself), 51 percent if he has ten salaried employees (including himself), and he loses the majority beyond ten salaried employees. A single, unsalaried stockholder has 45 percent of voting rights if the company has fewer than ten salaried employees, and then this share declines regularly and reaches 5 percent with 100 salaried employees.

Note: Salaried employees (whether or not they are stockholders) share 50 percent of voting rights, and within that 50 percent, an individual stockholder cannot hold more than 90 percent (or 45 percent of the votes) in a company with fewer than ten salaried employees; this fraction falls linearly to 10 percent (or 5 percent of the votes) in companies with more than ninety salaried employees (the unattributed stockholders' votes are reattributed to the salaried employees). *Sources and series:* piketty.pse.ens.fr/equality

clear that the establishment of such a system would require very strong popular support. In most countries, as in France, such a transformation would also involve a substantial revision of the constitution, which could probably be made only during moments of crisis, as has often happened in the past. We shall see that such profound changes would also have to be accompanied by a complete revision of the fiscal system, so as to allow a true circulation of property and economic power, as well as the redefinition of multiple international treaties, in particular those that concern the movement of capital. I am not suggesting that such a system could easily be set up next month, but simply insisting on the fact that no less gigantic transformations of the legal, fiscal, and social system continually occurred between 1780 and 2020, and that this process is not going to stop suddenly now. It is therefore not pointless to inquire into the subsequent stages of participatory socialism on the basis of the experience available.

Concerning the question of power-sharing in enterprises, and more generally the debate on the transformation of the economic system and the emergence of new forms of democratic socialism, it is striking to note to what point discussions have gained new vigor since the financial crisis of 2008. In several countries, especially in the United States and Britain, some important political movements have set out to formulate unprecedented proposals intended to establish rules that are inspired, in one way or another, by the Germanic and Nordic systems of comanagement.[33] If approved, the conditions for their adoption worldwide could be created. Within the intellectual and syndical world, ambitious collective and international projects like the "Manifesto for Labour Law" remind us to what extent there are several ways of organizing the economic system, and in particular the power relationships within enterprises.[34] In addition to the question of comanagement, the whole of syndical law must be rethought

---

33. See, for example, two bills introduced by Democratic senators in the United States in 2018–2020. The Reward Work Act of 2018 proposes that employees may elect one-third of the board of directors of listed companies; the Accountable Capitalism Act requires that 40 percent of the directors of all large companies be elected by salaried employees, and that political donations be approved by boards of directors by a 75 percent majority (since Supreme Court rulings make it impossible to forbid such political donations). See Reward Work Act of 2018 (S. 2605 and HR 6096; S. 915, introduced March 27, 2019; HR 3355, introduced October 17, 2019 S. 2605 and HR 6096); Accountable Capitalism Act S. 3348, introduced August 15, 2018; S. 3215, introduced January 16, 2020). On the new platform of the British Labour Party, see K. Ewing, G. Hendy, and C. Jones, *Rolling out the Manifesto for Labour Law* (Liverpool, UK: Institute of Employment Rights, 2018).

34. I. Ferreras, J. Battilana, and D. Méda, eds., *Le Manifeste Travail. Démocratiser, démarchandiser, dépolluer* (Paris: Seuil, 2020). Compare I. Ferreras, *Firms as Political Entities: Saving Democracy through Economic Bicameralism* (Cambridge: Cambridge University Press, 2017). See also McGaughey, "A Twelve-Point Plan for Labour," which

at the European and transnational level, thereby facilitating the support and participation of employees, reserving public markets for enterprises that sign collective agreements, and finally generalizing labor unions' right to enter the workplace and to organize meetings there.[35] Although it is too soon to know their impact, these initiatives indicate the liveliness of the debates. We shall also see that the discussions initiated in Sweden in the 1970s and 1980s on the subject of "employee funds" (called Meidner funds) have recently picked up again. But before we analyze in greater detail the prospects for future transformations, we have to understand better how the very intense compression of economic inequalities that took place in the twentieth century in many countries, and in particular in the world's main capitalist powers, was produced.

---

proposes that administrators be elected by assemblies composed of both employees and stockholders.

35. See the platform of the labor federation UNI Global Union. Compare S. Block and B. Sachs, "Clean Slate for Worker Power: Building a Just Economy and Democracy," a project of the Labor and Worklife Program, Harvard Law School, n.d.

6

THE "GREAT REDISTRIBUTION"

1914–1980

Between 1914 and 1980, inequalities in income and wealth decreased markedly in the Western world as a whole (the United Kingdom, Germany, France, Sweden, and the United States), and in Japan, Russia, China, and India, although in different ways, which we will explore in a later chapter. Here we will focus on the Western countries and improve our understanding of how this "great redistribution" took place.

The first factor was the welfare state's spectacular rise in power. This long-term development was in large measure the result of social struggles and mobilization of the socialist and labor movements since the end of the nineteenth century. Nevertheless, it was greatly accelerated by the two world wars and the Depression following the stock market crash of 1929—three events that in the three decades between 1914 and 1945 completely overturned the power relationships between labor and capital. The second factor was the development of a very progressive tax on income and inheritance, which made it possible to massively reduce the concentration of wealth and economic power at the apex of the social hierarchy while at the same time favoring increased mobility and greater prosperity. The progressive tax played a decisive role in defining a new social and fiscal contract. Finally, we shall see the essential role played by the liquidation of foreign and colonial assets, and how the dissolution of public debt helped to reduce inequalities and destroy perceptions of private property as sacred. Rivalries among European powers and the intolerable character of the inegalitarian colonial regime were critical ingredients in the subsequent fall of Belle-Époque societies dominated by property owners. The way in which Europe was reconstructed after World War I, by cancellation of its debts, also imparted lessons for the future.

The Invention of the Welfare State: Education, Health Care, and Social Security

Between 1914 and 1980, the power of the fiscal and social state was to undergo an unprecedented expansion in all Western countries. At the end of the nineteenth century and at the beginning of the twentieth century, total tax receipts, including taxes, contributions, and obligatory levies of all kinds, represented less than 10 percent of the national income in Europe and the United States. Between 1914 and 1980, this tax burden tripled in the United States and more than quadrupled in Europe. In France, Germany, Sweden, and the United Kingdom, tax receipts have amounted to between 40 and 50 percent of the national income since the 1980s and 1990s. Numerous studies have shown that the fiscal state's rise in power made a major contribution to the process of economic development. The new receipts did in fact make it possible to finance expenditures that proved indispensable not only for reducing inequalities but also for encouraging growth. These expenditures included a massive and relatively egalitarian investment in education and health care (or, at least, a much more massive and egalitarian investment than any previous); expansion of transportation and other community infrastructure; the replacement income, such as retirement pensions, necessary for supporting an aging population; and reserves, such as unemployment insurance, for stabilizing the economy and society in the event of a recession.[1]

---

1. See especially P. Lindert, *Growing Public: Social Spending and Economic Growth since the Eighteenth Century* (Cambridge: Cambridge University Press, 2004).

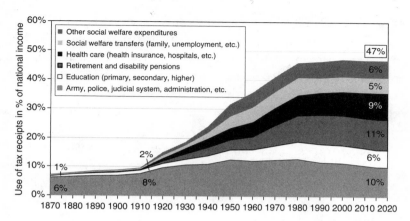

FIGURE 19. The Rise of the Welfare State in Europe, 1870–2020

In 2020, tax receipts represented on average 47 percent of the national income in Western Europe and were spent as follows: 10 percent of the national income went for state expenditures (army, police, judicial system, administration, and basic infrastructure, such as roads); 6 percent for education; 11 percent for pensions; 9 percent for health care; 5 percent for social welfare transfers (excluding pensions); 6 percent for other social welfare expenditures, such as housing. Before 1914, state expenditures absorbed virtually all the tax receipts.

Note. "Europe" is an average of France, Germany, Sweden, and the United Kingdom.
Sources and series: piketty.pse.ens.fr/equality

If we examine the main European nations, we find that the increase in tax receipts is explained almost entirely by the rise of social welfare expenditures related to education, health care, retirement pensions, and other transfers (see Figure 19). This transformation of the role of the state through increased tax receipts and expenditures accelerated between 1914 and 1950. On the eve of World War I as in the nineteenth century, the focus of the European state was centered on the maintenance of order and respect for the right of property, on the domestic terrain as well as on the interstate and colonial scene. State expenses, for the army, the police, the judicial system, general administration, and basic infrastructure, consumed almost all the tax revenues, or about 8 percent of the national income out of a total of scarcely 10 percent. Other expenses, notably social welfare expenses, had to make do with a bare 2 percent of the national income, of which less than 1 percent went for education. Conversely, at the beginning of the 1950s, the essential components of the welfare state were in place in Europe, with total receipts exceeding 30 percent of the national income, and a diversified set of expenditures for education and welfare that then consumed two-thirds of the total. This upward trend for social welfare expenditures continued between 1950 and 1980.

We must emphasize the capital importance of expenditures for education, both as a factor of equality and as a force driving development. At the end of the nineteenth century and the beginning of the twentieth, schools were extremely elitist and hierarchized. Only a small minority of the population could hope to receive more than a primary education and the first years of secondary education. Expenditures for education began to grow between 1870 and 1910, while generally remaining between 0.5 percent and 1 percent of the national income, with the United States clearly ahead and the United Kingdom just as clearly behind.[2] Then the investment in education grew almost tenfold in the course of the twentieth century and reached about 6 percent of the national income in all Western countries during the 1980s and 1990s, making it possible to finance almost universal access to secondary education, with a clear advance in access to higher education. Within this general landscape marked by the expansion of education, the United States' edge was particularly prominent around the middle of the twentieth century. In the 1950s, the propor-

---

2. See T. Piketty, *Capital and Ideology* (Cambridge, MA: Belknap Press of Harvard University Press, 2020), 517–522. In 1870 public expenditures for education (all levels taken together) represented 0.7 percent of the national income in the United States, 0.4 percent in France, and 0.2 percent in the United Kingdom. In 1910, they rose to 1.4 percent in the United States, 1 percent in France, and 0.7 percent in the United Kingdom. In comparison, military budgets reached or exceeded 4 to 5 percent of the national income in Europe in the nineteenth century and at the beginning of the twentieth century. On the global level, military expenditures fell from more than 6 percent of the national income in 1960 (colonial wars, the Cold War) to 3 percent in 2020 (2 percent in Europe, 4 percent in the United States, 10 percent in Saudi Arabia).

tion of children aged twelve to seventeen (boys and girls taken together) enrolled in secondary education was already almost 80 percent
in the United States. At the same time, the rate of enrollment in
secondary schools was between 20 and 30 percent in the United
Kingdom and France, and barely reached 40 percent in Germany
and Sweden. In these four countries, the high rates of enrollment in
secondary schools seen in the United States in the 1950s were not
reached until the 1980s and 1990s.[3] Japan, in an exacerbated competition with Western powers, had already distinguished itself by its accelerated educational expansion between 1880 and 1930, and soon
matched and exceeded Western figures with secondary school enrollments reaching 60 percent in the 1950s and more than 80 percent in
the early 1970s.

Generally speaking, at the end of the nineteenth century, governments were beginning to realize that education and training are a
factor in national power, and not simply a matter of equality and
individual emancipation. The second industrial revolution, which
unfolded between 1880 and 1940 in chemical industries, the steel
industry, the production of electricity, the automobile industry, and
the manufacture of household appliances, required much more job
training. During the first industrial revolution, and particularly in the
textile and coal industries, one could get along with a relatively mechanized workforce, overseen by foremen and a few engineers. During
the second industrial revolution, it became essential that an increasingly large part of the labor force be capable of mastering manufacturing processes that required technical and digital education, and the
ability to understand detailed equipment manuals. That was how the
United States—followed by Germany and Japan, who were newcomers
on the international scene—gradually surpassed the United Kingdom

---

3. In the nineteenth century, we find the same gap in primary school enrollments.
Around 1850, enrollments exceeded 80 percent in the United States, whereas in Germany, France, and the United Kingdom similar rates of enrollment were not reached
until 1890–1910.

in the new industrial sectors. The considerable gap observed between the United States and the rest of the Western world in terms of the productivity of labor in the middle of the twentieth century can be explained to a considerable extent by the United States' lead in education. This lead was overcome in the course of the following decades, as was the lead in productivity: since the 1980s–1990s, the GDP per hour worked is almost exactly the same in the United States, Germany, and France. Note in passing the importance of the choice of socioeconomic indicators. Time spent at work is ignored in this kind of comparison—a debatable if widespread choice that fails to account for immense historical progress toward increased leisure time, paid vacations, and a reduced work week, even though this question has been at the heart of popular and labor union mobilizations over the past two centuries.[4]

The Fiscal State's Second Leap Forward: An Anthropological Revolution

We must also emphasize the deep difference in nature between the fiscal state's first leap forward and its second. At the time of the first leap forward, between 1700 and 1850, when the principal European powers had moved from about 1–2 percent of the national income in tax receipts to approximately 6–8 percent, this advance corresponded chiefly to the growth of military and state expenditures.[5] The state was controlled by the aristocratic and bourgeois elites and was situated in the vanguard of interstate competition and commercial and colonial expansion. Between 1914 and 1980, growth of the state was led by social welfare expenditures. Considerations of power were never entirely absent, but this unprecedented extension of the state's role

---

4. Piketty, *Capital and Ideology*, 514–515. The historical movement demanding a reduction of the length of the workweek was also very important in the United States, but considerably weaker than in Europe, a fact which can be connected with the more limited development of the welfare state in general in the United States.

5. See Chapter 3, Figure 8.

took place primarily for the benefit of the lower and middle classes, and in large measure under their control, or at least under that of the political movements that represented them and that they had elected, under conditions entirely unprecedented in history.

In the United Kingdom, the Labour Party thus won an absolute majority of the seats in the elections of 1945. The National Health Service (NHS) and a vast system of social welfare insurance followed. The most aristocratic country in Europe, which until the constitutional crisis of 1909 had been governed by the House of Lords, it became a country in which a party both authentically popular and labor-focused came to power and put its reforms in place. In Sweden, the country where until 1910 property owners had a hundred voting rights, workers kept the Social Democrats in power more or less continuously starting in 1932. In France, in 1936, the Popular Front set up paid vacations, and the strong presence of communists and socialists in the parliament and the government made it possible to establish a system of social security in 1945. In the United States, a popular coalition carried the Democrats and the New Deal to power in 1932, and posed a long-lasting challenge to the dogmas of laissez-faire and the power of economic and financial elites.[6] The anthropological revolution was twofold. For the first time in history on this scale, the state escaped the exclusive control of the dominant classes. This was a result of universal suffrage, parliamentary and representative democracy, the electoral process, and frequent changes of power among different political parties, the whole spurred on by an independent press and the labor union movement. This political system remains eminently perfectible, if necessary by means of major constitutional revisions, but everyone

6. From 1950 to 1980, the Labour, Social Democratic, Socialist, Communist, and Democratic parties continued to bring together the popular vote, no matter which dimension of social stratification is selected (income, education, property). These coalitions gradually fell apart starting in 1980–1990, and this can be connected with the fact that the redistributive platforms became less ambitious. See A. Gethin, C. Martinez-Toledano, and T. Piketty, *Political Cleavages: A Study of Fifty Democracies, 1948–2020* (Cambridge, MA: Harvard University Press, 2021).

now knows that progress must emanate from egalitarian roots and electoral democracy. Acknowledgment of this fact in the 1970s–1980s contributed to the final delegitimation of the communist counter-model: if the latter produces both less political freedom and less social and economic well-being, then what's the point?

The second lesson is that it is possible to move beyond not only censitary government, but also capitalism and generalized commodification.[7] Vast sectors of the economy, starting with education and health care, and to a considerable extent transportation and energy as well, have been organized outside commercial logic, with various systems of public employment, mutualist or nonprofit structures, subsidies and investments financed by tax revenues. Not only has this worked, but it has worked much more efficiently than in the private capitalist sector. Even if some lobbyists in the United States continue to claim the contrary (for obvious reasons, and unfortunately sometimes with a certain efficacy), everyone who cares about facts now knows that public health-care systems on the European model are both less expensive and more efficient, in terms of well-being and life expectancy, than the private companies in the United States.[8] In the education sector, hardly anyone is proposing to replace elementary schools, secondary schools, or higher education with corporations governed by the logic of capitalism.[9] Whatever the legitimate criti-

---

7. On the importance of the processes of decommodification in the construction of different types of welfare state, see G. Esping-Andersen, *The Three Worlds of Welfare Capitalism* (Princeton, NJ: Princeton University Press, 1990). Compare K. Polanyi, *The Great Transformation* (New York: Farrar and Rinehart, 1944), on the generalized commodification of life in the nineteenth and twentieth centuries and its role in the collapse of European societies from 1914.

8. See, for example, P.-C. Michaud et al., "Differences in Health between Americans and Western Europeans," *Social Science and Medicine* 73, no. 2 (2011): 254–263; M. Roser, "Link between Health Spending and Life Expectancy: The US Is an Outlier," Our World in Data, updated May 26, 2017; A. Case and A. Deaton, *Deaths of Despair and the Future of Capitalism* (Princeton: Princeton University Press, 2020).

9. Something like this was tried in Chile after 1973, and also in the United States more recently with for-profit universities such as Trump University. In both cases the quest for profit undermined the ethical motivations on which education is founded.

cisms and debates regarding improvements to be made or whether a further expansion is advisable, no political movement of significant scope in countries that have experienced the rise of the fiscal and welfare state in the course of the twentieth century is proposing a return to a pre-1914 situation, when tax receipts represented less than 10 percent of the national income.

The Invention of the Progressive Tax on Income and Inheritance

Let us now come to the question of progressive taxation. Until the beginning of the twentieth century, almost all the world's fiscal systems were clearly regressive, in the sense that they were usually based on sales taxes and indirect taxes representing a proportionately heavier burden on the poorest people than on the wealthiest. The most extreme case of a regressive tax is the poll tax or capitation, which is a tax of a fixed amount for everyone. By definition, it represents a proportion of a low-paid employee's income ten times larger than that of a manager with a salary ten times higher.[10] A proportional tax is a tax representing a set percentage of income or assets, to be paid by all social classes. Conversely, a progressive tax is characterized by a rate of taxation that rises as income or wealth rises.[11]

The debates regarding progressive taxes have a long history. They became more important in the eighteenth century, especially during the French Revolution, when many pamphlets proposed systems quite close to the taxes on income that would finally be implemented on a

Similar results are found in health care and many other sectors, such as media and culture.

10. The poll tax in the United Kingdom, defended in 1988 by Margaret Thatcher, was so unpopular that the Tory Party had to abandon the project in 1990 and choose a new prime minister.

11. It will be noted that the regressivity or progressivity of a tax can be defined in relation to the level of income or the level of wealth. Both approaches are pertinent and complement one another, because income and wealth constitute two complementary indicators of an individual's ability to contribute.

TABLE 1

Progressive Tax Proposals in Eighteenth-Century France

Graslin: Progressive Income Tax (*Essai analytique sur la richesse et l'impôt*, 1767)		Lacoste: Progressive Inheritance Tax (*Du droit national d'hérédité*, 1792)	
Multiple of average income	Effective tax rate	Multiple of average estate	Effective tax rate
0.5	5%	0.3	6%
20	15%	8	14%
200	50%	500	40%
1,300	75%	1,500	67%

Note: In the progressive income tax proposed by Graslin in 1767, the effective tax rate rose gradually from 5 percent on an annual income of 150 *livres tournois* (roughly half the average income of the time) to 75 percent on an income of 400,000 *livres tournois* (roughly 1,300 times the average). Lacoste's proposed inheritance tax exhibits similar progressivity. *Source:* piketty.pse.ens.fr/equality

large scale in the twentieth century. In 1767, the town planner Jean-Joseph-Louis Graslin defended the idea of a tax scale in which an income equal to half the average income would be subject to an effective tax rate of 5 percent, whereas a taxpayer with an income equal to 1,300 times the average income would have to pay a tax of 75 percent. In 1792, the tax official Lacoste proposed a similar system for the inheritance tax: small legacies would pay a 6 percent tax and the larger ones a tax of 67 percent (see Table 1). But with the exception of 1793–1794, when progressive tax scales were briefly implemented, the Revolution finally adopted proportional or regressive taxes. All through the nineteenth century, parents' legacies to their children were taxed at a rate of 1 percent, no matter what the amount. Taxes were higher for legacies to brothers and sisters, cousins, and persons outside the family, but remained independent of the amount. This rejection of progressivity helps explain the increase in the concentration of property up to 1914.

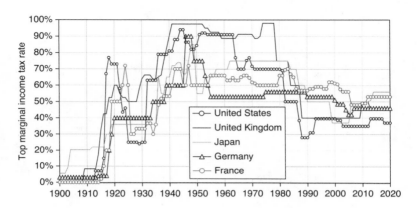

FIGURE 20. The Invention of Progressive Taxation: Top Income Tax Rates, 1900–2020

The marginal tax rate applied to the highest incomes was on average 23 percent in the United States from 1900 to 1932, 81 percent from 1932 to 1980, and 39 percent between 1980 and 2020. In the same periods, the top rates were 30, 89, and 46 percent in the United Kingdom; 26, 68, and 53 percent in Japan; 18, 58, and 50 percent in Germany; and 23, 60, and 57 percent in France. Progressive taxation was greatest in the middle of the century, particularly in the United States and the United Kingdom. *Sources and series:* piketty.pse.ens.fr/equality

It was not until the beginning of the twentieth century that progressive taxes were established more or less everywhere within the space of a few years. In the United States, the top tax rate for the federal income tax, that is, the rate applicable to the highest incomes, rose from 7 percent in 1913 to 77 percent in 1918, and eventually reached 94 percent in 1944 (see Figure 20). From 1932 to 1980, nearly half a century, the average top rate was 81 percent. Although the United States took the lead, we also see spectacular development of both progressive income taxes and progressive inheritance taxes in the United Kingdom, Germany, France, Sweden, and Japan (see Figure 21).

Could progressive taxes have been so quickly established without the shock of World War I, and without the Bolshevik regime's pressure on the elites in capitalist countries? Strictly speaking, it is impossible to answer that question. The history of the world since 1914

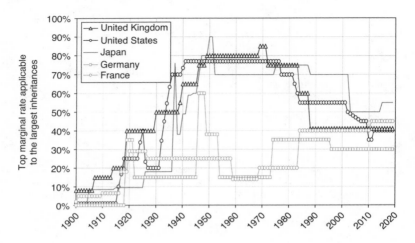

FIGURE 21. The Invention of Progressive Taxation: Top Inheritance Tax Rates, 1900–2020

The marginal tax rate applied to the largest inheritances was on average 12 percent in the United States from 1900 to 1932, 75 percent between 1932 and 1980, and 50 percent between 1980 and 2020. During the same periods, the top rates were 25, 72, and 46 percent in the United Kingdom; 9, 64, and 63 percent in Japan; 8, 23, and 32 percent in Germany; and 15, 22, and 39 percent in France. Fiscal progressivity was maximal at the middle of the century, particularly in the United States and the United Kingdom. *Sources and series:* piketty.pse.ens.fr/equality

has been so completely altered by World War I and the events that issued from it, starting with the Russian Revolution in 1917, that it no longer makes sense to imagine a twentieth century without the interwar period, the USSR, and the Cold War.[12] The invention of progressive taxation must nevertheless be seen as the consequence of both a social and political movement and a long-term protest movement. This process was accelerated, of course, by multiple events (wars, revolutions, economic crises), but the relative importance of the latter varies greatly depending on the country, and we must remember, above all, that these events themselves did not just appear out of the blue: they were in large measure the product of the enormously strong social and inegalitarian tensions of the time.

In the case of France, it is striking to note that parliamentary groups decided to raise the top tax rate to 60 percent in the early 1920s, even with power held by a conservative majority, the National Bloc, one of the most right-wing political groups in the history of the French Republic. Before the war, the same groups rejected a 5 percent income tax and then used every means at their disposal to block its adoption.[13] A few years later, it almost seemed as if political affiliation mattered little in a political context completely transformed by war and destruction, with millions dead and wounded. Postwar workers' wages still had not recovered the purchasing power they possessed in 1914, nor did they when several waves of strikes threatened the country with paralysis in May and June 1919, nor again in the spring of 1920. Remedies had to be found, and no one imagined that the richest people would be spared. The socialist and communist danger played an obvious role here: elites considered it safer to accept a very progressive tax than to run the risk of someday being faced with general expropriation. But that does not mean, of course, that this same threat might have materialized even without the assassination in Sarajevo or the seizure of the Winter Palace. Movements favoring fiscal progressivity were already becoming more powerful before the war, and the conflict that followed probably only lit the match.[14]

---

13. Before World War I, the republican elites used and abused this argument: France had been made egalitarian thanks to revolution in 1789, and thus didn't need a progressive tax, even though data available at the time clearly demonstrated the extreme concentration of wealth. If we include the 25 percent supplement that unmarried people had to pay, and the 10 percent supplement for married couples with no children after two years of marriage (proof of governments' fiscal imagination), also adopted in 1920 by the National Bloc, then the top rate reaches 75 percent in 1923 and 90 percent in 1924 (after final supplements approved by the Coalition of the Left, for good measure). For a history of progressive taxation in France, see T. Piketty, *Top Incomes in France in the Twentieth Century* (Cambridge, MA: Harvard University Press, 2018).

14. The creation of a progressive tax on inheritance (law of 25 February 1901) preceded that of the progressive tax on income (law of 15 July 1914, which was long blocked

The crucial importance of social and political movements is confirmed by studies on other countries. Sweden's hypercensitary system was challenged as early as 1909–1911. The country was relatively little affected by the two world wars, and it was above all the Social Democrats' coming to power that was decisive for the establishment of both the welfare state and progressive taxation. In the United Kingdom, the People's Budget of 1909 combined strongly progressive taxation with social welfare programs, overcoming opposition from the House of Lords and ultimately limiting their power in 1911. In the United States, the federal income tax was established in 1913. This event had nothing to do with World War I; rather, it was the outcome of a long process of constitutional amendment that began in 1895. Its passage testifies to the strength of the Progressive movement and the demand for fiscal and economic justice that was being expressed in the country at that time.[15] We must also stress the central role played by the stock market crash of 1929, an event more decisive and traumatizing in the United States than World War I or the Russian Revolution. The crisis made clear to everyone the need to regain control of capitalism, and led Roosevelt to push fiscal progressivity to unprecedented levels in the 1930s and 1940s.

Real Progressivity and the Social Contract: The Question of Consent to Taxation

What were the real economic effects of fiscal progressivity? Here we must put an end to a widely accepted notion, that the highest tax rates were never applied to anyone and had no substantial effect. It is true

---

by the Senate after it was adopted by the deputies in 1909, and finally passed to finance the war).

15. The process of revision was represented both by the Democrats (who had been censured by the Supreme Court in 1895) and the People's Party (or Populist Party), which was then defending a platform of land sharing, credit for small farmers, and opposition to the takeover of the country's government by stockholders, property owners, and large corporations.

that the 70 percent or 80 percent tax rates affected only a small minority, generally the richest 1 percent (or even 0.1 percent).[16] But the fact is that at the beginning of the twentieth century, the distribution of incomes and especially of properties was extremely concentrated: the richest 1 percent held more than half the total wealth in France, and almost two-thirds in the United Kingdom. The richest .01 percent held more than a quarter of the wealth in France, and more than a third in the United Kingdom. If we exclude housing and focus on the ownership of the means of production, the concentration appears even greater. In other words, even if the 70 and 80 percent tax rates concerned only the top hundredth or thousandth, these very restricted groups had considerable weight in the inegalitarian regime that characterized the property-owning societies of the Belle Époque. A meticulous examination of French inheritance archives on the individual level enables us to see to what point progressive taxation of incomes and inheritances has weighed heavily in favor of the deconcentration of property that occurred between 1914 and 1950.[17]

In the case of the United States, if we take into account all the levies (the federal income tax, but also all the other taxes and duties at all levels of government), we can see that the fiscal system was very strongly progressive between 1914 and 1980. Concretely, the effective tax rates paid by the least wealthy 90 percent were considerably lower than the country's average tax rate, whereas the effective rates paid by the richest thousandth and ten thousandth reached 60 to 70 percent,

---

16. The rate higher than 70 or 80 percent may be either a marginal rate (that applies to the fraction of income or assets above this threshold) or an effective rate (which then applies to total income or assets). Tax scales expressed directly in an effective rate were used, notably, by the Popular Front in its fiscal reform of 1936. They have the immense advantage of being more transparent and democratic: everyone understands more clearly who pays what and sees that income or assets must be very high indeed for effective rates to reach substantial levels.

17. T. Piketty, G. Postel-Vinay, and J.-L. Rosenthal, "The End of Rentiers: Paris 1842–1957," January 2018, WID.world.

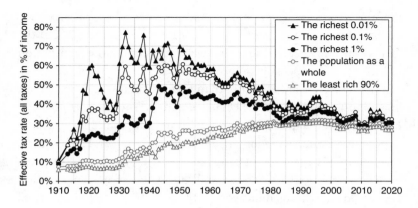

FIGURE 22. Effective Tax Rates and Progressivity in the United States, 1910–2020
From 1915 to 1980, the fiscal system was very progressive in the United States, in the
sense that the effective tax rates paid by the highest incomes (all taxes combined, in
percent of total pretax income) were significantly higher than the average effective
rate paid by the population as a whole (and in particular by the least rich 90 percent).
Since 1980, the fiscal system has been weakly progressive, with limited differences
between effective tax rates. *Sources and series:* piketty.pse.ens.fr/equality

or more than three times the average rate (see Figure 22).[18] The data
available for European countries confirm this conclusion. In other
words, during this period effective fiscal progressivity was a massive
and inescapable reality.

This strong progressivity had several consequences. First, it reduced inequality and led to a decline in the concentration of income
and property among the most well-off, and second, it altered overall
the social contract and increased collective acceptance of higher taxes
and greater socialization of wealth. Between 1914 and 1980, modest
and middle-level taxpayers (salaried employees, independent workers,
or owners of small and medium-sized companies) could be certain
that the most well-off economic actors (individuals with large incomes,
many assets, and more prosperous companies) would be asked to pay

---

18. Here we also take into account the tax on corporations (attributed to the different
centiles of the stockholders concerned), property tax (attributed to the centiles of property owners), taxes on consumption (attributed to the centiles of consumers), and so on.

taxes at a rate considerably higher than theirs. Today, the situation is completely different: real progressivity has disappeared when it has not been transformed into regressivity, in the sense that the wealthiest people sometimes succeed in paying taxes at effective rates lower than those paid by the middle and lower classes, and large companies often succeed in paying at a tax rate lower than that of small and medium-sized companies.[19] This poses a serious risk to the political acceptability of taxation and the legitimacy of the system of social solidarity as a whole.

Progressive Taxation, a Tool for Reducing Inequalities before Taxes

Here we must underline another essential lesson to be learned from the period 1914–1980, namely that fiscal progressivity made it possible to reduce inequalities not only after taxes, but also and especially before taxes (sometimes called *predistribution,* in contrast to redistribution).[20] This conclusion may seem paradoxical, but in reality, it is rather obvious. It is particularly clear in the case of progressive inheritance taxes, which reduce inequalities in fortune to the following generation. It would be even clearer if the inheritance tax were used to redistribute the legacy to the benefit of all those who inherit next to nothing, and if the annual wealth tax were also used to implement a permanent redistribution of capital. That is also the case for the progressive income tax, especially with almost confiscatory rates of 80 to 90 percent for the highest incomes. If high incomes proceeded from capital (dividends, interest, rents, etc.), as many of them did during the Belle Époque and the interwar period, then such rates

---

19. Thus, in 2018–2019 the effective rate paid by the 400 largest taxpayers in the United States fell below that paid by less wealthy taxpayers. See E. Saez and G. Zucman, *The Triumph of Injustice* (New York: W. W. Norton, 2019). These estimates do not take into account what is directly observable, and largely ignore the sophisticated strategies for optimizing and avoiding taxes.

20. A. Bozio, B. Garbinti, J. Goupille-Lebret, M. Guillot, and T. Piketty, "Predistribution vs. Redistribution: Evidence from France and the U.S.," October 2020, WID.world.

compelled the very wealthy to adopt a less extravagant way of life, because if they did not, they ran the risk of finding themselves forced to amputate their capital irremediably by selling off an increasing portion of their enterprises and goods. This effect played a role in the gradual deconcentration of wealth and the replacement of the very top wealth holders by the patrimonial middle class. If we examine incomes from work, and in particular the high remunerations paid to managers, we find that these tax rates drastically decrease the possibility of accumulating large fortunes, and above all, they radically transform the conditions for negotiating and setting these very generous remunerations, and thus in the end benefit those with the smallest remunerations.

The available data show that this second effect was very important, especially in the United States. Concretely, the 80–90 percent tax rates implemented under Roosevelt and during the postwar period led companies to put an end to the most astronomical remunerations, whose cost increasingly appeared to be excessive when compared with the real benefit to the manager and with alternative uses. These super-remunerations melted away, which left more funds to be invested and used to raise lower salaries. The data show that the redistributive effect of confiscatory tax rates was principally the result of predistribution, which also implies that a simple examination of the effective tax rates paid by the various centiles allows us to measure only part of the total effect. Comparison of different countries also indicates that this fiscal mechanism was even more efficient when employees became involved in setting and monitoring remunerations and salary scales (for example, through union representatives on boards of directors in Germanic and Nordic Europe or on the War Labor Board in the United States).[21] The data available at the level of the companies and of the different sectors and countries concerned also allow

---

21. This was a tripartite authority (government, unions, employers) set up to monitor salaries and smooth social relations. See C. Goldin and R. A. Margo, "The Great Compression: The Wage Structure in the United States at Mid-Century," *Quarterly Journal of Economics* 107, no. 1 (1992): 1–34.

us to establish that beyond a certain level, there is no meaningful relation between managers' salaries and their economic performance, and that these remunerations have mainly negative effects on low and middle-level salaries.[22]

On this subject, let us add that the rise in power of strongly progressive taxation seems in no way to have discouraged innovation or productivity. In the United States, the national income per inhabitant rose at a rate of 1.8 percent per annum between 1870 and 1910 without an income tax, and then at 2.1 percent between 1910 and 1950 after its introduction, and at a rate of 2.2 percent between 1950 and 1990, when the top tax rate reached, on average, 72 percent. The top rate was then cut in half, with the announced objective of boosting growth. But in fact, growth fell by half, reaching 1.1 percent per annum between 1990 and 2020 (see Figure 23). Beyond a certain level of inequality, repeatedly increasing differences in income and wealth has clearly had no positive effect on economic dynamism.[23] In sum, all the data at our disposal today suggest that virtually confiscatory tax rates have been an immense historical success. They have made it possible to greatly reduce the divergences of fortunes and incomes, while at the same time improving the situation of the middle and lower classes, developing the welfare state, and stimulating better economic and social performance overall. Historically, it is the battle for equality and education that has made economic development and human progress possible, and not the veneration of property, stability, and inequality.[24]

---

22. Piketty, *Capital and Ideology*, 532–534.

23. We find the same results in Europe: fiscal progressivity was maximal during the period between 1950 and 1990, and so was growth, which later decreased, along with progressivity. The results, however, are harder to interpret in the case of Europe. Growth there was particularly weak between 1910 and 1950 owing to the wars, leading to a catch-up effect later on. There is no catch-up effect of this kind in the United States (growth from 1910 to 1950 is intermediary between those of the periods 1870–1910 and 1950–1990), and this makes the comparison more meaningful. See Piketty, *Capital and Ideology*, 543–547, figs. 11.12–11.15.

24. On this subject, note the stagnation of educational investment since 1980–1990 (Figure 19), an evolution that is paradoxical on the historical scale, given the increase in

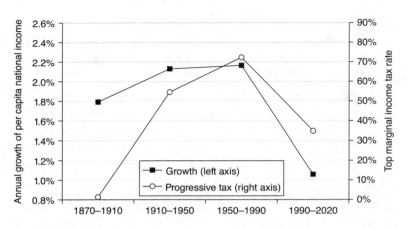

FIGURE 23. Growth and Progressive Taxation in the United States, 1870–2020
In the United States, growth of per capita national income increased annually by
2.2 percent from 1950 to 1990, and by 1.1 percent from 1990 to 2020, whereas during
the same period the top marginal tax rate applied to the highest incomes fell from
72 percent to 35 percent. The promised resurgence of growth when the top marginal
tax rate was lowered did not occur. *Sources and series:* piketty.pse.ens.fr/equality

The Liquidation of Colonial Assets and Public Debts

After the welfare state and progressive taxation, the third factor characterizing the "great redistribution" of the 1914–1980 period is the
liquidation of foreign and colonial assets and then of the public debts
that had been incurred during that period. On the eve of World War I,
property owners' prosperity seemed unshakeable. The total value of
private assets ranged from six to eight years of national income in
the United Kingdom, France, and Germany (see Figure 24).[25] More-

the number of university students, and that appears to be one of the most plausible explanations for the decline of growth.

25. The available sources allow us to estimate that the total value of private properties was located at about this level from 1700 to 1914 in the United Kingdom and France,
but with a radical transformation of the forms of property: agricultural land represented two-thirds of goods at the beginning of the eighteenth century, and then was
gradually replaced by industrial and international unmovable assets. See T. Piketty,

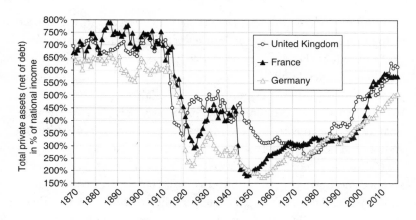

FIGURE 24. Private Property in Europe, 1870–2020

The market value of private property (real, occupational, and financial assets, net of debt) was around six to eight years of national income in Western Europe from 1870 to 1914, before collapsing from 1914 to 1950 and settling at around two to three years of national income from the 1950s to the 1970s, and then increasing again to around five to six years in the period between 2000 and 2020. *Sources and series:* piketty. pse.ens.fr/equality

over, these assets were very concentrated: the richest 10 percent held between 80 and 90 percent of the total. Between 1914 and 1950, we see a veritable collapse of private property: the total value of goods was between two and three years of national income in the 1950s, and then began to increase slowly again up to our own time, without, however, fully returning to its starting point, and especially without ever regaining its earlier concentration.[26] This collapse of private property is explained, first, by the destruction of goods (such as factories, buildings, and houses) caused by battles and bombardments during the two world wars: this represented between a quarter and a third of the

---

Capital in the Twentieth Century (Cambridge, MA: Belknap Press of Harvard University Press, 2014), 116–118, figs. 3.1–3.2.

26. See Chapter 2, Figure 6.

decline in France and Germany (and a few percent in the United Kingdom). It is also explained by a set of policies that sought deliberately to reduce the power of property owners (rent freezes, nationalizations, financial and economic regulation, and labor union rights, among others). These very diverse policies all sought to reduce the monetary value of goods for private property owners but not their social value for consumers: thus it was a question of redistributing power and not of losing real value. Finally, the third and most important reason—responsible for between a third and half of the collapse in France and Germany (and almost two-thirds in the United Kingdom) was the liquidation of foreign assets and then of public debts.[27] There, too, it is essentially a question of redistribution and not destruction: colonized peoples and postwar taxpayers became freer as a result.

This liquidation took place in two phases: the foreign assets were destroyed or transformed into public debts, and then the latter were themselves liquidated. To properly understand these events, we must first recognize that at the beginning of the twentieth century international assets had reached a level completely unprecedented in history and never attained since (see Figure 25). For instance, in 1914, net foreign assets rose to almost two years of national income for British property owners (or more than a quarter of what they owned), and almost a year and a half for French property owners (nearly a fifth of their possessions). These assets were held in the colonial empires, such as the rubber plantations in Indochina and the timber industry in the Congo, but also in many territories that were not, strictly speaking, colonies, but with which the United Kingdom and France maintained very hierarchized relations—for example, the oil wells in the Ottoman Empire and Persia, the railroads and public and private debt securities in Russia, China, and Latin America. The importance of colonial and international assets is clearly visible at the individual level in Parisian inheritance records. Between 1872 and 1912, foreign investments rose

---

27. For a more detailed analysis, see Piketty, *Capital and Ideology*, 432–441.

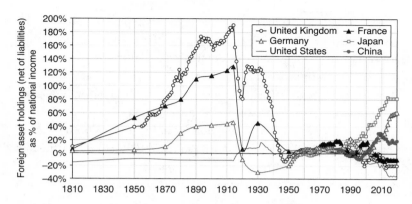

FIGURE 25. Foreign Assets in Historical Perspective: The Franco-British Colonial Apex

Net foreign assets, that is, the difference between foreign asset holdings by residents of each country (including the government) and assets held in each country by property owners in the rest of the world, rose in 1914 to 191 percent of national income in the United Kingdom and to 125 percent in France. In 2020, net foreign assets reached 82 percent of national income in Japan, 61 percent in Germany, and 19 percent in China. *Sources and series:* piketty.pse.ens.fr/equality

from 6 percent to 21 percent in the total of goods transmitted after a death, with a still greater increase in the largest inheritances.[28]

These international investments returned considerable income in the form of profits, dividends, interest, rents, and royalties to their owners: about 5 percent of supplementary income for France (or the equivalent of the total industrial production of the departments in the country's north and east, which are the most industrialized), and almost 10 percent for the United Kingdom.[29] This is also what allowed the two principal powers of the time to be almost constantly in commercial deficit with regard to the rest of the world between 1880 and

---

28. Piketty, *Capital and Ideology,* 133–137, table 4.1.

29. This way of accounting in terms of money is revealing, but it underestimates the actual size of colonial extraction, which can be correctly gauged only by favoring a multidimensional approach expressed in terms of material flows (such as cotton, wood, and oil). See Chapter 3.

1914, between 1 and 2 percent of the national income, on average: the revenues derived from foreign assets largely covered this deficit, while at the same time leaving considerable financial means that made it possible to continue colonizing the rest of the world and accumulating new assets. In reality, the pace of the accumulation of foreign assets by France and Britain between 1880 and 1914 was so excessive that it simply became untenable in the long term, for reasons both external and internal. The accumulation was so rapid that had it continued a few decades longer, European powers would have been in a position to colonize almost the whole planet. The logic of colonial extraction and of these international possessions was often accompanied by violence. This considerable brutality took the form of virtually forced or poorly paid labor, degraded working conditions, discrimination, and more generally a great indifference to human suffering.[30] This treatment could only help feed national liberation movements and favor their final victories, a process the two world wars merely accelerated.

Within Europe, the magnitude of the financial flows and of the profits realized was known to everyone, and colonial assets aroused increasingly ferocious greed and rivalries.[31] Germany—which had become, at the end of the nineteenth century and the beginning of the twentieth, the continent's leading power, demographically and industrially—was much less well endowed with foreign assets than the United Kingdom and France were. The Moroccan crisis of 1911 almost

---

30. See Chapter 4. The Irish famine of 1845–1848, which left around 1 million dead and sent 1.5 million emigrants abroad from a total population of 8 million, has often been compared, in its magnitude, to the Bengal famine of 1943–1944, which killed 4 million out of a population of 50 million. In Ireland, as in Bengal, the British elites knew what was happening and refused to take the steps required to avoid a tragedy, in some cases with the almost explicit goal of a Malthusian regulation of an impoverished population, and a rebellious one at that. During the following decades, the Irish famine fed a deep resentment toward British property owners, refusal to pay rents, and occupation of plots of land, followed by a powerful movement that led first to the redistribution of land and then to that country's independence.

31. In his classic book *Imperialism, The Highest Stage of Capitalism* (1916), Lenin had used, of course, the statistics on financial investments available at that time to show the enormity of the colonial powers' race to seize natural resources.

triggered hostilities, but Germany finally accepted the Franco-British agreement of 1904 regarding Morocco and Egypt, while at the same time obtaining a compensation in Cameroon. This made it possible to delay war for a few years. The next spark ignited the conflict.

The beginning of hostilities led to the collapse of foreign assets. British and French possessions were reconstituted to some extent during the 1920s, partly thanks to the distribution of German colonial assets, but then disappeared definitively following World War II. Between 1914 and the 1950s, history's greatest international possessions totally disappeared (see Figure 25). This is explained in part by a series of expropriations following revolutionary processes and wars of independence. After the 1917 revolution, the new Soviet state decided to repudiate all the debts accumulated by the czarist regime. In 1918–1920, a military expedition was conducted in northern Russia by the United Kingdom, France, and the United States, in the hope of crushing the revolution, but it failed. At the other end of the period, Egypt decided in 1956 to nationalize the Suez Canal, which had given its Franco-British stockholders solid dividends ever since it was constructed in 1869. Once again, the United Kingdom and France envisioned a military operation, as they had so often done in the past. But this time they were let down by the United States, which could not take the risk of allowing the global South to fall into the hands of the Soviet Union. The colonial powers no longer existed.

In addition to the expropriations, the wars themselves were to cost European property owners dear. To finance an unprecedented level of violence, holders of foreign assets sold an increasing share of their credits to make loans to their governments, which, as was only proper, promised to repay them, cash on the barrelhead, after the war. This promise could never be kept. In the hope of being able to bail out its property owners, the French state imposed an incredible war debt on Germany in the Treaty of Versailles: around 300 percent of the German national income, at a time when the country was already on its knees. (It will be noted that this is approximately the same proportion of the national income as the debt imposed on Haiti in 1825, about 300 percent, with the difference being that Germany had the means to defend itself.) The French authorities considered the amount justified: in 1871, France was obligated to pay the equivalent of 30 percent of its national income to Germany, and the damage caused by the fighting between 1914 and 1918 was far more extensive. In reality, the system had reached the point of breakdown. In *Mein Kampf*, written in 1924 when French troops were occupying the Ruhr to recover their property, Adolf Hitler constantly refers to this infamous tribute—which was imposed, moreover, by a people in demographic decline—and concludes that only the formation of a superior state power would make it possible for the German people to hold their heads high and finally carve out their own colonial empire.[32] The financial crash of 1929, followed by the battles of World War II, led to the ultimate collapse of colonial assets and the powers that had dominated the world until 1914, powers that were inseparably connected to property ownership and colonialism.

The Reconstruction of Europe through the Cancellation of Public Debts

Around 1945–1950, the principal European states were saddled with enormous public debts: between 200 and 300 percent of the national income (see Figure 26). In large part, these were the result, thirty years later, of foreign assets that had been gradually sold to finance wars (see Figure 25). Most of these countries chose not to repay these debts. They instead turned to other economic and social priorities, combining three series of measures that had already been tried after World War I: cancellations pure and simple, inflation, and exceptional levies

---

32. Along with its pathological anti-Semitism, the text's other great obsession was the "hordes of blacks" that the French occupying force had brought to the banks of the Rhine. Hitler suspected the French of preparing to wipe out "the last remains of pure blood" and seeking to constitute "an immense mixed-blood state that would extend from the Congo to the Rhine." The fear of the "great replacement" was already accompanied by a fear of a great mixing of blood. See Piketty, *Capital and Ideology*, 471–479.

on private wealth. In France, inflation exceeded 50 percent per annum for four consecutive years, from 1945 through 1948. The public debt was destroyed, as surely as a factory could be destroyed by bombardment. The problem was that millions of ordinary people with small savings accounts were also ruined, whereas wealthier individuals who had sold their public debt securities at the right time and bought stocks or real estate instead were affected little or not at all. This inflation aggravated a poverty already endemic among elderly people in the 1950s and aroused a deep feeling of injustice. In West Germany, where the traumatic memory of the hyperinflation of 1923 was still very near, more sophisticated solutions were tried. The monetary reform of 1948 replaced old debt securities worth a hundred German marks with securities worth 1 mark in the new money, while at the same time protecting the smallest savings with the help of a scale. The debt disappeared without provoking inflation. Above all, in 1952, the Bundestag adopted a mechanism known as "burden-sharing" (*Lastenausgleich*), which consisted in a levy of up to 50 percent on the largest financial, business, and real estate assets (whatever their nature), making it possible to finance compensations for holders of small and middle-sized fortunes crippled by the destructive effects of war and monetary reform. The system was far from perfect, but it involved considerable sums (about 60 percent of the German national income in 1952, with payments spread over thirty years), and it represented an ambitious and largely successful attempt to reconstruct the country on a more just basis of social equality.[33] Germany also benefited from a cancellation of its foreign debt during the London Conference of 1953, which helped increase the margins available for reconstruction, social welfare expenditures, and investments in

---

33. See the fascinating book by M. L. Hughes, *Shouldering the Burdens of Defeat: West Germany and the Reconstruction of Social Justice* (Chapel Hill: University of North Carolina Press, 1999). Compare S. Bach, "Die Linke Capital Levy: Revenue and Distributional Effects," DIW Berlin, German Institute for Economic Research, October 30, 2020, for a similar, stimulating comparison recently debated in the Bundestag with the goal of extinguishing the Covid debt.

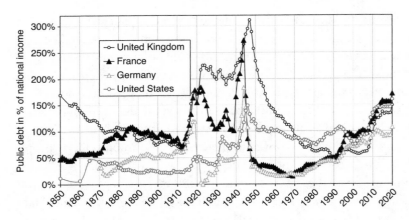

FIGURE 26. Fluctuations in Public Debt, 1850–2020

Public debt grew rapidly following the two world wars, reaching between 150 and 300 percent of national income in 1945–1950. It then fell suddenly in Germany and France (debt cancellations, exceptional taxes on private wealth, high inflation), and more gradually in the United Kingdom and the United States. The debt increased sharply again following the financial crises and epidemics of 2008 and 2020.

Note: The German debt issuing from the Treaty of Versailles (1919) is not taken into account here. It amounted to more than 300 percent of the national income at the time, and reimbursement never really began. *Sources and series:* piketty.pse.ens.fr/equality

infrastructure and training.[34] In Japan, the exceptional levy implemented in 1946–1947 affected 90 percent of the largest portfolios and also made it possible to accelerate the settlement of war-related accounts.

Retrospectively, these policies were very successful, in the sense that they made it possible to get rid of the debts of the past in just a few years and turn toward the future and reconstruction. If it had been necessary to pay off these debts by ordinary means, without

34. More precisely, the internal debt was suspended in 1953, and then finally cancelled when Germany was reunited in 1991. See G. Galofré-Vilà, C. Meissner, M. McKee, and D. Stuckler, "The Economic Consequences of the 1953 London Debt Agreement," *European Review of Economic History* 23, no. 1 (2018): 1–29.

cancellation or inflation, without exceptional levies on private wealth, and with budgetary deficits accumulating year after year, then we would still be reimbursing interest to heirs who received colonial and domestic assets from the period before 1914. This strategy of reimbursing property owners over the long term was the one chosen by the United Kingdom in the nineteenth century, though it is true that it is hard to see what government could have imposed this after the war, or, moreover, what government could establish it in future decades. However, we must remember that the decisions made in 1945–1950 involved gigantic political battles and were bitterly debated. After a long and conflict-ridden process, the liquidation of international assets and public debts ultimately played a major role in the reduction of income and property inequalities, enabling the "great redistribution" that took place between 1914 and 1980.

7

DEMOCRACY, SOCIALISM, AND
PROGRESSIVE TAXATION

Let us turn now toward the future. The "great redistribution" of the period between 1914 and 1980 was no piece of cake, much less a banquet, but from it we've gleaned some valuable lessons. The main lesson is the following: the welfare state and progressive taxation are powerful tools allowing us to transform capitalism. The movement toward equality can be resumed only if these institutions become the object of a vast movement and a collective appropriation. It is also crucial to gauge correctly the limits of what these institutions accomplished in the twentieth century and the factors that led to their weakening since 1980. I will emphasize in particular the damage done by financial liberalization and the free circulation of capital, as well as the strategic conclusions that will be required to escape this framework.

The Limits of Equality:
The Hyperconcentration of Property

First, we must remember the limited extent of the march toward equality that took place in the course of the past century. The most striking fact is the persistence of a hyperconcentration of property (see Figure 27). Granted, in Europe we see the emergence, over the long term, of a patrimonial middle class. The 40 percent of the population between the poorest 50 percent and the richest 10 percent owned

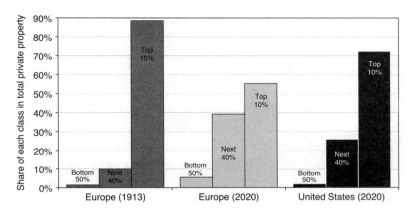

FIGURE 27. The Persistence of Hyperconcentration of Property

The share of the richest 10 percent of total private property owners reached 89 percent in Europe (average of France, Sweden, and the United Kingdom) in 1913 (compared to 1 percent for the poorest 50 percent), 56 percent in Europe in 2020 (compared to 6 percent for the poorest 50 percent), and 72 percent in the United States in 2020 (compared to 2 percent for the poorest 50 percent). *Sources and series:* piketty.pse.ens.fr/equality

scarcely more than 10 percent of property in 1913; in 2020, they held 40 percent, especially in the form of real estate.[1] It remains that in Europe in 2020 the poorest 50 percent still own nothing tangible (5 percent of the total), whereas the richest 10 percent own 55 percent. In other words, the average wealth of the former is 50 times smaller than the average wealth of the latter (their share in the total is more than ten times smaller, even though they are five times more numerous). In the United States, the situation is still more extreme: the poorest 50 percent owned barely 2 percent of the total in 2020, as opposed to 72 percent for the richest 10 percent, and 26 percent for the patrimonial middle class. In terms of the concentration of wealth, in 2020 the United States is in a position between Europe in 1913 and Europe in 2020, and is trending closer to the Europe of 1913.

---

1. See Chapter 2, Figure 5.

It is striking to note the extent to which the United States and Europe inverted their relative positions in terms of inequality over the course of the twentieth century (see Figure 28). European fortunes were based above all on colonial and international assets (United Kingdom and France) and on inegalitarian, censitary sociopolitical systems (Sweden). When they could, members of the European working class emigrated to the United States to find better wages there. After two world wars, however, European labor unions and political movements established new rules and transformed the face of the Continent. A more extensive and more ambitious welfare state emerged, and this made possible a greater reduction of inequalities than in the United States. In Figure 28, we see the curves cross between 1960 and 1970, reversing the positions of the United States and Europe. Since 1980, the gap has deepened in the other direction. In the United States, the patrimonial middle class, which in wealth was almost equal to its European counterpart at the beginning of the 1980s, was to see its share of the country's total wealth reduced by more than a quarter between 1985 and 2020. The share of the poorest 50 percent fell to lower and lower levels. In Europe, the deepening of wealth inequality has been less marked, but we also see a gradual weakening of the position of the middle 40 percent and especially of the poorest 50 percent, who had little wealth at any time. No country, no continent is in a position to strut or to lecture others on this subject. Almost everywhere, the economic and financial deregulation at work since the 1980s has favored the largest financial portfolios and benefited hardly at all those in the poorest groups, who have often been saddled with debt.

We find similar developments in inequalities of income, which have also started growing again since 1980, with an appreciably more marked movement in the United States (see Figure 29). There again, all the available data suggest that these developments are explained by a set of political reversals on the social, fiscal, educational, and financial levels. In the United States, the virulence of politicians opposed to labor unions and the collapse of the federal minimum wage have been decisive in the fall of the lowest incomes. The US federal

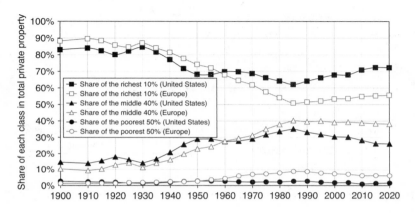

FIGURE 28. Property in Europe and the United States, 1900–2020: The Birth and Fragility of a Patrimonial Middle Class

In Europe as in the United States, we see between 1914 and 1980 a steep decline in the share of the richest 10 percent in total private property (real, occupational, and financial assets, net of debt), to the benefit principally of the middle 40 percent. This movement is partially reversed between 1980 and 2020, notably in the United States.

Note: "Europe" is an average of France, Germany, Sweden, and the United Kingdom. *Sources and series:* piketty.pse.ens.fr/equality

minimum wage has fallen, when adjusted for inflation, from almost 11 dollars per hour in 1970 to 7.25 dollars in 2020, although many Democratic officials would like to raise it. Taking into account transfers in kind connected especially with public health insurance (Medicare and Medicaid) attenuates this diagnosis only minimally.[2] The very strong growth of the largest fortunes and the explosion of remunerations for top executives, which is particularly marked in the United States, are explained above all by the obstruction of progressive taxation. Progressive tax rates had climbed from 1932 to 1980 before reversing with the same vigor after 1980, during the "conservative revolution." In Europe, the welfare state and the fiscal state made it possible to contain

---

2. T. Piketty, *Capital and Ideology* (Cambridge, MA: Belknap Press of Harvard University Press, 2020), 522–535, figs. 11.5–11.10.

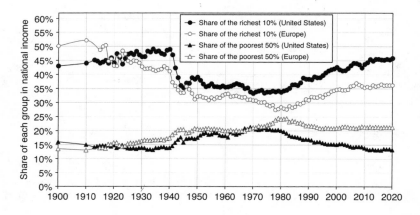

FIGURE 29. Income Inequality: Europe and the United States, 1900–2020

In Europe, income inequality has started rising again since 1980, although remaining at levels clearly lower than those of 1900–1910. The increase in inequality has been much greater in the United States. In both cases, inequality has remained high: the richest 10 percent, though five times fewer, still receive a share of total income much larger than the poorest 50 percent receive.

Note: "Europe" is an average of France, Germany, Sweden, and the United Kingdom.
Sources and series: piketty.pse.ens.fr/equality

the resurgence of inequalities. The share of the richest 10 percent dropped from 52 percent of total income in 1910 to 28 percent in 1980, before climbing to 36 percent in 2020. The share going to the poorest 50 percent increased from 13 percent in 1910 to 24 percent in 1980, and then fell again to 21 percent in 2020. In the end, inequalities of income were thus appreciably smaller in 2020 than in 1910—all this with a considerable increase in the average income in the course of the past century. There again, this must not make us forget that inequalities still remained very great in absolute terms.

European societies have never ceased to be hierarchical, and the range of material disparities has again begun to broaden significantly over recent decades. Achievements to date must be used to spur future progress, not to fuel self-congratulation, which too often serves as an excuse to justify all kinds of hypocrisies and renunciations.

The Welfare State and Progressive Taxation: A Systemic Transformation of Capitalism

To continue the march toward equality, the most natural path seems to be already blazed: we have to deepen and generalize the institutions that made the movement toward equality, human progress, and prosperity possible over the course of the twentieth century, starting with the welfare state and progressive taxation. But to move forward on this path, it is essential to arrive at a better understanding of the limitations encountered by the institutions, as well as the factors that have weakened them since 1980. Between 1914 and 1980, it was social and political struggles that made institutional change possible. Without a powerful social and collective movement supporting further change, the latter will not happen. If the Reagan-Thatcher revolution had such an influence after 1980, it was not only because it benefited from broad support within the dominant classes and a powerful network of influence through the media, think tanks, and political financing (even if these factors obviously played a role). It was also because of the weaknesses of the egalitarian coalition, which failed to produce a convincing alternative narrative and nurture a sufficiently strong popular movement rallying around the welfare state and progressive taxation.

That is why it is vital to construct such a narrative and to show in what way the welfare state and progressive taxation do in fact constitute a systemic transformation of capitalism. When their logic is allowed to fully unfold, these institutions represent an essential stage on the way to a new form of democratic socialism, decentralized and self-managing, ecological and multicultural, making it possible to structure a different world that is far more emancipatory and egalitarian than the present one. Historically, the socialist and communist movements have been constructed around a significantly different platform, namely state ownership of the means of production and centralized planning, both of which have failed and have never really been replaced by an alternative. In comparison, the welfare state and especially progressive taxation have often appeared to be "soft" forms of socialism, incapable of challenging the deep logic of capitalism. Before World War I, progressive taxation was advocated in France by the Radical Party, which called for "social reform respecting private property." The socialists were skeptical about a reform that was limited to retroactively reducing the inequalities produced by the capitalist system without really getting to the heart of the process of production, without questioning its social relationships—a process and relationships that might even halt workers' advance toward proletarian revolution. These historical origins and debates continue to permeate representations of democratic socialism. It seems to me urgent to challenge them, for several reasons.

First of all, everything clearly depends on the degree of fiscal progressivity. A progressive tax with a maximal rate of 2 percent is not the same thing as a progressive tax with a rate of 90 percent. Our experience with progressive taxation in the twentieth century has shown us that it is possible to implement successfully almost confiscatory tax rates at the highest level of the wealth hierarchy, but this essential historical lesson remains largely unacknowledged. Second, the question of progressive taxation must be envisioned as inseparable from the question of the welfare state. As we have seen, in the course of the twentieth century the construction of the welfare state took the form of a powerful movement to socialize wealth, with tax receipts increasing from less than 10 percent of the national income before 1914 to about 40–50 percent since the 1980s and 1990s in the main European nations. It thereby demonstrated that it was completely possible to organize, beyond commercial logic, vast sectors of activity, notably in health care and education, but also in culture, transportation, energy, and so on. No one can decide in advance how far such a process will go, whether regarding the list of sectors concerned, the forms of decentralized and participatory organizations that will be developed in these different sectors—hospitals and clinics, schools and universities, associations and foundations, local and state administrations, cooperatives and local, state-owned companies—or how and to what extent they will be collectively financed (perhaps someday 60 or 70 percent of the national income, or even more).[3] What seems certain, however, is that it is impossible to envisage a new stage in the socialization of wealth if we do not succeed in reestablishing the conviction that the system of collective financing is based on a rigorous conception of fiscal and social justice. Unless the highest incomes and fortunes are subjected to certified and verifiable levies, and thus unless there is a genuine renewal of progressive taxation, no new stage in the construction of the welfare state and in the historical process of de-commodification is conceivable.

We must also remember that progressive taxation, as it functioned in the course of the twentieth century, enabled us not only to more fairly distribute taxes on wealth and income but also to impose narrow limits on inequalities before taxes. This role of predistribution and not just redistribution was absolutely central. It shows to what extent progressive taxation is also a form of intervention at the very heart of the process of production—together, of course, with other practices, such as labor law or the presence of employees on boards of directors. Let us stress that the drastic reduction of the salary scale that progressive taxation permits, particularly the 30–90 percent rates applied to the highest incomes, is also an indispensable tool for confronting the commercial sector on equal terms. If capitalist enterprises in the information technology sector pay extravagant remunerations in

---

3. The debates on organizational forms that make it possible to reconcile centralization and regulation optimally in the various sectors of the welfare state are endless and can be only touched upon here. In health care, it is often thought that the French system constitutes a better compromise than the British model. That may be true in part, but on the condition that access to care and physician incomes be genuinely regulated. In higher education, the autonomy of individual institutions and decentralization is probably a good thing, if they are accompanied by an appropriate system of public financing. In the realm of culture and show business, the status of casual workers includes interesting elements, again on the condition that financing is adequate and accepted as cultural policy. In the domain of water, energy, or transportation, much is to be learned from the new forms of municipal management developed in several cities in Europe and other parts of the world.

order to poach almost all the most expert computer scientists on the market, that can seriously complicate the task of the public agencies entrusted with regulating them (unless they choose to encourage the race toward ever greater differences in pay). The same holds true in finance or law. The fact that salaries have been reduced to a scale of one to five and no longer one to twenty, or even one to a hundred, is not only a matter of distributive justice. It is also a matter of efficiency for public regulation, and it contributes to the construction of alternative modes of economic organization.

Finally, we must take into account the limits of what the welfare state and progressive taxation have allowed us to accomplish in terms of reducing inequalities of income and especially of wealth, and to find ways of moving beyond them. Regarding differences in income, we have already noted that the increase in income inequality since 1980 was explained in part by the thwarting of progressivity. Such levels of inequality would be difficult to justify by considerations of incentives or efficiency. In fact, this development was accompanied by a 50 percent decline in growth. The return of greater fiscal progressivity would make it possible to narrow the range of salaries once again. This action would have to be accompanied by many other tools that would support equality of access to training and negotiating power for employees and their representatives. The basic income systems currently in place in most European countries suffer from multiple insufficiencies, notably regarding access for the youngest and for students, as well as for persons who are homeless or who do not have bank accounts. Moreover, it is essential that the basic income scheme also cover people with low wages and income from work, along with a system of automatic payment on pay stubs and the progressive income tax system, without forcing recipients to ask for a handout. In addition, we must emphasize that the modest amount envisaged for the basic income, generally between half and three-quarters of the minimum wage for full-time work, depending on the offers, can by construction be no more than a partial tool for combating inequalities. This enables us to set a floor, which is essential, but on the condition that we do not stop there.[4]

A more ambitious tool that could be used along with basic income is the system of guaranteed employment recently proposed in the context of discussions of the Green New Deal. The idea is to make available to all a full-time job at a minimum salary set at a decent level ($15 an hour in the United States). The financing would be provided by the federal government, and the jobs would be offered by public employment agencies in the public and nonprofit sectors. Following in the footsteps of the Economic Bill of Rights proposed by Franklin D. Roosevelt in 1944 and the March on Washington for Jobs and Freedom at which Martin Luther King Jr. spoke in 1963, such a system could contribute powerfully to the process of decommercialization and to the provision of public services, the transition to alternative energies, and the renovation of infrastructure.[5]

Property and Socialism: The Question of Decentralization

Let us now come to the question of wealth inequality and the property system. If we adopt a long-term perspective, we may be struck by the persistence of hyperconcentration of property. In particular, the poorest 50 percent have almost never had any substantial possessions. If it were possible to wait until growth diffuses wealth, we would have seen the effects long ago: that argument falls flat. The most

---

4. Taking into account its limited, minimalist amount, it seems to me more appropriate to speak of "basic income" rather than a "universal income." On the automatic payment of the basic income on pay slips, see P.-A. Muet, *Un impôt juste, c'est possible!* (Paris: Seuil, 2018). In addition, this system makes it possible to defend the salaried status and to oppose the fragmentation of labor.

5. P. Tcherneva, *The Case for a Job Guarantee* (Cambridge: Polity Press, 2020). Compare the system of guaranteed employment proposed by A. B. Atkinson, *Inequality: What Can Be Done* (Cambridge, MA: Harvard University Press, 2015).

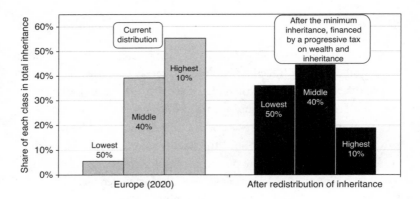

FIGURE 30. Redistribution of Inheritance

The share of the poorest 50 percent in total inheritance was 6 percent in Europe in 2020, as opposed to 39 percent for the middle 40 percent and 55 percent for the richest 10 percent. After implementing an "inheritance for all" (minimum wealth equal to 60 percent of the average inheritance, paid at the age of twenty-five), financed by a progressive tax on wealth and inheritance, it would be 36 percent (as opposed to 45 percent and 19 percent).

Note: "Europe" is an average of France, Sweden, and the United Kingdom. *Sources and series:* piketty.pse.ens.fr/equality

natural way of escaping this situation would be to imagine a system of inheritance redistribution that enabled everyone to receive a minimal inheritance (see Figure 30). For example, this minimal inheritance could be equal to 60 percent of the average wealth per adult (120,000 euros if the average is on the order of 200,000 euros, as it currently is in France), paid to each person at the age of twenty-five. This capital endowment could be financed by a combination of a progressive tax on wealth and on inheritances, levying approximately 5 percent of the national income, whereas the financing of the welfare state and ecological programs (including basic income and guaranteed employment) would be financed by a unified system of progressive income taxes, including contributions for social welfare and a tax on carbon emissions, levying about 45 percent of the national income (see Table 2).

TABLE 2

Circulation of Property and Progressive Taxation

Progressive property tax (financing the capital endowment to each young adult)			Progressive income tax (financing basic income, guaranteed employment, and welfare and ecological benefits)	
Multiple of average wealth	Annual property tax (effective rate)	Inheritance tax (effective rate)	Multiple of average income	Effective tax rate (including social taxes and carbon tax)
0.5	0.1%	5%	0.5	10%
2	1%	20%	2	40%
5	2%	50%	5	50%
10	5%	60%	10	60%
100	10%	70%	100	70%
1,000	60%	80%	1,000	80%
10,000	90%	90%	10,000	90%

Note: The proposed tax system includes a progressive tax on property (annual tax on net wealth and inheritance tax) financing a capital endowment for each young adult and a progressive income tax (including social contributions and a progressive tax on carbon emissions) financing basic income, social welfare, and ecological measures. These might include health care, education, retirement pensions, unemployment insurance, energy, and so on. This system of circulating property is one of the constituent elements of participatory socialism, with voting rights on corporate boards shared between workers and stockholders.

In the example shown here, the progressive tax on property brings in roughly 5 percent of national income (4 percent for the annual income tax and 1 percent for the inheritance tax, allowing a capital endowment equivalent to 60 percent of average wealth at age twenty-five) while the progressive income tax brings in roughly 45 percent of national income (allowing an annual basic income equivalent to 60 percent of average income after taxes—5 percent of national income) and the state's welfare and ecological programs (40 percent of national income). *Source:* piketty.pse.ens.fr/equality

The primary objective of an inheritance for all is to increase the negotiating power of everyone who owns almost nothing (that is, about half the population). If you have nothing, or worse yet, if you have only debts, then you must accept whatever wages and working conditions you can get, or almost. Basic income and guaranteed employment are valuable tools for changing this situation and rebalancing power relationships, but unfortunately they do not suffice. Having 100,000 or 200,000 euros as a complement to basic income, guaranteed employment, and all the rights associated with the most extensive welfare state possible (free education and health care, retirement pensions and highly redistributive unemployment benefits, labor law, and so on) changes the situation substantially.[6] Recipients could reject certain job offers, buy an apartment, engage in a personal project, or create a small business. This freedom, which is certain to delight some, may well frighten employers and property owners.

Several points must be clarified. First, the factors expressed in figures here are purely illustrative and might be set at more ambitious levels. With the parameters used here, those who currently inherit nothing (approximately, the poorest 50 percent) would receive 120,000 euros, while those who inherit a million euros (which corresponds to the average inheritance received by the richest 10 percent, with enormous disparities) would receive 600,000 euros after taxes and endowment. We see that we are still very far from equality of opportunity, a principle often defended at an abstract and theoretical level, but one which the privileged classes fear like the plague as soon as any concrete application is envisaged. In theory, it would be completely pos-

---

6. Regarding retirement pensions, the extension of life expectancy and the challenge of dependency render even more obsolete the idea that pensions must be limited to reproducing unto the last breath the inequalities characterizing a person's working life. On the contrary, a unified and renovated retirement system ought to do all it can to guarantee a better rate of replacement for the lowest salaries than for average and high salaries, while at the same time being financed by a progressive tax on all incomes. This subject, among others, also shows that the egalitarian coalition needs to formulate new, more ambitious programs, and must not continue to limit itself to defensive postures.

sible (and in my opinion, desirable) to increase much further the re-distribution of inherited wealth.

It will be noted that the proposed system of financing is based on tax scales similar to those that were already used during the twentieth century, with rates ranging from a few percentage points for assets and income lower than average to 80–90 percent for the highest assets and income. The main novelty is the recourse to a similar scale for taxes for the annual wealth tax, and not solely for taxes on income and on inheritance.[7] This is absolutely essential if we want to expand the redistribution of property beyond what was achieved during the twentieth century. Correctly applied and monitored, the annual wealth tax makes it possible to levy receipts far more substantial than those of the inheritance tax, and to improve redistribution in proportion to each individual's ability to contribute.[8] A specific tax scale should ideally be applied to endowments held by foundations and other nonprofit organizations as well, in order to avoid an excessive concentration of power within a small number of entities and to enable less wealthy entities to develop.[9]

---

7. Very progressive tax scales have already been applied to property during major historical episodes (in postwar Germany or Japan, or at the time of agrarian reforms in numerous countries), but not as a permanent system. Most of the long-lasting annual taxes on assets have been strictly proportional or slightly progressive. Strictly proportional taxes like the US property tax or the French *taxe foncière* have remained virtually unchanged since the end of the eighteenth century. These are applied to both moveable and immoveable property without any progressivity and without taking into account financial assets and liabilities. Their rather heavy receipts—about 2 percent of the national income—are very unfairly distributed. Slightly progressive taxes include the annual wealth taxes applied in Germanic and Nordic Europe during most of the twentieth century, or in France intermittently since 1981. They feature rates not exceeding 2–3 percent, multiple exemptions, and virtually no fiscal auditing, and so result in low receipts. See Piketty, *Capital and Ideology*, 558–571.

8. Concretely, if a person has become a billionaire at the age of thirty or forty, it is hard to understand why we have to wait until that individual is eighty or ninety to tax that wealth. In addition, prioritizing the annual wealth tax (more popular than the inheritance tax, because it is better able to target the largest fortunes) would enable us to ensure more efficiently that the middle classes benefited from the reform.

9. If the foundation is only an instrument in the service of a private person, then its endowment must naturally be taxed as such. If it is a nonprofit structure pursuing a general interest, a specific scale must be provided. The available data show that the

We must also explain that redistribution of property alone does not suffice to transcend capitalism. If the objective were simply to replace large property owners with small and middle-sized property owners who are just as greedy and careless of the social and environmental consequences of their actions, then it would be of limited interest. The project described here is of a quite different nature. The redistribution of property is accompanied by very progressive tax scales that prevent individuals from accumulating or polluting without limits, and that can be made more demanding, if necessary.[10] We could also imagine that the function of the inheritance for all might be regulated, for instance by limiting its use to housing purchases or the creation of an enterprise devoted to social or environmental goals. The debate is legitimate, as long as the same rules are applied equally to all inheritances and all heirs, and not only to the lower classes benefiting from a minimal inheritance.

In addition, I assert that the idea of an inheritance for all presented here is meaningful only if it is added to systems of basic income and guaranteed employment, which ought to be established first, and more generally, only if the inheritance for all is added to an existing welfare-state system whose objective is the gradual decommercialization of the economy. In particular, fundamental goods and services in do-

---

largest endowments (for example, those of the richest universities in the United States) have grown at a pace on the order of 7–8 percent per annum (over and above inflation) between 1980 and 2018, figures close to those seen for the largest private fortunes, but incommensurate with the growth of the world economy or smaller endowments (like those of other universities or small associations). See T. Piketty, *Capital in the Twenty-First Century* (Cambridge, MA: Belknap Press of Harvard University Press, 2017), 447–450; and Piketty, *Capital and Ideology*, 685–686.

10. In particular, the carbon card for individuals, a credit card that tracks one's carbon footprint, is supposed to enable us to enforce respect for the limits on the amount of global emissions set collectively, while at the same time concentrating our efforts on the largest emissions and the richest taxpayers. It is crucial that the carbon credit card be structurally connected with the scale of the progressive income tax, so as to be able to neutralize automatically, for the lower and middle classes, the negative impact on purchasing power of the measures occasioned by more restrictive emissions targets. See Piketty, *Capital and Ideology*, 1004–1007.

mains such as education, health care, culture, transportation, or energy are by nature to be produced outside the commercial sphere, in the context of public, municipal, group, or nonprofit structures. This vast nonprofit sector is destined to grow, whereas the for-profit sector, in which the inheritance for all might be invested, would gradually be reduced to a limited number of activities, such as housing and small businesses (notably in the craft industry, commerce, hotels and restaurants, repairs, consulting, and so on).

Finally, we must emphasize that the small- and middle-sized properties involved in the inheritance for all must be designed more as social, temporary properties than as strictly private ones. Inheritance would take place within a legal framework based on sharing power with other users of capital, and within the framework of a tax that drastically limits opportunities for accumulation and perpetuation. Regarding power sharing in enterprises in the for-profit sector, as I have already said, I propose to apply the system of "participatory socialism" described above, with the individual voting rights divided 50–50 between employees and stockholders and strict limits on the voting rights of individual stockholders depending on the size of the enterprise, so that a single employee who is also a stockholder would retain the majority of votes in a very small company but would lose it as soon as the company had more than ten employees.[11] It could also be imagined that the voting rights would depend on the seniority of the employees, in the same way that renters in an apartment building gradually accumulate rights that give them almost a permanent right of usage.[12] The recent debates have also included a renewal of discussion of the proposals for "employee funds" imagined by Rudolf Meidner and his colleagues in the Swedish trade union federation,

---

11. See Chapter 5, Figure 18. The parameters can be adjusted, of course.

12. This is partly the case in the numerous legal systems that grant particular protection to longtime renters or give them a preferential purchase right, sometimes with a discount or subsidy. Furthermore, whatever the status of the housing, it is indispensable to apply strict, verifiable, and sanctionable rules of social mixture that prevent ghettoization.

Landsorganisationen i Sverige (LO), in the 1970s and 1980s. According to this system, reserved mainly for the largest enterprises, employers would be expected to pay part of their annual profits into a fund that enables employees to gradually take control of 52 percent of the capital after twenty years.[13] Intended to complete the system of comanagement (which guarantees that employees will have a share of voting rights, independently of any participation in the capital), this proposal aroused fierce opposition among Swedish capitalists, and could not be adopted. It has recently been put back on the agenda by some Democrats in the United States, notably Bernie Sanders and Alexandria Ocasio-Cortez, and included in the official program of the British Labour Party.[14] Other innovative proposals have also been formulated to allow for the development of public investment funds at the local and communal levels.[15] The objective is not to close the discussion but rather to widen it: the concrete forms of power and economic democracy still require reinvention, and always will.[16]

For a Democratic, Self-Managing, and Decentralized Socialism

Let us sum up. The welfare state and progressive taxation, pushed to their logical conclusions, allow us to lay the foundations for a new form of democratic socialism: self-managing, decentralized, and

---

13. One might also imagine that the progressive tax on property described in Table 2 might be paid in part in the form of stocks put into the employee fund.

14. R. Meidner, *Employee Investment Funds: An Approach to Collective Capital Formation* (London: Allen and Unwin, 1978); G. Olsen, *The Struggle for Economic Democracy in Sweden* (Farnham, UK: Ashgate, 1992); J. Guinan, "Socialising Capital: Looking Back on the Meidner Plan," *International Journal of Public Policy* 15, no. 1–2 (2019): 38–58.

15. J. Guinan and M. O'Neill, *The Case for Community Wealth Building* (Cambridge: Polity Press, 2020).

16. For an imaginative discussion of a society based on "melting" property, defined as property whose value for the owner is gradually reduced until end of life, at which point it is returned to a common fund and resold, and the equalization of all powers, rather close in certain ways to the "participatory socialism" outlined here, see E. Dockès, *Voyage en misarchie. Essai pour tout reconstruire* (Paris: Editions du Détour, 2017).

based on the continual circulation of power and property. This system differs entirely from the kind of centralized, authoritarian state socialism that was tried within the Soviet bloc during the twentieth century. It is situated mainly within ongoing social, fiscal, and legal transformations begun in many Western European countries in the past century, through a hard-earned history of changing power relations, popular movements, and multiple crises and moments of great tension.

The democratic socialism described here is only an outline. It includes many weaknesses and limitations. For example, some readers may think that by allowing the continued existence of a limited form of private ownership of the means of production (at the level of small businesses) and housing, we are taking the risk that these changes will be ephemeral, and that the strict limitation of differences in wealth will not last, given the considerable efforts that some people will deploy to ensure that the tax scales are modified and to reject all limits. This fear is legitimate, but must not be instrumentalized: it was this fear that led the Soviet authorities, who at the time talked about "capitalist gangrene," to criminalize in the 1920s any form of property, including property for very small businesses with a tiny number of employees, and to descend into now well-known authoritarian and bureaucratic excesses. The proper response is to consider a deeper conception of democracy: when we redistribute property, we must also adopt a system of egalitarian financing for political campaigns, the media, and think tanks, in order to prevent electoral democracy from being co-opted by those who are better off. More generally, we have already noted that the system of redistributing property outlined here would require substantial constitutional revisions.[17]

---

17. A constitutional formulation allowing for the redistribution of property and protecting progressivity might be: "The law determines the conditions for the exercise of the right of property and takes care to promote its diffusion and its role in the service of the common interest, if necessary through a system of progressive taxes on property, capital endowment, and voting rights for employees. If total direct and indirect taxes are paid in proportion to the goods of all kinds held by taxpayers, this proportion cannot be lower for the richest taxpayer than for the poorest. It may be higher, depending on the terms set by law."

A supplementary protection would be to assign these collected taxes to a fund that manages the inheritance for all, in the same way that social security contributions are managed by specific social security funds in most countries. Historical experience has shown that strengthening administrative structures makes it difficult for politicians to renege on these choices (for example, by promising decreases in taxes or contributions), because it forces them to make explicit the withdrawal of benefits granted.

Moreover, nothing forbids us to reflect on systems that reject any form of private property, including social and temporary property like the one envisaged here. I am thinking, for example, of the system of "salarial socialism" defended by Bernard Friot.[18] To simplify, Friot proposes to extend the model of the social security funds set up in 1945 in France to other socioeconomic arenas, especially those of retirement and health insurance. That would involve in particular the creation of a "salary fund" and an "investment fund," the former entrusted with classifying people, according to their qualifications, in different levels of "salary for life" (with a scale ranging from one to four), and the latter entrusted with attributing investment credits and rights to use real and business capital in the various units of production and in multiple individual and collective projects. Insofar as these funds would be managed in a participatory and democratic way, in precise forms that would have to be, however, made more explicit (which Friot does not do), such a proposal is full of potential. Generally speaking, the development of new organizational forms based on common property and Friot's category of "property for use" is to be encouraged, for it complements the system of social and temporary property defended here.[19]

18. See in particular B. Friot, *Puissances du salariat*, new enlarged ed. (Paris: La Dispute, 2012). The expression "salarial socialism" is not used by Friot, but it seems to me apt to express his (justified) insistence on the emancipatory potential of the *"déjà-là,"* i.e., a "salary for life" and the extension of social security.

19. On the diversity of the forms of organization developed in history to make common use of natural, material, or cognitive resources, see D. H. Cole and E. Ostrom,

I simply want to draw attention to this point: the salary and investment funds Friot imagines (or their equivalent in other proposals depriving small private property, social and temporary, of any role) would hold a considerable power over millions of lives and everyday decisions, bearing notably on salary levels and the use of capital with regard to housing and small businesses. The internal organization of these quasi-state, hypercentralized authorities is not at all clear, in particular how they might function in a truly democratic and emancipatory way. It would be premature, to say the least, to assume in advance that this question has been settled and that any risk of bureaucratic and authoritarian excess can be ruled out. Explanations must be given for the systems of voting and power-sharing that might be applied in such institutions and comparisons made with better-known sociohistorical experiences (parliaments, parties, labor unions, social welfare funds, public banks, etc.) and the potential for learning and improvements they may contain.[20] In the current state of our knowledge and experience, it seems to me more appropriate to recognize a lasting role for small private properties, particularly in the sector of housing and small businesses, while at the same time encouraging the development of collective and cooperative structures when they correspond to the needs of the actors concerned. Generally speaking, the sometimes excessive faith in the ability of large, centralized organizations to handle internal deliberation and democratic decision-making

---

eds., *Property in Land and Other Resources* (Cambridge, MA: Lincoln Institute of Land Policy, 2012); B. Coriat, ed., *Le Retour des communs* (Paris: Les Liens qui Libèrent, 2015); T. Boccon-Gibod and P. Cretois, *État social, propriété publique et biens communs* (Lormont: Le Bord de l'eau, 2015).

20. Friot says that the salary and investment funds will be managed by authorities who are elected or chosen by lots, without indicating his opinion as to which is preferable, and without specifying the connection with state authorities, whose identities are left vague. See B. Friot and J. Bernard, *Un désir de communisme* (Paris: Textuel, 2020), 32. Compare F. Lordon, *Figures du communisme* (Paris: La Fabrique, 2021), who supports the system proposed by Friot but proposes to rename the "salary for life" the "general economic guarantee." Lordon says nothing more than Friot about the system of governance (elections, parties, labor unions, media, etc.).

can lead us to underestimate the emancipatory potential of institutional systems such as small private property, properly supervised and limited in its scope and the rights it confers. The same goes for progressive taxation. If all the major organizational decisions regarding the distribution of salaries and investments are made within a salarial fund and an investment fund at the national level, then the form of the tax matters little: its base and its progressivity have hardly any importance because in any case the distribution of value will be defined collectively at the centralized level.[21] Conversely, if we accept the principle of a permanently decentralized socioeconomic organization involving a great diversity of actors, collectivities, and mixed structures, then the concrete forms of taxation are important: they help determine the distribution of value, alongside, of course, other institutional mechanisms such as the systems of voting rights within the different structures.

The Free Circulation of Capital:
The New Censitary Power

We now come to an absolutely essential point. The challenge to the welfare state and progressive taxation since the 1980s was not based solely on talk. It was also materialized in a set of rules and international treaties seeking to make the change as irreversible as possible. The heart of the new rules is the free circulation of capital, without any compensation in the form of regulation or common taxation. In sum, states have instituted a legal system in which economic actors have won a quasi-sacred right to enrich themselves by using a country's

---

21. This explains why Friot is not interested in the question of taxation and fiscal progressivity. But that does not prevent him from adopting, at times, more gradualist proposals, such as the idea of a food security program that would be financed by a new welfare contribution and would grant everyone a monthly subsidy to buy food from certified producers, a proposal that could certainly be included in the decentralized framework defended here.

public infrastructures and social institutions (such as the educational and health-care systems), and then, with the stroke of a pen or the click of a mouse, to move their assets to another jurisdiction, without any arrangement to follow the wealth in question and to tax it in a way that is fair and coherent with the rest of the tax system. This is, *de facto,* a new form of censitary power, in the sense that the states that have signed such treaties can, from the moment that they refuse to reconsider the commitments made by earlier governments, wind up explaining in all sincerity to their people that it is strictly impossible to tax the first beneficiaries of international integration (billionaires, multinationals, those with high incomes), and that consequently they must turn once again to taxpayers in the lower and middle classes who have had the good taste to remain quietly where they were. The logic claims to be unanswerable. The reaction of the classes that don't move their assets around is just as unanswerable: all this leads to a feeling of abandonment and a hatred of globalization.

It is natural to wonder how we got into this situation. Research has revealed a long period of preparatory work by banking lobbies after the war, the role played generally by employers' groups, banks, and wealth managers in the co-production of the law, and finally implementation of the law in the most advantageous means possible, including evasions and optimizations.[22] This level of control exerted over the economy by financiers and investors and the deregulation of financial flows must also be analyzed in the context of a stockholders' strategy, seeking to restore managers' control (or rather, to align their interests with those of the stockholders) and to allow more rapid and more profitable reconfigurations of the major units of production

---

22. S. Weeks, "Collective Effort, Private Accumulation: Constructing the Luxembourg Investment Fund, 1956–2019," in *Accumulating Capital Today: Contemporary Strategies of Profit and Dispossessive Policies,* ed. M. Benquet and T. Bourgeron (London: Routledge, 2021). Compare C. Herlin-Giret, *Rester riche. Enquête sur les gestionnaires de fortune et leurs clients* (Lormont: Le Bord de l'eau, 2019); S. Guex, "L'emergence du paradis fiscal suisse," in *Pour une histoire sociale et politique de l'économie,* ed. D. Fraboulet and P. Verheyde (Paris: Editions de la Sorbonne, 2020).

(mergers and acquisitions, transfer of assets).[23] The idea of using international treaties to depoliticize the economy, to protect property, and to prevent redistribution was, moreover, one of the Hayekian and ordoliberal theses formulated as early as 1940 with a view to structuring the postwar world, theses that ended up being adopted in 1980–1990, thanks to private lobbyists.[24] We must also emphasize the central and sometimes paradoxical role played by European governments at the end of the 1980s in the movement to liberalize capital flows. Having had their fingers burned by their economic difficulties, starting in 1984–1985 French socialists decided to stake everything on the construction of Europe. In order to accelerate the implementation of the common currency, they agreed to the demands of the German Christian Democrats, who sought a complete liberalization of capital flows. This demand materialized in a European directive of 1988 that was retranscribed in the Maastricht Treaty of 1992. The terms of this treaty were then adopted by the Organisation for Economic Cooperation and Development (OECD) and the International Monetary Fund (IMF) and were to serve as the new global standard. One of the motivations of the actors of that time was also to lower the cost of public borrowing by means of a call for international investments,

---

23. P. Francois and C. Lemercier, *Sociologie historique du capitalisme* (Paris: La Decouverte, 2021). On the way, the themes of agility and flexible, reactive structures have been used to make old public and private bureaucracies seem obsolete and to reconfigure the ideology of capitalism in the 1970s and 1980s; see L. Boltanski and E. Chiapello, *The New Spirit of Capitalism,* trans. G. Elliott (London: Verso, 2006). The generalized financialization has also resulted in a multiplication of cross-ownerships between companies and between countries: the total of private financial assets and liabilities held by banks, enterprises, and households has risen from 200 percent of GDP in 1970 to 1,000 percent of GDP in 2020 (without even including derivatives), whereas real wealth (that is, the net value of enterprises' immoveable assets) rose from 300 percent to 500 percent of GDP.

24. O. Rosenboim, *The Emergence of Globalism* (Princeton, NJ: Princeton University Press, 2017), shows that other theses were formulated in the 1940s, like those of Barbara Wooton and William Beveridge regarding a future European federation based on social protection, progressive federal taxation, and democratic socialism.

without there having really been time to explain and discuss these different objectives.[25]

What is certain is that it seems impossible to resume the movement toward equality without leaving this framework behind. Concretely, each state that wants to do that must free itself from these obligations and set explicit conditions in terms of fiscal and social justice for the circulation of capital and for free trade. The process has already begun, in part. In 2012, at the urging of the Obama administration, Switzerland rewrote its banking laws to require transmission of information about US taxpayers who had accounts in Swiss banks; if they did not, the banks in question would immediately lose their licenses to operate in the United States. In 2021, the Biden administration announced its intention to levy direct taxes on profits in countries with low taxes, billing the enterprises and subsidiaries concerned for the difference between a minimal tax rate set by the United States and the one practiced in the country in question (for example, in Ireland or Luxembourg). In both cases, these unilateral decisions made by the United States openly violated all the earlier rules, and especially intra-European rules: if France or Germany had made similar decisions, the targeted states would easily have had them invalidated by European courts, in the name, precisely, of treaties signed in the past by the French and German states.[26] But the fact is that it appears to be the only way to move forward. The problem is twofold. On the one hand, the steps taken up to this point by administrations in the United

---

25. R. Abdelal, *Capital Rules: The Construction of Global Finance* (Cambridge, MA: Harvard University Press, 2007). The inquiry is based especially on the testimony of officials of the time (in particular, J. Delors and P. Lamy). Compare B. Lemoine, *L'Ordre de la dette. Enquête sur les infortunes de l'État et la prospérité du marché* (Paris: La Découverte, 2016).

26. The European Court of Justice (ECJ) has gone particularly far in defending the absolutely free circulation of capital (including via the creation of offshore structures making it possible to evade *de facto* any regulation), but this development would not have been possible had the Maastricht Treaty correctly taken into account the right of the states to set rules and to levy taxes. See K. Pistor, *The Code of Capital: How the Law Creates Wealth and Inequality* (Princeton, NJ: Princeton University Press, 2019).

States are in reality minuscule in comparison with what would be necessary, and it would be completely illusory to wait for the solution to come from the United States alone, given how political life is financed in that country.[27] On the other hand, the European states continue to do nothing and to rely on a hypothetical, unrealistic future unanimity to change the rules within the European Union or the OECD. By legalism, or else out of fear of being blacklisted by other countries, financial lobbies, or the media and the think tanks that they influence, they refuse to withdraw unilaterally from the existing framework and to impose anti-dumping sanctions on public and private actors who are making it possible to perpetuate this new censitary power.

There is no other way of escaping this dead end, however. The redefinition of international rules is critical not only for the global North, but also for the global South and the entire planet. The current economic system, based on the uncontrolled circulation of capital, goods, and services, without social or environmental objectives, is akin to a neocolonialism that benefits the wealthiest. We will see that only a project of global transformation, to which each country can make its contribution by practicing a new form of sovereignism with a universalist vocation, that is, by relying on explicit indicators of social justice, can make it possible to overcome these contradictions.

---

27. For example, the minimal rate of 21 percent envisaged by the Biden administration (as opposed to the current 12 percent rate in Ireland) could play a useful role if it were merely a first step in initiating a global financial register, one that would reestablish fiscal progressivity (with rates potentially reaching 80–90 percent on the highest incomes from capital and labor). Things are very different if it is a final rate (which could, moreover, be further lowered to about 15 percent, to judge by OECD-level discussions).

8

REAL EQUALITY AGAINST

DISCRIMINATION

Let us now return to the question of social and racial discrimination, and especially to equality of access to training and employment. One of the major limits of the movement toward equality that occurred in the course of the past century is that it was too often limited to a formal equality. In short: we have proclaimed the theoretical principle of the equality of rights and opportunities, independent of origins, but without giving ourselves the means to determine whether this principle corresponds to reality or not. If we want to attain real equality, we must develop indicators and procedures that will allow us to fight gendered, social, and ethno-racial discrimination, which is in practice endemic nearly everywhere, in the global North as well as in the South. In practice, one of the biggest difficulties is to succeed in combating tenacious prejudices without rigidifying identities. There is no single answer to this dilemma, and the solution may depend on the national and postcolonial context in question. Only a calm examination and comparison of experiences in Europe, the United States, India, and other parts of the world can allow us to sketch out avenues for understanding, while at the same time resituating the struggle against discrimination in the more general framework of a social policy with universalist objectives.

Educational Equality:
Always Proclaimed, Never Realized

We will begin with the question of educational justice: the diffusion of knowledge has always been the central tool enabling real equality, beyond origins. But the problem is that almost everywhere there is a monumental gap between official statements regarding equality of opportunities and the reality of the educational inequalities that the disadvantaged classes face. Access to elementary education, and then secondary school, was extended to the whole of the population in the course of the twentieth century, at least in the global North, and this constitutes considerable progress. But in reality, inequalities of access to the most advantageous courses of study and schools remain very deep, especially in higher education. In the United States, researchers have been able to correlate a student's educational path with parental tax information. The results are depressing: the parents' income predicts almost perfectly the child's chances of going to a university. Concretely, the probability of being admitted to an institution of higher learning is scarcely 30 percent among the 10 percent of young adults whose parents have the lowest income, increasing linearly to more than 90 percent for the young adults whose parents have the highest incomes (see Figure 31).

In addition, the two groups do not go to the same institutions of higher education: the former usually have to be content with summary courses of study in badly financed public universities and community colleges, whereas the latter have access to highly specialized curricula in extremely rich private universities. These latter institutions are, moreover, characterized by the opacity of their admission procedures and a near-absence of public regulation. Although these universities have benefited from multiple sources of governmental financing, they have succeeded in convincing powerful political figures that it is normal to let them do as they please with their admissions algorithms, including giving priority for admission to "legacy students" (that is, the children of alumni or rich donors). In other words, not

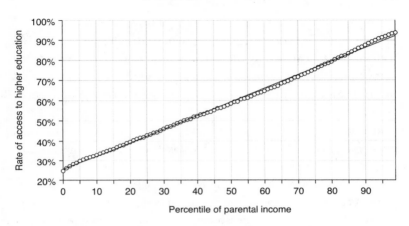

FIGURE 31. Parental Income and Access to Higher Education, United States, 2018

In 2018, the rate of access to higher education (the percentage of persons aged nineteen to twenty-one enrolled in a university, college, or other institution of higher learning) was scarcely 30 percent for children of the poorest 10 percent in the United States, and more than 90 percent for children of the richest 10 percent. *Sources and series:* piketty.pse.ens.fr/equality

only do fabulously high tuition fees put the best universities out of reach for the least well-off students (unless they have exceptional grades granting them access to scholarships), but the richest parents can pay a kind of supplement to make up for their offspring's insufficient grades. Universities explain that the rate of legacy admissions is minimal, even as they deny access to this information and to the formulas used to assess grades and donations.[1]

It is striking to see the number of academics in the United States who have become used to this reality: after all, if it provides supplementary funds from generous billionaires who want to have their offspring admitted, why not? It would be simpler, however, to make

---

1. Nonetheless, we know that donations made by rich alumni to universities are abnormally and massively concentrated in the years when their children are of an age to apply for admission, which suggests that purchasing admission is more common than universities claim. J. Meer and H. S. Rosen, "Altruism and the Child Cycle of Alumni Donations," *American Economic Journal* 1, no. 1 (2009): 258–286.

them pay the same amount in the form of taxes intended to finance education for all, and principally those most disadvantaged (and not the contrary). In any event, these delicate questions should be decided democratically, after transparent discussion of the pros and cons, and not in the smoke-filled rooms of governing boards dominated by donors.

It would be quite wrong to believe that this massive educational hypocrisy exists only in the United States. Even if education is almost free of charge in many countries, that does not in any way protect it from social selection. The pursuit of extensive training in institutions of higher learning in the absence of an adequate system of minimum income represents a considerable investment for people with lower incomes. Moreover, these students have not always had access to the preliminary training, the social codes, and the networks that provide opportunities for certain courses of study. The French system is an extraordinarily hypocritical one. Under cover of "republican" equality—low to no tuition fees, no official privilege for any rank—it manages to spend three times more in public resources per student for those who have had access to selective courses of study (the *grandes écoles*) than for those who pursue degrees in ordinary universities. It happens that the former have, on average, social origins far more privileged than the latter, especially within the most sought-after schools.[2] That

2. According to the most recent data available, students from disadvantaged social categories (36 percent of an age group) represent 20 percent of those studying in baccalaureate + 3 or baccalaureate + 5 programs, but only 8 percent of those enrolled at Sciences Po in Paris, 7 percent of those at ENS Ulm, 3 percent of those at HEC, and 0 percent of those at Polytechnique. Conversely, students from very privileged social categories (23 percent of an age group) constitute 47 percent of the students in baccalaureate + 3 or baccalaureate + 5 programs (the US equivalents of a bachelor's degree and master's degree, respectively), but 73 percent at Sciences Po Paris, 75 percent at ENS Ulm, 89 percent at HEC, and 92 percent at Polytechnique. See C. Bonneau, P. Charousset, J. Grenet, and G. Thebault, "Quelle démocratisation des grandes écoles depuis le milieu des années 2000?" IPP Report no. 30, Institut des Politiques Publiques, Paris, January 2021. Moreover, this study notes that no measurable progress in the area of social mixture has been achieved since the 2000s, despite the repeated claims of governments and schools.

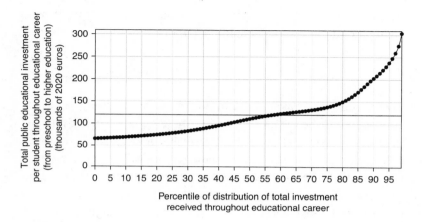

FIGURE 32. The Inequality of Investment in Education in France

Students reaching the age of twenty in 2020 have benefited, from primary school to higher education, from an average public investment of about 120,000 euros (or about fifteen years of education for an average cost of 8,000 euros each year). Within this generation, the 10 percent of students who benefited from the smallest public investment received about 65,000 to 70,000 euros, whereas the 10 percent who benefited from the largest public investment received between 200,000 and 300,000 euros.

Note: The average costs by track and by year in the French educational system in 2015–2020 ranged from 5,000 euros to 6,000 euros in nursery/primary school, 8,000 to 10,000 euros in secondary school, 9,000 to 10,000 euros in higher education, and 15,000 to 16,000 euros in preparatory classes for advanced studies (at the *grandes écoles*). *Sources and series:* piketty.pse.ens.fr/equality

is why people can, with a clear conscience, use public means to strengthen existing social inequalities. On the whole, if we take into account all education expenditures, from nursery school to university, we find considerable inequalities within an age group: the 10 percent of students who benefit from the lowest expenditures receive around 65,000 to 70,000 euros each, whereas the 10 percent who benefit from the highest expenditures receive between 200,000 and 300,000 euros each (see Figure 32). This concentration of expenditures for education to the benefit of a minority is, to be sure, less extreme than it used to be, but it remains considerable, and is hardly in conformity with contemporary talk about equality of opportunity.[3]

For an Affirmative Action Based on Social Criteria

There is only one way to move beyond these hypocrisies: we have to give ourselves the means to measure these realities collectively and democratically, to set quantified, verifiable goals, and to constantly adjust the policies used to reach them. In terms of fiscal justice, it took centuries to define an objective understanding of inequality, with conceptions of income, property, tax scales, and tax rates that would make it possible to construct norms and a common language for comparison. This process is still very far from having reached its end. With regard to educational justice, it is sometimes imagined that we can rely on general principles and declarations of good intentions. Figures 31 and 32 show that this is not the case. To begin, full transparency by public authorities is critical: such quantified facts must made publicly available on an annual basis, not just revealed from time to time by individual researchers. Specifically, it is important that we make public every year the distribution of expenditures for education and the rates of access to the various courses of study in relation to social origins and percentile of parental income, breaking down this information by level of schooling. Broad access to these data would ensure that this information will provide food for a balanced, democratic debate, free of manipulation. The road ahead is long: in practice, governments and public administrations display, regarding these questions, an opacity hardly less extreme than that of private universities. Too often, these actors continue to rely on a vertical conception of public policy and the common interest, and to arrogate to

---

3. See Chapter 4, Figure 14. Compare T. Piketty, *Capital and Ideology* (Cambridge, MA: Belknap Press of Harvard University Press, 2020), 1007–1012. Taking into account the expenditure per student over recent decades, the goal is not to reduce the means available for selective courses of study, but rather to raise other courses of study to the same level.

themselves, without restraint, the monopoly on expertise and information that accompanies it.

The production of universally accepted indicators is central, but not sufficient. What matters most is that this exercise in transparency be directly connected with levers of action and policies that permit change on all educational levels. In the case of higher education, many countries have begun to establish centralized procedures for assigning students at the regional or national level (for example, the Parcoursup platform in France). In comparison with systems in which each university does whatever it pleases, this is potentially an improvement, in the sense that it becomes possible to escape from the logic of networks and individual relations (or even, in the United States, donations of money) and to define democratically neutral admission criteria and goals that apply to all in the same way. Thus, we can imagine a system based on students' wishes, their grades, and their social origins. Inclusion of the latter takes into consideration the fact that poorer secondary school students encounter more difficulties.

It goes without saying that finding the best compromise is not easy: a certain dose of affirmative action based on social criteria may be justified, but if we go too far, it can become counterproductive for everyone. No one can claim to know the ultimate truth regarding such complex judgments. This makes it all the more indispensable to organize the conditions for a vast democratic debate based on transparency and experimentation. Unfortunately, algorithms are regularly applied to students and their parents without any prior consultation or evaluation of the pros and cons. As a result they run the risk of arousing a generalized distrust with regard to such systems, or even to the very idea of educational justice. In France, the Parcoursup platform is supposed to have implemented, since 2018, a form of affirmative action for scholarship students in secondary schools (between 15 and 20 percent of the students, based chiefly on parental income) who are asking for admission to preparatory classes. However, how this is configured remains obscure: no quantified objective was set, and no evaluation has been carried out. In 2021, there was talk about the possibility of introducing more places for scholarship students (between 50 and 60 percent of an age group) in schools of administration, but there again no explanation was given that would make it possible to evaluate the real impact of such a plan.[4] Although governments and administrations should without saying respond to the need for transparency and disengage themselves from their vertical and sometimes manipulative culture, the success of such a process requires the participation of citizens, associations, labor unions, elected government officials, and political parties, who must demand full access to data and use it constructively to make policy proposals for improvement. Things will really change only when this new democratic space for public participation has been fully occupied.

Beyond the question of higher education, the exercise in transparency must also enable a radical review of the allocation of resources in primary and secondary education. When a student is entering university, it is generally too late to reduce inequality of opportunities radically: we have to act much earlier. But on this point educational hypocrisy reaches a pinnacle. In many countries, governments claim to have set up systems seeking to "give more to those who have less," that is, to send supplementary resources to the most socially disadvantaged schools. The problem is that the data often suggest exactly the reverse. For example, when we examine public middle schools in and around Paris, we see that the proportion of teachers who are tem-

---

4. If 10 or 20 percent of the places are reserved for a group representing 50–60 percent of an age group, then it is possible that the actual effect would be limited or even negative, in the event that a group was stigmatized without increasing the number of places. The discussion is sometimes obscured by the fact that the notion of a scholarship student in secondary school (in France, roughly speaking, the 15–20 percent of lycée students whose parents have the lowest incomes) is much more restrictive than that of a scholarship student in higher education, which has eight levels and applies, in all, to about 40 percent of the students (and between 50 and 60 percent of an age group, taking into account the fact that the parental incomes of students in higher education are higher than those of their generation as a whole). These distinctions illustrate the need for precise, neutral, and independent information to feed informed democratic debate on these questions.

porary contract employees (less trained and lower paid than teachers holding permanent positions) or beginners is barely 10 percent in the wealthiest departments (Paris, Hauts-de-Seine) and reaches 50 percent in the most disadvantaged departments (Seine-Saint-Denis, Val-de-Marne). Studies conducted by Asma Benhenda using National Education payroll files have made it possible to confirm the extent to which the proposed system has been reversed. If we calculate the average salary of teachers in the various elementary, middle, and secondary schools, taking into account the paltry premiums paid in priority zones and other forms of remuneration (connected with seniority, degrees held, status as tenured or temporary, and so on), we see that the higher the percentage of privileged students enrolled, the higher the average remuneration.[5] In addition, we find this reality in most of the OECD countries: young people coming from advantaged backgrounds are more likely to have tenured, experienced teachers than those from disadvantaged backgrounds, who more often have substitute teachers or teachers hired with short-term contracts, and the small premiums intended to correct this situation are generally insufficient to compensate for the systemic inequality.[6]

Here we see that in practice the first issue is not to achieve affirmative action using social criteria, but simply to avoid negative discrimination: in primary and secondary schools, as in higher education, we often end up allocating higher public expenditures

---

5. In middle schools in France, the teachers' average remuneration is less than 2,400 euros per month in the 10 percent of the schools having the lowest percentage of socially privileged students, and then rises steadily to reach 2,800 euros in the schools having the highest percentage of these students. In the lycées, this same average remuneration rises from less than 2,700 euros per month in the 10 percent of the most disadvantaged schools to almost 3,200 euros per month in the 10 percent of the most privileged. See A. Benhenda, "Teaching Staff Characteristics and Spending per Student in French Disadvantaged Schools," unpublished manuscript, April 2019, http://piketty.pse.ens.fr/files/Benhenda2019.pdf; A. Benhenda, *Tous des bons profs. Un choix de société* (Paris: Fayard, 2020).

6. OECD, "Effective Teacher Policies: Insights from PISA," Programme for International Student Assessment, Organisation for Economic Co-operation and Development, June 11, 2018.

for privileged students than for others. In theory, it would not be so difficult to adjust the amount of the premiums to ensure that the average salary cannot in any case be an increasing function of the percentage of socially privileged students in a school, at least at the level of the educational system as a whole. We can escape from this situation only through objective, verifiable demographic data and complete transparency regarding government funding of schools, combined with collective action focused on the highly political issue of educational equality.

On the Persistence of the Patriarchy and Productivism

As central as it may be, the question of educational justice does not settle everything. When prejudices concerning certain groups are too deeply rooted, we must resort to other means of acting, including quotas making certain offices and professions—and not only certain courses of study—more accessible. Historically, women have undoubtably been subjected to the most massive and systematic discrimination, in the North as in the South, in the East as in the West, in all dimensions and in all latitudes. Nearly all human societies have been patriarchal societies, in the sense that they were constructed on the foundation of a sophisticated set of gendered prejudices that assigned certain rules to each of the two sexes. The development of the centralized state in the eighteenth and nineteenth centuries was even accompanied, at times, by a kind of hardening and systematization of the patriarchy. Gendered rules were codified and generalized throughout nations and among social classes, such as the asymmetry of rights between spouses in the framework of the Napoleonic Code or inequality of electoral rights in many countries. Women's suffrage was obtained as a result of long struggles and battles whose outcome was uncertain: in New Zealand in 1893, in Turkey in 1930, in Brazil in 1932, in Switzerland in 1971, and in Saudi Arabia in 2015. In France, after decades of feminist rallies, and after hopes betrayed in 1789, 1848, and 1871, the Chamber of Deputies approved women's right to vote in 1919, but the Senate vetoed the law. In France, not until 1944 did women's suffrage become a reality.[7]

Despite the establishment of formal equality before the law for women during the second half of the twentieth century, cultural norms promoted the presence of a housewife in the family as a measure of social and financial success during the three postwar decades known as *les Trente Glorieuses*. In 1970, women received hardly more than 20 percent of total payroll in France. Money matters were seen as issues for men.[8] All investigations show, however, that if we include domestic tasks, women have always provided more than 50 percent of total hours spent working (commercial and domestic). If incomes had been distributed between the sexes on the basis of work time, that would have represented a radical transformation of the distribution of income and power in society and within families. The important point is that we are just now exiting this golden age of patriarchy. Women's share of the payroll reached barely 38 percent in France in 2020, as compared with 62 percent for men, or 50 percent more monetary power for the latter. We point out once again the importance of the choice of indicators. If we limit ourselves to noting that the salary gap is 14 percent for a given job, then we are indulging in understatement, because one of the most important aspects of gendered inequalities is precisely that women and men do not occupy the same jobs.

This is particularly striking with respect to political offices or managerial positions. It is true that in France, the proportion of women among the 1 percent of those receiving the highest remunerations has risen from 10 percent in 1995 to 19 percent in 2020. The problem is that this advance is extremely slow: if we continue at this pace, parity will not be achieved until 2107 (see Figure 33). The data available elsewhere in Europe, in the United States, and in other parts of the world lead to similar conclusions. A central element of the explanation has to do

7. B. Pavard, F. Rochefort, and M. Zancarini-Fournel, *Ne nous libérez pas, on s'en charge! Une histoire des féminismes de 1789 à nos jours* (Paris: La Découverte, 2020).

8. Piketty, *Capital and Ideology,* 690–691.

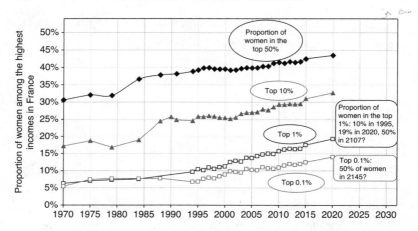

FIGURE 33. The Persistence of the Patriarchy in France in the Twenty-First Century

The proportion of women in the top centile of the labor income distribution (salaries and income from unsalaried work) rose from 10 percent in 1995 to 19 percent in 2020, and is expected to reach 50 percent between now and 2107 if the 1995–2020 trend continues. For the top thousandth, parity could be reached by 2145. *Sources and series:* piketty.pse.ens.fr/equality

with the strength of certain prejudices against women. In India, research has made it possible to quantify these prejudices by measuring, on a large scale, the reactions aroused by male and female voices reading the same political speeches. The same argument, for example concerning a municipal budget or the construction of a school, is systematically judged less credible when it is given by a female voice. This research has also shown that placing women in leadership roles reduces negative gender stereotypes, which may constitute one of the most convincing proofs of the necessity and potential efficacy of affirmative action policies for overcoming ancient prejudices.[9]

Quotas favoring women have multiplied over recent decades, not without arousing strong opposition. An initial law was adopted in

9. L. Beaman, R. Chattopadhyay, E. Duflo, R. Pande, and P. Topalova, "Powerful Women: Does Exposure Reduce Bias?" *Quarterly Journal of Economics* 124, no. 4 (2009): 1497–1540.

France by the Socialist majority in 1982. The measure was modest, since it simply provided that no sex could occupy more than 75 percent of the seats in elections that follow a closed proportional list system, and in particular in municipal and regional elections. That would already have represented a significant advance for women, who at that time represented less than 10 percent of elected officials, but the law was struck by the Constitutional Council for violating the principle of equality, and could not be revisited until the constitutional revision of 1989. For elections based on lists, the law passed in 2000 established complete parity (that is, lists that include equal numbers of men and women and penalize parties that propose too few women in district elections—penalties that have proven insufficient). The government at that time tried to require parity on admission panels as well, but was again overruled by the judges. A second constitutional revision adopted in 2008 extended parity to executive functions in regional and municipal councils. A series of laws adopted between 2011 and 2015 set quotas for women on companies' boards of directors (20 percent of the seats), and then on juries and the managerial organs of public institutions. In 2021 there are ongoing parliamentary discussions regarding possible extensions of quotas or incentivizing targets for all management positions in private enterprises (which could end up having a measurable impact on the share of women in the upper centile or upper decile of remunerations). Although it is too early to evaluate the complete effect of these measures, this sequence bears witness to the fact that it is possible to move toward real equality and, if necessary, to rewrite constitutional texts when the political will to do so exists.[10]

Although such measures may prove to be indispensable for advancing toward parity at the level of the highest offices, we must

---

10. It will be noted that the first great French experiment with affirmative action is the law of April 26, 1934, which required all companies with more than ten employees to have wounded war veterans on their payrolls at a rate of 10 percent, or pay the equivalent of a day's salary per day and per missing veteran. This law then evolved toward the system favoring handicapped workers that is currently in force (with less dissuasive sanctions and lower targets).

nonetheless underline the limits of an approach that is focused on the top of the hierarchy. Such an approach ignores the issue of parity in less well-paid jobs, which are the common lot of the immense majority of women. In other words, opening up positions for women in management groups must not serve as an excuse to maintain for everyone else a social system that is extremely hierarchized and gendered. The central issues here are wages and salaries, the length of the workday, and working conditions for millions of cashiers, waitresses, housekeepers, and dozens of other jobs usually filled by women. Traditionally female working-class occupations have not always received the same attention from labor unions or in public debate as have traditionally male working-class occupations.[11] We must add that many fiscal and social systems that proceeded from *les Trente Glorieuses* (such as the conjugal quotient, which for tax purposes divides household income by the number of people in the household, or else systems of parental leave) continue today to reinforce a highly gendered distribution of roles and jobs.[12] In reality, the exit from social patriarchy can occur only through a general transformation of the connection between production and social reproduction, between occupational life, on the one hand, and family and personal life, on the other. So many who earn the highest salaries hardly ever see their children, their families, or their friends; they often lack time for civic

---

11. C. Arruza, T. Bhattacharya, and N. Fraser, *Feminism for the 99%* (London: Verso, 2019). Compare M. Benquet, *Encaisser! Enquête en immersion dans la grande distribution* (Paris: La Découverte, 2015); F.-X. Devetter and J. Valentin, *Deux millions de travailleurs et des poussières. L'avenir des emplois du nettoyage dans une société juste* (Paris: Les Petits Matins, 2021).

12. H. Perivier, *L'Économie féministe* (Paris: Sciences Po, 2020). New inequalities have also appeared: an increase in separations and the maintenance (or sometimes deepening) of very unequal systems of dividing up goods have led to a paradoxical increase in wealth gaps between men and women. See C. Bessiere and S. Gollac, *Le Genre du capital. Comment la famille reproduit les inégalités* (Paris: La Découverte, 2020); C. Bessière, "Reversed Accounting: Legal Professionals, Families and the Gender Wealth Gap in France," *Socio-Economic Review* (2019), https://doi.org/10.1093/ser/mwz036; N. Frémeaux and M. Leturcq, "Inequalities and the Individualization of Wealth," *Journal of Public Economics* 184 (2020), 104–145.

participation, but contribute actively to the consumer rat-race and its resulting environmental damage. Resolving the problem of gender inequality by encouraging women to pursue the same lifestyle is not the solution: instead, we must find a different balance. The issue requires far more attention than enacting a few quotas, even if the latter are part of the solution.

Fighting Discrimination without Rigidifying Identities

Long contested, gender parity and quotas benefiting women have spread in many countries and are now broadly accepted. The same cannot be said about quotas benefiting those who have experienced social, ethno-racial, or religious discrimination, which continue to arouse strong reservations. This reticence is not entirely without foundation and does not proceed solely from the selfishness of those who do not want to give up their jobs (even if this factor can never be neglected). Before considering the application of social or racial quotas, the first priority has to be opposing discrimination as such. In other words, we have to equip ourselves with the means to identify and end discriminatory and racist practices, notably by pursuing legal action against those who engage in them, whether these be employers, the police, sports fans, demonstrators, internet users, or others.

Social or racial quotas involve two serious risks. On the one hand, they can lead to questions about whether those who benefit have "earned" the opportunity, especially from those who believe they would have received the benefit otherwise. On the other, they may pin social or ethno-racial identities, which are by nature plural, mixed, and mutable, and even reinforce the antagonisms connected with identity.[13] For all that, there may be countries or regions where prejudices are so deeply rooted (as in the case of prejudices against women) that only quotas can open up the situation. The question is extremely

---

13. The first risk applies to quotas favoring women; the second much less.

delicate, and there is no single answer: only a detailed, case-by-case examination can enable us to form an opinion.

Let us begin with the case of India, which is the country that has gone furthest in the use of quotas. The "reservations" (the term used in the Indian context) were first applied to the benefit of the "scheduled castes" (SC) and "scheduled tribes" (ST), that is, the former Dalits and Indigenous peoples who were the objects of discrimination in traditional Hindu society. These castes, which represent about 20–25 percent of the population, have benefited since 1950 from quotas granting access to universities and public employment. Starting in 1980–1990, the system was extended to the intermediary classes ("other backward classes, OBC"), or about 40–45 percent of the population, so that in all, 60–70 percent of the Indian population currently benefits from quotas at the federal level (see Figure 34).[14] The Constitution of India extended civil protections against discrimination that should have benefited the OBC after 1950, but the establishment of commissions entrusted with defining the corresponding social categories raised major difficulties, so the process took several decades. In 1993, a constitutional amendment also forced the states that had not yet done so to reserve for women one-third of leadership roles in village councils (the *panchayat*). Discussions are still ongoing to decide whether the Constitution would have to be amended to reserve seats for women in elections for parliament and state legislative assemblies, as was already done for the scheduled castes and tribes in 1950 (in proportion to their share in the population).

The available data lead to a qualified judgment on this experiment. The extreme prejudices and discriminations against socially disadvantaged classes in India are a consequence of both an ancient inegalitarian system and its rigidification by the British colonial government, which relied extensively on caste divisions to establish its domination but also gave them a permanent administrative existence

---

14. In terms of numbers, the SC-ST correspond roughly to secondary-school scholarship students in the French context, whereas the SC-ST-OBC correspond to the scholarship students in higher education.

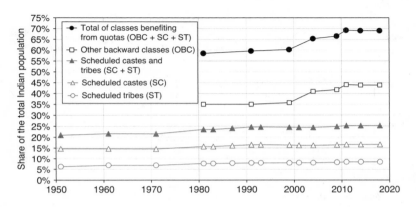

FIGURE 34. Affirmative Action in India, 1950–2020

Quotas for access to universities and public employment were put in place in 1950 for the "scheduled castes" (SC) and "scheduled tribes" (ST), former Dalit and Indigenous peoples subject to discrimination, and then extended, during the 1980s, to "other backward classes" (OBC) (former Shudras), by the Mandal Commission in 1979–1980. In all, these quotas benefited about 70 percent of the Indian population between 2010 and 2020. The SC-ST also benefit from quotas for elected positions. *Sources and series:* piketty.pse.ens.fr/equality

that had not existed previously. Taking into account these ingrained prejudices, it is probable that the members of scheduled castes and tribes would not have gained access as quickly to elective offices, higher education, and public employment without the establishment of quotas. From an economic point of view, the inequalities separating the scheduled castes from the rest of the population remain very strong, but they have been reduced significantly since 1950—more significantly, for example, than the inequalities between Blacks and Whites in the United States (see Figure 35).[15] Several studies have also shown that the quotas were a major factor in the construction of Indian electoral democracy: all the parties were led to promote elected

15. The comparison with the United States (where Blacks comprise 10–15 percent of the population) is more meaningful than the comparison with South Africa (where Blacks comprise more than 80 percent).

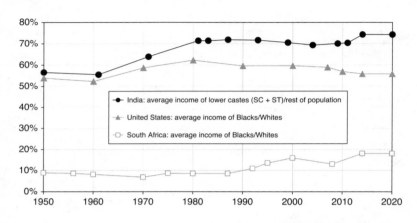

FIGURE 35. Discrimination and Inequality in Comparative Perspective
The ratio between the average income of the lower castes in India (scheduled castes and tribes, SC + ST, former Dalit and Indigenous peoples subject to discrimination) and that of the rest of the population rose from 57 percent in 1950 to 74 percent in 2018. During the same period, the ratio between the average income of Blacks and Whites rose from 54 to 56 percent in the United States, and from 9 to 18 percent in South Africa. *Sources and series:* piketty.pse.ens.fr/equality

officials who came from the scheduled castes, and the reservations played, *de facto,* an integrating and mobilizing role.[16]

If the balance sheet on Indian quotas is on the whole positive, this experiment also illustrates the limits of such a policy. This kind of system is not sufficient for eliminating inequality; it must be accompanied by social policies that are more ambitious and have universalist goals. By construction, the places in universities, elected assemblies, and public offices can concern only a small minority of

---

16. F. Jensenius, *Social Justice through Inclusion: The Consequences of Electoral Quotas in India* (Oxford: Oxford University Press, 2017). Compare C. Jaffrelot, *Inde: la démocratie par la caste. Histoire d'une mutation sociopolitique 1885–2005* (Paris: Fayard, 2005). Note that Muslims (15 percent of the population) were excluded from the SC-ST quotas but were able to benefit from the OBC quotas, which resulted in a *de facto* solidarity between the Hindu and Muslim disadvantaged classes, even as quotas nourished the rise of the BJP's conservative nationalists, who were anti-Muslim and anti-low castes. See Piketty, *Capital and Ideology,* 929–953.

the socially disadvantaged classes. In the Indian context, quotas were often used by the elites as an excuse for not paying the taxes necessary to finance investments in infrastructure, education, and health care that would have been necessary to really reduce social inequalities in India and increase equality for all the disadvantaged classes (and not only a minority within them). In the absence of a sufficiently well-financed welfare state, inequalities did in fact begin to increase quickly again after 1980, despite their decrease over the first decades following independence.[17] In addition to education and health care for all, the redistribution of property, particularly in the form of agrarian reform, is another systemic policy that would have made it possible to thwart India's heavy inegalitarian heritage. That is what was done in certain states run by communist governments, notably in Kerala and West Bengal, with very good results on the social and economic level.[18] But nothing like that was tried at the federal level in India: leaders counted heavily on quotas, without even asking the property-owning classes to pay the taxes and cede the properties that would have been necessary for a genuine social redistribution.

Reconciling Social Parity and the Redistribution of Wealth

We come now to lessons for other countries. Note first of all that the Indian system of quotas was itself capable of evolving. In 1993, the Supreme Court introduced an income criterion for the application of quotas: if a caste is included among the OBC, then members of the group whose annual income exceeds a certain threshold are excluded

---

17. L. Chancel and T. Piketty, "Indian Income Inequality, 1922–2015: From British Raj to Billionaire Raj?" *Review of Income and Wealth* 65, no. S1 (2019): S33–S62. Compare J. Dreze and A. Sen, *An Uncertain Glory: India and Its Contradictions* (Princeton: Princeton University Press, 2013); C. Jaffrelot and A. Kalaiyarasan, "Post-Sachar Indian Muslims: Facets of Socio-Economic Decline," unpublished manuscript, 2021.

18. Piketty, *Capital and Ideology*, 357–359.

from the benefit of quotas.[19] It is possible that the whole system will very gradually evolve toward a system of affirmative action based on other social criteria such as parental income, education, or wealth, and no longer on membership in a caste that has historically been targeted for discrimination. That may be the best that we can hope for it. Ideally, in order to avoid rigidifying categories and antagonisms, a system of quotas should foresee the conditions of its own transformation, to the extent to which it allows the reduction of prejudices against groups that have been discriminated against. For example, in view of the almost complete absence of the disadvantaged classes in elected assemblies in Western democracies, we might imagine the introduction of a form of social parity as a complement to gender parity (finally applied). In other words, half the candidates nominated by political parties for election would come from the disadvantaged classes.[20] To the extent that the policies adopted would permit a systematic reduction of differences in wealth, it could be hoped that these rules would gradually become less and less necessary and that the thresholds could be lowered without reducing the equality of representation in the assembly.[21]

We must emphasize that up to this point, no Western country has ever implemented social or racial quotas in a way comparable to what has been done in India, and that many systems regarding these ques-

---

19. In 2021, the threshold is 800,000 rupees, which in practice excludes about 10 percent of the population.

20. J. Cagé, *Libres et égaux en voix* (Paris: Fayard, 2020). Cagé proposes forcing parties' nominees to include, at a rate of 50 percent, candidates who are salaried employees or working class (social categories that represent about 50 percent of the working population) and to apply dissuasive sanctions in the event of evasion (for example, if these categories represent less than 40 percent of their elected officials). The working classes could also be defined on the basis of the average annual income over the previous ten years or on the basis of wealth.

21. Note that there exists a kind of reverse social parity in the German comanagement system: managers have a right to a quota among the representatives of salaried employees. This rule has always been attacked by the labor unions, who see in it (not without foundation) an employers' strategy for dividing them and increasing stockholders' power. See S. J. Silvia, *Holding the Shop Together: German Industrial Relations in the Postwar Era* (Ithaca, NY: Cornell University Press, 2013).

tions remain to be invented. In the United States, promises of reparations were made to former slaves after the Civil War, but they were never fulfilled. When legal racial discrimination was ended by passage of the Civil Rights Act of 1964, the Johnson administration took additional steps, for example, requiring by executive order that federal contractors ensure equal job opportunities. Subsequent amendments have made these protections more inclusive. But contrary to what is sometimes thought, no federal legislation has mandated a specific and formal system of quotas for access to universities, government jobs, or elected offices. Very strong political support and mobilization would be required before the issue of quotas could be considered by Congress, nor is it certain that the Supreme Court, which had upheld the constitutionality of racial segregation in *Plessy v. Ferguson* in 1896, would have upheld such an initiative. In any case, the absence of any coherent and consistent federal policies of reparation or quotas explains in part the continuation of very strong racial inequalities in the United States.[22] Some states tried to introduce quotas in the 1970s and 1980s, but they were overruled by judges or by referenda, like the one conducted in California in 1996 that forbade a system based on race (or, moreover, on gender). Several states then developed admissions policies in high schools and universities that timidly took into account the applicants' neighborhood or their parents' income.[23]

Generally speaking, affirmative action based on universal social criteria such as income, wealth, or territory has many advantages. In

---

22. On the magnitude and persistence of racial inequalities in the United States, see F. T. Pfeffer and A. Killewald, "Visualizing Intergenerational Wealth Mobility and Racial Inequality," *Socius* 5 (2019), https://doi.org/10.1177/2378023119831799.

23. However, the use of parental income has been forbidden by judges in several states, in which case the systems had to be limited to the neighborhood, which is insufficient to obtain the desired social targeting. It is often the most privileged individuals in a disadvantaged neighborhood who benefit from this measure. See G. Ellison and P. A. Pathak, "The Efficiency of Race-Neutral Alternatives to Race-Based Affirmative Action: Evidence from Chicago's Exam Schools," NBER Working Paper no. 22589, National Bureau of Economic Research, Cambridge, MA, September 2016.

addition to enabling us to put together more easily those political majorities that favor it, it has the merit of avoiding the rigidification of ethno-racial identities. We have also noted that this kind of affirmative action is in its infancy in most countries, including France and the United States. In practice, it would be significant if we were able to avoid negative discrimination. Disadvantaged social classes almost everywhere receive fewer and poorer educational benefits than the privileged classes. The same can be said for the paucity of funding for infrastructure and public services in disadvantaged communities. We begin from a place in which communities have vastly unequal resources. Should we then noisily congratulate ourselves for setting up a few meager compensatory systems that ameliorate only a small part of the systemic inequality that we refuse to challenge? Too often, the concept of affirmative action has been instrumentalized to avoid having to finance broader social policies supporting equality. The idea of affirmative action on the basis of social criteria can be saved, but only if it is supported by an ambitious program of wealth redistribution and if it complements universal measures such as the welfare state, guaranteed employment, or the inheritance for all.

Measuring Racism: The Question of Ethno-racial Categories

No matter how useful it is, affirmative action on the basis of social criteria cannot by itself overcome discriminatory practices that have ethno-racial foundations. These practices can be fought only if we adopt indicators and procedures allowing us to measure and correct them explicitly and directly. For some observers, the only way to proceed is to import in Europe ethno-racial categories like the ones used for many years by the US Census. Whether or not these categories are helpful is uncertain, however. They were initially introduced and used to support racial discrimination, not to combat it. To be sure, for a few decades now they have been used to measure the pervasiveness of racism, and sometimes to fight it, but the results obtained in terms of social and racial equality in the United States are not such as to make the rest of the planet squirm with envy. For all that, however, the rejection of these categories and the ritual critique of the US model do not suffice to define a policy. The truth is that no country is in a position to lecture others regarding racial discrimination or, for that matter, regarding educational justice. For centuries, people of different ethno-racial origins have lived almost without contact with each other except through the intermediary of military domination or slaveholding and colonial relations. The fact that recently we have for some years been cohabiting within the same political communities constitutes a major advance in civilization. But it continues to arouse almost everywhere prejudices and political exploitation that cannot be overcome solely with more democracy and more equality. Everyone has things to learn from the experience of other countries, and it would be wiser to spend more time finding solutions than using this question as a pretext for nationalist self-satisfaction or contrasting different national models without any genuine concern for their efficacy and the problems that they do or do not allow us to solve.

The United Kingdom is the only European country that has introduced ethno-racial categories of the type used in the United States, with the goal of fighting discrimination.[24] Since the 1991 census, people have been asked to check a box to indicate their race. Similar categories are used in many investigations and in documents connected with police checks. Even if that has probably helped draw more public attention to certain abuses and excesses, to date no study allows us to say that it has truly made it possible to reduce the amount of racial discrimination in the United Kingdom as compared with

---

24. Z. Rocha and P. Aspinall, *The Palgrave International Handbook of Mixed Racial and Ethnic Classification* (London: Palgrave, 2020).

other European nations.[25] We can also note that there is no single model, and that everything depends on the migratory and postcolonial context in question. In Germany and France, populations of extra-European origin come for the most part from Turkey and the Maghreb. But the fact is that the differences in physical appearance are relatively small all around the Mediterranean: the variations are gradual and continuous, especially since people of different national origins are constantly mixing—far more than in the United States, for example.[26] Many individuals with Mediterranean origins have difficulty choosing a single White/Black racial classification,[27] and investigations have shown that they often feel ill at ease with having to identify themselves using ethno-racial categories in general.[28]

25. See A. F. Heath and V. Di Stasio, "Racial Discrimination in Britain, 1969–2017: A Meta-Analysis of Field Experiments on Racial Discrimination in the British Labour Market," *British Journal of Sociology* 70, no. 5 (2019): 1774–1798; and L. Quillian et al., "Do Some Countries Discriminate More Than Others? Evidence from 97 Field Experiments of Racial Discrimination in Hiring," *Sociological Science* 6 (2019): 467–496, which find discrimination greater in France and Sweden than in Britain and Germany, with differences between countries that are nonetheless below the threshold for statistical significance.

26. In France, the proportion of intermarriages is as high as 30 to 35 percent for persons having an ancestor of North African origin in the preceding generation, or about the same percentage as for those having a Portuguese parent or grandparent. It reaches 60 percent for persons with Spanish or Italian origins. C. Beauchemin, B. Lhommeau, and P. Simon, "Histoires migratoires et profils socioeconomiques," in *Trajectoires et origines. Enquête sur la diversité de la population française* (Paris: INED, 2015). In 2015, 15 percent of intermarriages in the United States included persons identifying themselves as Black (compared with 2 percent in 1967). The proportion of intermarriages reaches 25 to 30 percent for Latinos and Latinas and minorities with Asian ancestry. It is about 10 percent for Whites. See G. Livingston and A. Brown, "Intermarriage in the U.S. 50 Years after Loving v. Virginia," Pew Research Center, May 18, 2017.

27. In British censuses, between a quarter and half of people born in Turkey, Egypt, or the Maghreb classify themselves as "White," a category with which they identify more than with "Black/Caribbean" or "Indian/Pakistani." Others choose "Asian," and still others "Arab" (a category introduced in 2011, without attracting all those targeted).

28. See P. Simon and M. Clement, *Rapport de l'enquête "Mesure de la diversité,"* Institut Nationale d'Études Démographiques (INED), 2006. The discomfort expressed in the face of ethno-racial questionnaires is much stronger among people of North African descent than among those of sub-Saharan or West Indian origin. See also P. Ndiaye, *La Condition noire: Essai sur une minorité française* (Paris: Calmann-Levy, 2008).

Under these conditions, we can legitimately imagine that the introduction of these categories in censuses would have mainly negative effects. But in fact, it is possible to go very far in measuring racism and in detecting and correcting discriminatory practices (or in any case much further than we have so far) without asking people to put themselves in a box based on ethno-racial identities. Concretely, France, Germany, and all the other countries concerned by this question should establish a center that would monitor discrimination objectively and draw up a yearly assessment of the state of the situation to guide policies. In France, researchers have sent false CVs to employers in response to thousands of job advertisements and observed the rates of response in the form of a proposal for a hiring interview. When the name sounds Arab-Muslim, the rate of response is divided by four. Names that sound Jewish are also discriminated against, though less massively.[29] The problem is that this study has not been repeated, so that no one knows whether the situation has improved or deteriorated since 2015. Repeated testing on a large scale by a trusted government agency would allow us to make reliable comparisons over time and between regions and sectors. Similar measures could be taken to monitor traffic stops and other police activity for forms of discrimination based on appearance.[30] This agency could also compile data and issue annual reports on discrimination inside companies, measuring salaries, rates of promotion, availability of training, and so forth. By combining census data about parents' country of origin (although currently this data is not recorded in France and several other countries) with salary information provided anonymously by companies

---

29. M.-A. Valfort, "Discriminations religieuses à l'embauche: une réalité," study, Institut Montaigne, Paris, October 2015.

30. In the French context, the High Authority for Combating Discrimination and for Equality (Haute Autorité de lutte contre les discriminations et pour l'égalité, HALDE) was replaced in 2011 by the Défenseur des droits (an independent official entrusted with defending rights and combating discrimination), but these authorities have never had the means necessary to organize annual monitoring on a grand scale. The same goes for the corresponding agency at the European level (Agency for Fundamental Rights).

under the supervision of a public authority, it would be possible to produce detailed breakdowns by the region, sector, and size of companies.[31] These indicators could be used in connection with labor unions to identify possible discriminatory practices and to provide material for further investigation. This system might lead to lawsuits or sanctions in the event of clear under-representation of certain countries of origin in companies of sufficient size. In theory, if it proves indispensable, we could envision introducing a general question about ancestry into the census.[32] But international experience suggests that the real goal is not to multiply statistics, but to use the available indicators in the service of a genuine antidiscrimination policy, firm and resolute, transparent and reliable, and involving all the actors (labor unions and employers, political movements and citizen associations). So far, beyond national models, this has never really been done.

Religious Neutrality and the Hypocrisies of French-Style Secularism

Let us conclude by noting that the battle against ethno-racial discrimination also involves the invention of new forms of religious neutrality. There again, no country can claim to have achieved a satisfactory balance. The model of French-style secularism likes to present

---

31. There has long been a question about the parents' country of origin on many French public forms ("Employment," "Training and Professional Qualification," or "Trajectories and Origins"). But their periodicity and size are insufficient to produce detailed breakdowns. In 2010 an official report had proposed, without success, to use the information provided by employees to produce these breakdowns (see "Inégalités et discrimination: Pour un usage critique et responsable de l'outil statistique," Rapport du Comité pour la mesure de la diversité et l'évaluation des discriminations (COMEDD), February 5, 2010. Working through the census would make it possible to simplify the procedure.

32. A possible formulation might be: "To the best of your knowledge, do you have ancestors in any of the following parts of the world?" This question would be followed by a series of Yes / No checkboxes: Southern Europe, North Africa, Sub-Saharan Africa, South Asia, etc.

itself as perfectly neutral, but the reality is more complex.[33] Places of worship are not officially subsidized, except when they were built before the law of 1905 separated church and state in France. In practice, this law concerns almost exclusively Christian churches and puts Muslim believers at a disadvantage in relation to Christians. Catholic elementary schools, middle schools, and lycées that were already established at the time the Debré law was approved (1959) continue to be massively financed by the taxpayers, in proportions found in almost no other country. These institutions have also retained the right to choose their pupils freely, without respecting any common rule in terms of social diversity, so that they make a powerful contribution to educational ghettoization.[34] Concerning the financing of religions (clergy and buildings), we must add the central role played by fiscal subsidies. In France, as in many countries, donations to religions entitle the giver to tax deductions that constitute, *de facto,* a mode of extremely inegalitarian public financing, because the public subsidy increases along with the proportion of the donation (in practice, this favors certain new religions with respect to others).[35]

The same is true for charitable donations in Italy, where every taxpayer can assign a fraction of his taxes to the religion of his choice, or

---

33. The younger generations are much more sensitive to anti-Muslim discrimination than are elderly persons, and this may bode well for positive developments. See "Enquête auprès des lycéens sur la laïcité et la place des religions à l'école et dans la société," International League against Racism and Anti-Semitism (LICRA), March 4, 2021.

34. See J. Grenet, "Renforcer la mixité sociale dans les collèges parisiens," presentation at the Paris School of Economics, June 22, 2016. France is also the only country that has chosen to close its primary schools one day per week (Thursday, from 1882 to 1972, and thereafter Wednesday) to study catechism. This day was about to be reinstated, but in 2017 it was decided to continue this French exception, despite a fragmented week and excessively long school days, and despite proven harmful effects on learning and gender inequalities. See C. Van Effenterre, "Essais sur les normes et les inégalités de genre" (PhD diss., École des Hautes Études en Sciences Sociales, 2017).

35. In France, after tax deduction, a donation of 100 euros costs the taxpayer only 34 euros; the remaining 66 euros are paid by the national collective. This subsidy applies to all charitable giving devoted to the general interest; tax relief is capped at 20 percent of taxable income (which excludes the poorest half of the population).

in Germany, where the mechanism takes the form of a supplementary tax collected for the churches. In both cases, there is a bias in favor of religions that have a unified national organization (which in practice excludes the Muslim religion). In comparison, the French model, which treats religious associations in the same way as other associations, is potentially more satisfactory. It amounts to seeing religion as a belief or a cause like others, and favors the renewal and diversity of structures. This system could be made more egalitarian by changing public subsidies into vouchers of equal amounts for all, and each person could then donate to the organization of choice, whether religious, cultural, or humanitarian, according to personal values and beliefs. Such a system would advance real equality and move away from the current climate of suspicion and stigmatization.

9

EXITING NEOCOLONIALISM

The battle for equality is not over. It must be continued by pushing to its logical conclusion the movement toward the welfare state, progressive taxation, real equality, and the struggle against all kinds of discrimination. This battle also, and especially, involves a structural transformation of the global economic system. The end of colonialism has made it possible to begin a process of equalization, but the world-economy remains profoundly hierarchical and unequal in its workings. Our current economic organization, which is founded on the uncontrolled circulation of capital lacking either a social or an environmental objective, often resembles a form of neocolonialism that benefits the wealthiest persons. This model of development is politically and ecologically untenable. Moving beyond it requires the transformation of the national welfare state into a federal welfare state open to the global South, along with a profound revision of the rules and treaties that currently govern globalization.

The *Trente Glorieuses* and the Global South: The Limits of the National Welfare State

If we examine the evolution of the differences in wealth between countries over the past two centuries, we find two clearly distinct phases: first, a long period of increasing inequality between 1820 and 1950, which corresponds to the Western powers' conquest of the world economy between 1820 and 1910, followed by the maximal extension

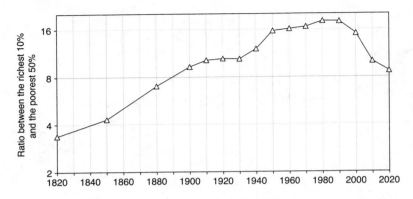

FIGURE 36. Differences in Income between Countries, 1820–2020: The Long Exit from Colonialism

The differences in income between countries, as measured by the ratio between the average income of the 10 percent living in the richest countries and the average income of the 50 percent living in the poorest countries, increased steadily between 1820 and 1960–1980, and then began to decrease.

Note: For the calculation of this ratio, the population of countries straddling deciles is distributed between these deciles as if they were several different countries.

Sources and series: piketty.pse.ens.fr/equality

of colonial empires between 1910 and 1950; then a phase between 1950 and 1980 in which inequalities between countries were highly stable (the *Trente Glorieuses* in the global North, independence in the global South), followed by an initial diminution between 1980 and 2020. In 1820, the 10 percent of the world population that lived in the world's richest countries had an average income that was a little over three times greater than that of the 50 percent that lived in the poorest countries. This was not complete equality, but it corresponded to a world in which the differences between countries were relatively small (and in which the average income of the population as a whole was very low). In 1960, the extent of the scale of worldwide incomes was five times greater: from one to sixteen. Despite a clear drop since 1980, the scale still ranges from one to eight in 2020 (see Figure 36).

Several points are worth stressing. First of all, it is clear that worldwide inequalities remain very great, and that they bear the scars of colonialism and the divergence between the West and the rest of the world between 1820 and 1960. Although inequalities have decreased in recent decades, led in part by gains in total income in China but also in South Asia and Sub-Saharan Africa, this process is very far from over.[1] Both the old powers and the new tend to make less wealthy countries permanently dependent on them, without granting them the means to develop autonomously, so that a relationship that is permanently hierarchical is in no way impossible unless there is adequate mobilization and sufficiently strong political opposition. We must also avoid idealizing the postwar period of the *Trente Glorieuses* (1950–1980), adorned with all the virtues of the global North, whereas the global South was above all marked by wars for independence and difficult struggles to establish sovereignty in situations characterized by great poverty and extreme demographic pressure. The social welfare state of the *Trente Glorieuses,* apart from the fact that it preferred to be social-patriarchal, was above all a nationalist social welfare state, in the sense that it was developed chiefly in northern nation-states with systems of social protection and investments in education and infrastructure conceived to benefit the people of those nations, without excessive concern about the international and colonial integration in the recent past—all too easily forgotten—that had allowed the West to get rich or about the development of the rest of the planet.[2] The populations of the South might be asked to supply the

---

1. Since 2010, China has ceased to be one of the poorest 50 percent of countries, and the decline of the ratio indicated in Figure 36 reflects above all the growth of India, Indonesia, Vietnam, and parts of Africa. We note that the inequality of income per hour worked is still greater than the inequality of total income: the poor countries have, on average, longer working hours per person, but that makes up only very partially for the smaller economic and educational capital at their disposal. See L. Chancel and T. Piketty, "Global Income Inequality, 1820–2020," July 20, 2021, WID.world.

2. On the notion of the "Keynesian-Westphalian" state (in Fraser's sense) or the "national-social" state (in Balibar's sense), see N. Fraser, *Scales of Justice: Reimagining Political Space in a Globalized World* (Cambridge: Polity, 2009); E. Balibar and I. Wallerstein, *Race, Nation, Class: Ambiguous Identities,* trans. C. Turner (London: Verso, 1991); E. Balibar, *Histoire interminable. D'un siècle l'autre* (Paris: La Découverte, 2020);

North's needs for labor, but no one envisaged any outcome other than immediately sending them home once the work was done, or raised the question of a model of codevelopment and the new forms of circulation and regulation that it would have implied.

When the colonies were winning independence, leaders like Léopold Senghor in Senegal were already aware of the fact that the newly created states were going to be much too weak to negotiate their place in the global division of labor. To gain some clout when confronting the multinationals and Western states, and also to avoid reproducing nationalist rivalries like those in Europe, Senghor envisaged the development of a vast federation of West Africa. This project materialized between 1959 and 1961 in the form of the ephemeral Federation of Mali, which briefly grouped together Senegal and the present states of Mali, Benin, and Burkina Faso, after Ivory Coast and Niger had finally withdrawn.[3] Other federal projects sporadically appeared, such as the United Arab States (Egypt, Syria, Yemen) or the West Indies Federation (which included Jamaica, Trinidad, and Barbados, among others) between 1958 and 1962.[4] When setting up the UN, several delegations tried to give more weight to the countries of the South and to public regulation of commercial flows and investments. The International Trade Organization (ITO) project supported by

L. Boltanski, N. Fraser, and P. Corcuff, *Domination et émancipation. Pour un renouveau de la critique sociale* (Lyon: Presses universitaires de Lyon, 2014).

3. France had a destabilizing effect on the project, insofar as between 1945 and 1960 it continued to entertain the illusion of a Franco-African federal union directed by Paris, to the detriment of West African federal projects. See F. Cooper, *Citizenship between Empire and Nation: Remaking France and French Africa, 1945–1960* (Princeton, NJ: Princeton University Press, 2014). The Federation of Mali, at its largest, was supposed to have had fewer than 20 million inhabitants in 1960, each of the six component countries contributing between two and four million.

4. The project for the West Indies was notably pushed by the Trinidadian C. L. R. James, known for his very influential book on the slave revolt in Saint-Domingue, *The Black Jacobins* (New York: Dial Press, 1938), and for his debates with Trotsky about self-organization of minorities within emancipation movements. See L. Trotsky, *Question juive, question noire. Textes choisis et commentés de Léon Trotsky,* foreword by D. Obono and P. Silberstein (Paris: Syllepse, 2011).

India and Brazil in 1947–1948 went so far as to propose a multilateral legal framework that would have made it possible to collectively regulate nationalizations and transfers of property. Worried about this interventionism, which could escape their control and threaten their interests, the rich countries rejected this project.[5] It was replaced by structures such as the General Agreement on Tariffs and Trade (GATT), then the World Trade Organization (WTO), which allowed rich countries to keep the upper hand and to impose their conditions on sensitive questions right down to the present day.[6]

Neocolonialism, Commercial Liberalization, and Tax Havens

The conservative revolution of the 1980s, with its regular attacks on progressive taxation in English-speaking countries and its obsession with the free circulation of capital (a new motto that came from Western Europe as well as from the United States) was also to help redefine the discourse of the wealthy countries and international organizations with regard to the global South. Starting in 1980–1990, what has been called the Washington Consensus permeated the policies the poor countries were advised to adopt: a smaller role for the state, budget austerity, commercial liberalization, and all-around deregulation. In view of the asymmetrical power relationships involved,

---

5. R. Toye, "Developing Multilateralism: The Havana Charter and the Fight for the International Trade Organization, 1947–1948," *International History Review* 25, no. 2 (2003): 282–305. Compare Q. Slobodian, *Globalists: The End of Empire and the Birth of Neoliberalism* (Cambridge MA: Harvard University Press, 2018). Note that the British Labour Party opposed projects for the ITO (judged to be contrary to imperial interests and violently stigmatized by the Tories) and that the French Socialists were directing the government at the time of the Suez expedition in 1956 (they were then allied with the center-right against the Communists).

6. The possibility for Western nations to veto any proposal that threatens them was illustrated in 2020–2021 during the Covid-19 crisis, when wealthy countries blocked a demand by India, South Africa, and about a hundred countries in the global South that the WTO temporarily suspend intellectual property rules regarding vaccines.

it is no exaggeration to say that these polices were imposed more than advised, and to see in them a form of neocolonialism (even if the mechanisms of persuasion were not the same as in the colonial period).[7] Since the 2008 crisis, it is fashionable to say that this consensus no longer exists, and that the IMF, the World Bank, and Western governments have become aware of the excesses of liberalization, the resurgence of inequalities, and the environmental crisis. In reality, because it has not been replaced by an alternative, liberal orthodoxy continues to have considerable influence, particularly regarding the South.

With the distance we can take on it today, it is clear that this policy of rapid deregulation and commercial liberalization has helped permanently weaken the fragile process of constructing a legitimate government and state power in the global South. Concretely, if we examine their tax receipts as a proportion of GDP, we see that the poorest states on the planet became poorer between 1970–1980 and 1990–2000, before gaining slightly between 2010 and 2020, though never reaching their starting point (which was very low to begin with). The fall in tax receipts is explained almost entirely by the loss of customs duties. Let us acknowledge that reducing taxes on international trade is not necessarily a bad thing in itself, especially if they are replaced by direct taxes on the profits of multinationals and the highest incomes and wealth. But that is not at all what happened: the suppression of customs duties was imposed very rapidly, without giving the countries concerned time to develop alternative receipts, and without any international support for that purpose—quite the contrary. In fact, the very principle of progressive taxation was at the same time denigrated by the Washington Consensus.[8] Finally, the divergence in

---

7. Without idealizing the Cold War period, recent studies have shown that at that time, competition between East and West was accompanied by greater attention to the global South than what followed. See S. Kott, *Organiser le monde. Une autre histoire de la guerre froide* (Paris: Seuil, 2021).

8. In the West, the loss of (historically very high) customs duties occurred in a much more gradual way in the course of the nineteenth and twentieth centuries, without ex-

fiscal capacity has clearly grown since 1970: the receipts of poor countries stagnated at about 15 percent of GDP, whereas those of wealthy countries rose from 30 percent to 40 percent (see Figure 37). These are very low levels, and they also conceal large disparities. In many African countries, such as Nigeria, Chad, or the Central African Republic, fiscal receipts amount to 6 to 8 percent of GDP. But as we have noted elsewhere, such receipts are barely sufficient to maintain order and build basic infrastructure. They do not make it possible to envisage financing a significant investment in education and health care, and they cannot adequately fund a social security system. If a state seeks to fulfill all these functions with such small tax receipts, the danger is that none of them will properly function (which is, unfortunately, often the case, so difficult is it to decide to abandon this or that essential function).[9] In view of the fact that the process of development in wealthy countries was based on a major increase in the power of the fiscal state (with receipts rising from less than 10 percent to more than 40 percent of the national income between 1914 and 1980), we can naturally wonder why these same countries imposed such a policy on poor countries. This may be explained by historical amnesia, or else by doubts regarding the ability of the ex-colonies to govern themselves on their own and to administer large receipts. Unfortunately, the solution proposed (the impoverishment of countries in the global South) does not exactly favor a virtuous dynamic.[10] More trivially, this may also reflect the fact that the rich

---

ternal pressure, and after taking care to prepare substitute receipts. See J. Cagé and L. Gadenne, "Tax Revenues and the Fiscal Cost of Trade Liberalization, 1792–2006," *Explorations in Economic History* 70 (2018): 1–24.

9. The absence of the registration and minimal taxation of real estate and business goods in poor countries has also resulted in a hypertrophy of the informal sector. See M. Chen and F. Carré, *The Informal Economy Revisited: Examining the Past, Envisioning the Future* (London: Routledge, 2020).

10. An additional difficulty for the construction of the state in the South is that the most educated there can compare their salaries with those of people with the same qualifications in the North (or with those of former colonial officials), especially since the option of emigrating is a little less closed to them than to others in the South. This

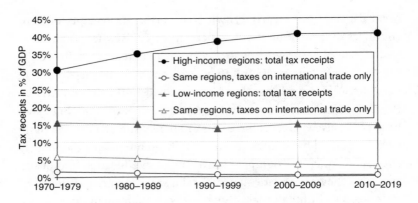

FIGURE 37. State Building and Trade Liberalization, 1970–2020

In low-income regions (the poorest third, such as Sub-Saharan Africa and South Asia), tax revenue fell from 15.6 percent of the GDP in 1970–1979 to 13.7 percent in 1990–1999 and 14.5 percent in 2010–2019, essentially because of the uncompensated decline of customs duties and other taxes on international trade (which brought in 5.9 percent of GDP in 1970–1979, 3.9 percent in 1990–1999, and 2.8 percent in 2010–2019). In high-income regions (the richest third, such as Europe and North America), customs duties were already very low at the beginning of the period and tax revenues continued to rise, and then stabilized. *Sources and series:* piketty.pse.ens.fr/equality

countries have been especially concerned to liberalize trade in order to open markets for their companies, and they have not been very interested in helping poor countries tax the profits of multinationals or regulate outflows of capital from the South, especially since these funds are usually invested in the banks and capitals of the North.

We must stress the magnitude of the damage done to the South by the increasing power of the free circulation of capital, tax havens, and international financial opacity over the last few decades. Of course, this damage is extensive almost everywhere, including in the North, where the uncontrolled circulation of capital has encouraged not only fresh challenges to progressive income taxes but also the establishment of a new censitary power. However, in addition to the fact that

complicates the process and makes all the more necessary the development of cooperation and a transnational norm of justice.

it was the states of the North that imposed this new legal system on the rest of the world, the southern countries have been particularly affected by it, given the weakness of the state and the administration. According to the available estimates, the financial assets held in tax havens represent between 10 and 20 percent of the total of the portfolios owned in Europe and in Latin America (which is already considerable), and this share is between 30 and 50 percent in Africa, in South Asia, and in oil-producing countries (Russia, the oil monarchies in the Middle East). In the case of the largest portfolios, everything indicates that the use of tax havens is even greater.[11] *De facto*, this amounts to a massive and generalized evasion of national legal systems to the benefit of offshore jurisdictions, all with the blessing of the highest global authorities, international law, and the local elites. Under such conditions, it is virtually impossible for the poorest states to launch into a viable process of state construction, which is necessarily based on the people's minimal consent to taxation, and thus on the construction of a credible norm of fiscal and social justice. If the wealthiest openly escape what are meant to be shared burdens, it is very difficult to advance in that direction.

The Pretenses of International Aid and Climate Policies

We must also emphasize the extreme hypocrisy that surrounds the very notion of international aid. First, public aid for development is much more limited than is often imagined: in all, it represents less than 0.2 percent of the global GDP (and scarcely 0.03 percent of the global GDP for emergency humanitarian aid).[12] In comparison, the

---

11. T. Piketty, *Capital and Ideology* (Cambridge, MA: Belknap Press of Harvard University Press, 2020), 601; A. Alstadsæter, N. Johannesen, and G. Zucman, "Who Owns the Wealth in Tax Havens?" *Journal of Public Economics* 162 (2018): 89–100.

12. P. Micheletti, *0,03 %. Pour une transformation du mouvement humanitaire international* (Paris: Éditions Parole, 2020). The OECD's official target for public aid for

cost of climatic damage inflicted on poor countries by past and current emissions from rich countries amounts by itself to several points of the global GDP.[13] The second problem, which is not a detail, is that in most of the countries supposedly "aided" in Africa, South Asia, and elsewhere, the amount of the outflow in the form of multinationals' profits and capital flights is in reality several times greater than the incoming flows from public assistance, even if we limit ourselves to outgoing flows registered in the official national accounts, and there is every reason to think that they underestimate the real flows.[14] Here we are talking about an essential point in the relations between center and periphery on the global scale, one that never ceases to amaze observers: the rich countries claim to be helping those countries from which they are deriving profits. We find this general reality not only in North-South relations, but also in regional relations, for example in Europe. If we examine the difference between the public funds received (for example, in the case of regional investment funds) and the contributions paid into the EU budget, we see that countries like Poland, Hungary, the Czech Republic, and Slovakia received net public transfers amounting to between 2 and 4 percent of GDP between 2010 and 2018. The problem is that the outgoing flows, in the form of profits, dividends, and other income from property, have been almost twice as high during the same period: between 4 and 8 percent of their GDP (see Figure 38). In Eastern Europe, it is justifiably pointed

---

development is 0.7 percent of the gross national product (GNP) for rich countries, but many countries like France give around 0.3–0.4 percent, so that the worldwide total is less than 200 billion euros (for a worldwide GDP of 100,000 billion in 2020, or less than 0.2 percent). Let us add that the Official Development Assistance (ODA) includes expenses such as salaries for Western consultants that some people would hesitate to include in the category of assistance.

13. See Chapter 1. On the amount of the minimal funds for adaptation according to the United Nations (between 0.5 and 1.0 percent of the annual GDP), see L. Chancel and T. Piketty, "Carbon and Inequality: From Kyoto to Paris," November 2015, WID.world.

14. In the period 1970–2012, the official outgoing flow of income from capital was on average three times greater in Africa than the incoming flow from international aid. See T. Piketty, *Capital in the Twenty-First Century* (Cambridge, MA: Belknap Press of Harvard University Press, 2014), 68–69.

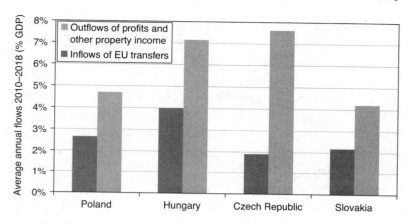

FIGURE 38. Economic Flows In and Out of Eastern Europe, 2010–2018
Between 2010 and 2018, the annual flow of EU net transfers (the difference between total expenditures received and contributions paid into the EU budget) averaged 2.7 percent of GDP in Poland; over the same period, the outgoing flow of profits and other capital income (net of corresponding inflows) averaged 4.7 percent of GDP. For Hungary, these same figures were 4.0 and 7.2 percent. *Sources and series:* piketty.pse.ens.fr/equality

out that investors from the West (especially the Germans and the French) have used the new member states as a reservoir of cheap labor where they have realized immense profits, while at the same time placing these territories in a state of permanent economic subordination. For their part, Germany and France prefer to ignore the private outgoing flows: they like to see them as a natural compensation for the investments made, and think that only the incoming public flows should be examined. There is a practical element to the dominant actors' propensity to "naturalize" economic forces and the "market balance" and to concentrate on the transfers set up *ex post* (that is, after this virtuous balance has been established), transfers that are then seen as an act of generosity on the part of the winners in the market. That the power relationships at work in property relations are in no way natural is sometimes forgotten. The level of salaries and profits depends on multiple mechanisms and social institutions, such as the existence or nonexistence of social and fiscal harmonization at the European level, the rules governing the circulation of capital, and so on, all of which should be included in the discussion.[15]

The same logic is at work on the global level. By focusing on public assistance, even though it is minuscule, and forgetting to inquire into the magnitude of private flows, a completely distorted view of the international economic system has been constructed. We must add that assistance is always given at the pleasure of the wealthy countries and under their supervision through the intermediary of development agencies or nongovernmental organizations. Although in absolute terms assistance is modest, the amounts are sometimes substantial when compared to the meager tax receipts supervised by the governments of the poorest countries. Studies have shown how the resources provided by agencies and NGOs through distribution networks that circumvent official state networks have helped weaken a little further the process of state construction, especially in the context of the Sahel, where the founding of a territorial sovereignty accepted by the various local actors and social groups has never really had time to establish itself after decolonization. Assistance given to supplement normal tax revenues would have had a positive impact, but intervention in a context of extreme state impoverishment, one which merely delegitimized the state a little bit more, probably did not help much.[16]

Rights for Poor Countries: Moving Away from the Center-Periphery Logic

To find a way back from these dead ends, we have to begin from the principle that every country should have an equal right to develop

---

15. On the necessity of renovating the analysis of social classes, working conditions, and the system they form at the European level, see C. Hugree, E. Penissat, and A. Spire, *Social Class in Europe: New Inequalities in the Old World* (London: Verso, 2020).

16. G. Mann, *From Empires to NGOs in the West African Sahel: The Road to Nongovernmentality* (Cambridge: Cambridge University Press, 2015).

itself, and more generally that the distribution of the wealth produced at the global level is an eminently political question that depends entirely on the rules and institutions that have been established. In particular, the poor countries should have the right to receive part of the taxes paid by the planet's multinationals and billionaires, on the one hand, because every human being has at minimum an equal right to health care, education, and development, and on the other hand, because the prosperity of the richest actors is entirely dependent on the global economic system and the international division of labor. For starters, we can imagine, for example, a worldwide tax of 2 percent on fortunes that exceed 10 million euros, which would bring in considerable sums: around 1,000 billion euros each year, or 1 percent of the global GDP, which could be allocated to each country in proportion to its population.[17] By placing the threshold at 2 million euros, it would be possible to levy 2 percent of the global GDP, or 5 percent with a very progressive scale for billionaires.[18] If we confine ourselves to the least ambitious option (letting each country make up the rest, when necessary, with its own tax scale on the largest fortunes), that would be amply sufficient to replace entirely all the current public assistance and to provide supplementary means that would make it possible to invest massively in health care, education, and infrastructure in the poorest countries. All this could be complemented by giving poor countries the right to receive part of the tax on the profits of multinationals, in connection with current discussions of that subject.[19]

---

17. Such a tax would concern less than 0.1 percent of the world population (around 3 million adults out of 5 billion), a group that holds about 15 percent of total wealth, or 75 percent of global GDP (75,000 billion euros). In comparison, the 3,000 billionaires listed by Forbes (less than 0.001 percent of the world population) hold about 2 percent of total wealth, or 10 percent of the world GDP (10,000 billion euros). In short, the potential receipts are much larger with a wealth tax starting at 10 million euros rather than 1 billion.

18. See Chapter 7, Table 2.

19. The BEPS project presently being debated in the OECD envisages requiring multinationals to make a single declaration of their profits on the global level, which would represent a major advance. The problem is that when the time comes to divide up this fiscal base among countries, the plan is to use a mixture of criteria (payrolls and sales

The rich countries could, of course, continue to finance their own development agencies and humanitarian organizations in the form of public and private assistance. But that would be in addition to poor countries' irrevocable right to develop themselves and build their state. To avoid money being misused, we must generalize the tracking of the excessive fortunes accumulated by the leaders of both the South and the North, not only in the government and the public sector but also in the private sector. But this fear must cease to be instrumentalized in order to constantly challenge the very legitimacy of states in the global South. For the fragile process of construction to resume its course in poor countries on a better basis, it is crucial that the states in question escape from the guardianship of northern lenders and that they have automatic fiscal receipts they can count on over the long term.

The biggest problem with the current conception of international assistance is that it presupposes the existence of a fundamentally fair market balance, in which each country is the legitimate owner of the wealth it has produced and accumulated in the past, in splendid isolation. But that is not at all how things happened. The enrichment of the West since the Industrial Revolution could not have occurred without the global division of labor and the frenetic exploitation of the planet's natural and human resources. In general, the rich countries would not exist without the poor countries and without the resources of the rest of the world: this also holds for both the former Western powers and the new Asian powers (Japan and China). After slaves, cotton, timber, and then coal in the eighteenth and nineteenth

---

made in the various territories), which in practice would lead to attributing to the rich countries more than 95 percent of the profits currently placed in tax havens, leaving only crumbs for poor countries. To escape this dead end, it is imperative that at least part of the receipts be prorated according to the population of each country (one person, one euro). Moreover, the receipts foreseen using a minimal rate of 15 to 20 percent on multinationals being considered by the OECD are scarcely 100 billion euros (0.1 percent of the global GDP). Rates of 25–30 percent would make higher receipts possible, but in any case what is at stake is less important than the progressive tax on the largest fortunes.

centuries, in the course of the twentieth century and the early twenty-first century, economic development has continued to be based on the large-scale use of the world's resources, through cheap labor in the peripheral countries and reserves of oil and gas that have accumulated underground over millions of years, and which we are burning at an accelerated pace that is threatening to make the planet uninhabitable, to the detriment chiefly of the poorest countries.[20]

The idea that each country (or worse yet, each person in each country) is individually responsible for its production and its wealth makes little sense from a historical point of view. All wealth is collective in origin. Private property was instituted (or ought to be instituted) only insofar as it serves the common interest, in the context of a balanced set of institutions and rights making it possible to limit individual accumulations, to make power circulate, and to distribute wealth more fairly. The fear of not knowing where to stop in such a political process is understandable, especially on the transnational scale, where prejudices are often considerable and where the social groups concerned do not know each other well and may have difficulty correctly perceiving their respective situations, which makes the quest for a common norm of justice even more complex and uncertain.[21] This fear is, however, a bad counselor, because in reality there is no option other than this political and institutional process, which is as fragile as it is indispensable. The compromises and devices that

---

20. Studies have also shown how the different energy-producing systems have themselves had an impact on the form of social conflicts and the distribution of wealth: coal and its accompanying concentrations of labor have made it easier to mobilize workers, whereas the fluidity of oil has, on the contrary, helped quash social movements. See T. Mitchell, *Carbon Democracy: Political Power in the Age of Oil* (London: Verso, 2011). Compare P. Charbonnier, *Abondance et liberté. Une histoire environnementale des idées politiques* (Paris: La Découverte, 2020).

21. During the interwar period, Gramsci emphasized the difficulties involved in constituting a popular bloc in a southern, peripheral context, including within Italy. He explains, for example, that the poverty of the Mezzogiorno region remains largely incomprehensible for most in the North, where some actors are tempted to constitute a common historical consciousness by appealing to a mystified nationalism of the fascist type. See A. Tosel, *Étudier Gramsci* (Paris: Editions Kimé, 2016).

will be found, like reparations or the worldwide taxes discussed here, will always be imperfect and provisional. But the alternative solutions consisting in making the market sacred and in absolute respect for property rights acquired in the past, whatever their magnitude or their origin, are only incoherent constructs seeking to perpetuate injustices and positions of power that are without foundation, and that in the final analysis merely pave the way for new crises.

From the National-Social State to the Federal-Social State

Beyond the poor countries' right to develop themselves and to receive part of the tax receipts of the multinationals and the billionaires, it is the whole of international organization that must be rethought. For several decades, the global economic system has been based on a two-fold postulate. On the one hand, the relations between countries are supposed to be based on the most absolutely free circulation of goods and capital, virtually without any conditions. On the other hand, the political choices made within countries, notably in terms of the fiscal, social, or legal system, concern only these countries, and must be the object of a strictly national sovereignty: that is the principle of the national-social state. The problem is that these two postulates are incompatible: the free, uncontrolled circulating of capital, without any taxation or common regulation, radically biases national choices in favor of the most mobile and most powerful actors, and thus constitutes *de facto* a new form of censitary power to the benefit of the richest. More generally, free trade without control is accompanied by an increase of inequalities within countries and a headlong rush toward global warming, both of which are now broadly recognized as the two main challenges of globalization.[22]

---

22. The rise of inequalities within countries since 1980 concerns not only the United States and Europe, but also the rest of the world, starting with India, China, and Russia. The only regions in which inequalities have not increased, or increased only a little, are

In theory, the solution is relatively simple. We have to replace the purely commercial and financial treaties that have up to now organized globalization with treaties that promote genuine, sustainable, and equitable codevelopment. The new types of treaties would set explicit, binding social and environmental goals, with quantified, verifiable targets. These targets would address, for example, tax rates for multinationals, the distribution of wealth, the volume of carbon emissions, and biodiversity. They would subordinate the pursuit of trade to the achievement of these objectives instead of making the former a precondition.[23] Obviously, the passage from one kind of treaty to the other will not happen overnight. Patience will be needed to build coalitions of countries that wish to go in this direction, and there is no guarantee that the transition will always go smoothly, even if there is widespread awareness that current globalization is at an impasse. Ideally, codevelopment treaties should also include a major transnational dimension that is democratic. In the case of the classic treaties, the logic of the whole is very vertical: heads of state and their administrations negotiate the rules of free trade among themselves. These rules may be the object of a ratification by parliament, and then everything works on autopilot, without any genuinely

---

the ones that did not really experience an egalitarian phase in the postwar period (in particular, the Middle East, Latin America, and Sub-Saharan Africa). In all, between 1980 and 2018, the richest 1 percent on the planet have appropriated a share of worldwide growth that is more than twice as high as that going to the poorest 50 percent. See F. Alvaredo et al., *World Inequality Report 2018* (Cambridge, MA: Belknap Press of Harvard University Press, 2018).

23. This also involves a profound change in the indicators used: the classic treaties appeal to the GDP or to the deficit and the debt, expressed as a percentage of GDP (as in the European treaties); the treaties of codevelopment would have to introduce indicators concerning inequalities, profit / salary sharing, or carbon emissions. This is partly the case in the climate accords, with the difference that they are not binding. On the need to include social justice goals in international law, see A. Supiot, *The Spirit of Philadelphia: Social Justice vs. the Total Market*, trans. S. Brown (London: Verso, 2012);; M. Delmas-Marty, *Aux quatre vents du monde. Petit guide de navigation dans l'océan de la mondialisation* (Paris: Seuil, 2016); S. Moyn, *Not Enough: Human Rights in an Unequal World* (Cambridge MA: Harvard University Press, 2018).

TABLE 3

A New Organization of Globalization: Transnational Democracy

Transnational Assembly

In charge of *global public goods* (climate, research, training, work, etc.) and *global fiscal justice* (common taxes on the largest fortunes and revenues and on the largest companies, carbon taxes)

National Assembly	National Assembly	National Assembly	National Assembly	[. . .]
Country A	Country B	Country C	Country D	

Note: According to the proposed organization, treaties regulating globalization (circulation of goods, capital, and persons) will henceforth provide for the countries concerned to create a transnational assembly in charge of global public goods (climate, research, training, labor laws, etc.) and global fiscal justice (common taxes on the largest inheritances, highest incomes, and largest firms, and carbon taxes). Countries A, B, C, and D may be states like France, Germany, Italy, Spain, and so on, in which case the transnational assembly would be the European Assembly; or else they could be regional unions like the European Union, the African Union, and so on, in which case the transnational assembly would be the Euro-African Union. The transnational assembly may consist of deputies of national assemblies and / or transnational deputies specially elected for the purpose, as the case may be. *Source:* piketty.pse.ens.fr/equality

democratic supervision. Even the settlement of disputes is possibly subcontracted to private arbitration courts, to the great satisfaction of the multinationals. In the case of codevelopment treaties, there are many genuinely political arbitrages concerning the social, fiscal, and environmental regulations to be applied, and these cannot be entirely determined in advance; they may be delegated, within certain limits, to transnational assemblies representing the different signatory countries (see Table 3).

Generally speaking, these assemblies can be of two types: they may consist of deputies drawn from the national parliaments of the countries concerned, or they may include transnational deputies specially elected for this purpose. The second formula may seem more ambitious on the democratic level, in the sense that from the outset the goal is to move beyond the political institutions of the nation-state. In practice, however, this may be a delusion. Since 1979, the European Parliament has been elected directly, with universal suffrage, but the real power continues to be exercised by the European Council of heads of states or the Council of ministers, which meet behind closed doors and with a single representative per country. Each country has a veto right on fiscal and budgetary issues, so that the supposed transnational parliamentary democracy is merely spinning its wheels.[24] If by some miracle unanimity makes it possible to make a decision, such as the plan to prime the economic pump adopted during the pandemic crisis of 2020, with common borrowing intended to come to the aid of the countries most affected, it will have to be approved by each of the national parliaments. In the current legal framework, national legislative bodies alone are allowed to commit their taxpayers, and this makes the process sluggish and not very reactive. One way out of this impasse could be for countries to establish voluntarily a European Assembly that consists of national deputies (in proportion, for example, to the size of populations and political groups) that would be permitted to make a certain number of budgetary, fiscal, and social decisions by majority vote within limits set by the countries concerned.[25]

---

24. From 1952 to 1979, the European Community had a parliamentary assembly consisting of national deputies, an assembly that in 1962 was renamed the European Parliament, but played primarily a consultative role (in large measure, like today's European Parliament).

25. In 2019, a bilateral treaty created a Franco-German Assembly of this kind, but it is purely consultative. For a projected treaty of the democratization of Europe that seeks to open such an assembly to all countries that wish to join it and to endow it with real powers (voting on a budget for a social and ecological jump-start, financed by progressive taxation), see "Manifesto for the Democratization of Europe," http://tdem.eu/en /manifesto/; and M. Bouju, A.-L. Delatte, S. Hennette, et al., *Changer l'Europe, c'est possible!* (Paris: Seuil, 2019).

For a Social and Democratic Federalism

The question of the federal-social state does not concern Europe alone—far from it. The construction of new forms of federal socialism, that is, democratic federalism driven by explicit, verifiable social objectives, is a challenge for the planet as a whole. For example, the countries of West Africa are presently engaged in a discussion to redefine their common currency and finally throw off colonial guardianship. This is an opportunity to put the West African currency in the service of a project of development based on investment in young people and infrastructure (and no longer serving solely to increase the mobility of the richest peoples' capital). This would involve the invention of new forms of fiscal and budgetary federalism, in West Africa and potentially someday in the African Union as a whole, absorbing all the lessons taught by earlier failures, and in particular by conflicts revolving around fiscal transfers that have frequently undermined federal projects in the post-independence period.[26]

The question of fiscal justice and the taxation of the wealthiest is naturally central to winning support for such projects. The ideal would be to develop a genuine public financial register making it possible to track holders of financial assets at the national and international levels.[27] Discussions have been going on since the crisis of 2008, with a

---

26. K. Nubukpo, *L'Urgence africaine. Changeons le modèle de croissance* (Paris: Odile Jacob, 2019). In 2008 the West African Economic and Monetary Union issued a directive instituting a common basis for taxing companies and obliging each country to apply a tax rate between 25 and 30 percent, which the European Union has been incapable of doing so far. The current project to transform the CFA franc (a currency that was issued by the Bank of Senegal founded in 1853 on the basis of indemnities paid to slaveholders in accord with the law of 1848) into a sovereign currency called Eco has a strong political and historical dimension.

27. Piketty, *Capital and Ideology,* 674–677. The problem is that countries have given over the function of registering financial assets (crucial for economic organization) to private financial depositories that are themselves not exactly transparent, such as the Depository Trust Company in the United States and Clearstream and Eurostream in Europe. The solution to the problem involves the creation of a Global Financial Register (GFR) that would play the role of a central depository.

view to fighting financial opacity and enabling the automatic transmission of international banking information, but so far little has come of them.[28] On this subject, as on others, future progress will also depend on unilateral actions that various countries can make right now, without waiting for worldwide or regional unanimity. In particular, each nation can require holders of real estate, business assets, or production units established on its territory (or involving users in its territory) to transmit the identity of the owners concerned and the profits made, so as to be able apply the tax scales that it has democratically adopted.[29] It is by combining unilateral action with federal-social proposals that we can hope to make progress, and not by opposing these different approaches.

On the transcontinental scale, for example on the Euro-African level, the idea of setting up common assemblies may seem naïve and out of reach. In reality, the growing importance of the common stakes in terms of economic development, migratory flows, and environmental degradation is going to make this kind of forum increasingly indispensable. The development of movements like Black Lives Matter, MeToo, and Fridays for Future also shows that many young people see things in a decidedly global and transnational perspective. If, for example, we set out to evaluate the activities of multinational companies like the Total oil group in Uganda or Congo with regard to issues

---

28. The Common Reporting Standards project discussed at the OECD has numerous defects, insofar as not all the assets are covered. The same goes for the registers of the actual beneficiaries of enterprises (that is, the true owners, beyond the principle of shell companies) developed in Europe, as was shown by the LuxLeaks inquiry in 2021. Generally, it is crucial that fiscal administrations publish indicators making it possible to verify the extent to which this transmission of information leads to better taxation of wealthy people who have up to now escaped paying taxes. See L. Chancel, "Measuring Progress towards Tax Justice," September 2019, WID.world.

29. If an enterprise does not provide the information requested, the simplest sanction is to apply to it the tax scale for the corresponding wealth of an individual owner. States can also apply an exit tax like the 40 percent tax proposed in 2020 by Bernie Sanders and Elizabeth Warren for US taxpayers who were seeking to escape their project of a federal wealth tax by giving up their nationality and transferring their assets abroad.

such as working conditions or attacks on biodiversity, then the existence of transnational parliamentary chambers making it possible to debate openly the most appropriate regulations is not necessarily a luxury. Similarly, it would make sense to debate in these protected spaces the circulation of people and the financing of higher education. For example, following a decision the French government made in 2019, European university students will continue to pay the same fees as French students (between 200 and 300 euros), whereas extra-European students will have to pay between 3,000 and 4,000 euros. In theory, why students from Mali or Sudan should pay between ten and twenty times more than students from Luxembourg or Norway is not at all clear. We can imagine that a public, transnational parliamentary debate might lead to adopting a more balanced solution, for example, by taxing the parents or taxpayers in Mali and Luxembourg in proportion to their respective incomes. The important point is that fundamental rights like freedom of movement cannot be conceived in isolation from the systems of public services and collective financing associated with them.

Let us conclude by noting that the refusal to engage with social and democratic federalism may help nourish reactionary projects aimed at compensating, in an authoritarian manner, for the limitations of the nation-state. In *The Origins of Totalitarianism*, Hannah Arendt as early as 1951 noted that the main weakness of European Social-Democrats during the interwar period was precisely that they had not fully taken into account the need for a world-politics to respond to the challenges of the world-economy.[30] In a certain way, they were the only ones: both the colonial empires and the Bolshevik and Nazi political constructions were based on postnational state forms that were adapted to the dimensions of the world-economy and to the internationalization of industrial and financial capitalism. Nature abhors a vacuum: if no democratic post-national project is formulated, then authoritarian constructions will take its place in order to propose more or less convincing solutions to the feelings of injustice engendered

---

30. Piketty, *Capital and Ideology*, 479–485.

by the unrestrained economic and state forces operating on a worldwide scale.

The most dramatic example of this kind of situation in the recent past is no doubt the emergence of ISIS in 2014 (and of its multiple resurgences in the Sahel and elsewhere). According to the available data, the Middle East is the most inegalitarian region of the world, in large part because its oil resources (which should be left in the ground) are concentrated in very thinly populated areas, where oligarchies accumulate unlimited financial reserves on the international markets, with the active support of the West, which is only too happy to be able to sell them weapons or recuperate part of the funds in their banking systems or their sports clubs. During this time, a few hundred kilometers away, a country with 100 million inhabitants like Egypt has completely inadequate resources to educate its youth and to invest in its infrastructure.[31] In theory, we could imagine a federal and democratic organization for the region that would make a better distribution and diversification of wealth and investments, as was envisaged in the past, and as a renovated form of the Arab League or the Arab Union might embody in the future. But if the actors involved close these discussions and cling to the economic and territorial status quo, then they will be helping to pave the way for reactionary projects to redefine colonial borders, such as that of ISIS, which hopes that by constructing a superior state power, a violently self-centered identity, and a totalitarian religious ideology, it will be able to respond to what its supporters see as a feeling of humiliation, like that of the Nazi state during the interwar period (but, fortunately, with less power and politico-military success up to this point). Today, as in the past, it is through projects of equitable development and credible objectives of social justice with a universal calling that identitarian and totalitarian excesses can be overcome.

---

31. F. Alvaredo, L. Assouad, and T. Piketty, "Measuring Inequality in the Middle East 1990–2016: The World's Most Unequal Region?" *Review of Income and Wealth* 65, no. 4 (2019): 685–711. Compare Piketty, *Capital and Ideology*, 653–655.

10

TOWARD A DEMOCRATIC, ECOLOGICAL, AND MULTICULTURAL SOCIALISM

The battle for equality will continue in the twenty-first century, basing itself chiefly on the memory of past struggles. If a historical movement toward more social, economic, and political equality has been possible over the last two centuries, that is above all thanks to a series of revolts, revolutions, and political movements of great scope. The same will be true in the future. In this last chapter, I would like to discuss certain factors that may help drive change in the course of the coming decades, beginning with the environmental catastrophes that are on our horizon and the competition between statist, ideological powers on the global scale. Specifically, I am interested in the challenges posed by the rise of "Chinese socialism," a statist, authoritarian model that is opposed on every point to the democratic, decentralized socialism defended in this book, and that, in my opinion, is far less emancipatory. However, the Western powers would be wise to take it seriously. If they persist in defending an obsolete, hypercapitalist model, it is not at all certain they will succeed. The true alternative is democratic socialism, participatory and federalist, ecological and multicultural. It is the logical end of a long-term movement toward equality that has been underway since the end of the eighteenth century. To ensure that everyone can contribute to it in a decentralized way, we must develop new forms of sovereignism with a universalist vocation.

Climate Change and the Battle between Ideologies

All the transformations discussed in this book, whether the development of the welfare state, progressive taxation, participatory socialism, electoral and educational equality, or the exit from neocolonialism, will occur only if they are accompanied by strong mobilizations and power relationships. There is nothing surprising about that: in the past, it has always been struggles and collective movements that have made it possible to replace the old structures with new institutions. Nothing prevents us from imagining peaceful developments, supported by new social and political movements that have succeeded in mobilizing a large majority of voters and rising to power on the basis of platforms proposing ambitious transformations. Nevertheless, past experience suggests that large-scale historical change often involves moments of crisis, tensions, and confrontations. Environmental catastrophes are, of course, among the factors that may help accelerate the pace of change. In theory, we could hope that the mere prospect of these catastrophes, whose future occurrence scientific research has increasingly confirmed, might suffice to provoke adequate mobilization. Unfortunately, it is possible that only tangible, concrete damage greater than that we have already seen will manage to break down conservative attitudes and radically challenge the current economic system.

At this stage, no one can predict the source from which these concrete manifestations will arise. We know that in the course of the twenty-first century the planet is probably heading for a temperature increase of at least three degrees Celsius compared with preindustrial levels, and that only actions much more vigorous than those envisaged up to now might make it possible to avoid such a prospect. With temperatures three degrees higher on the planetary scale, the only certainty is that no model is able to predict the whole set of chain reactions that might result, the speed with which coastal cities will be engulfed, or the desertification of entire countries. In view of the other damage that is already occurring, it is also possible that the first signals of impending cataclysm might come from other sources, such as the accelerated collapse of biodiversity, the acidification of the oceans, or loss of soil fertility.[1] In the darkest scenario, the signals will come too late to avoid conflicts between nations over resources, and it will take decades to realize possible, as yet hypothetical reconstructions.[2] We can also hope that the next waves of important signals, such as outbreaks of fires and natural calamities, will suffice to trigger a healthy public awareness of climate change and legitimize a profound transformation of the economic system, including new forms of intervention by public authorities, as did the crisis of the 1930s. As soon as enough people have seen the dramatic consequences of the processes occurring in their everyday life, attitudes toward free trade, for example, may change radically. We can also foresee hostile reactions toward countries and social groups whose ways of life have contributed most to the disaster, starting with the richest classes in the United States, but also in Europe and the rest of the world.[3]

Recall that the global North, despite a limited population (about 15 percent of world population for the United States, Canada, Europe, Russia, and Japan), has produced nearly 80 percent of the carbon emissions that have accumulated since the beginning of the Indus-

---

1. IPCC, *Global Warming of 1.5°C*, Special Report, Intergovernmental Panel on Climate Change, Geneva, 2018; IPBES, "Global Assessment Report on Biodiversity and Ecosystem Services," Intergovernmental Science-Policy Platform on Biodiversity and Ecosystem Services, Bonn, May 4, 2019; W. Steffen et al., "Planetary Boundaries: Guiding Human Development on a Changing Planet," *Science* 347, no. 6223 (2015), 1259855; J. Hickel, *Less Is More: How Degrowth Will Save Society* (London: William Heinemann, 2020).

2. In *Rouge impératrice* (Paris: Bernard Grasset, 2019), Léonora Miano imagines that in 2124 a powerful African Federation finally achieves unity and, after the climatic and nuclear catastrophes of the twenty-first century, succeeds in transcending the dead ends of Westerners' commercial globalization and ends up moving beyond its prejudices and resentments to offer a helping hand to European refugees.

3. See Chapter 1, Figure 3. After such catastrophes, it is possible that people will no longer smile at all at the whims, private jets, or space tourism of billionaires, who are always prompt to support the craziest geo-engineering hypotheses if these will allow them to avoid simple and rebarbative solutions, such as paying taxes and living modestly.

trial Age. This is explained by the fact that in Western countries, the annual emissions per inhabitant reached extremely high levels between 1950 and 2000: between twenty-five and thirty tons per person in the United States, and around fifteen tons in Europe. These levels have now begun to decline: in the early 2020s they neared twenty tons in the United States and ten tons in Europe. China's carbon emissions were below five tons until 2000, yet it emitted between five and ten tons per person between 2000 and 2020. Considering the trajectory we have seen up to now, China should succeed in reaching a Western standard of living without ever passing through a stage of carbon emissions levels as high as those in the West.[4] This is certainly to be explained in part by increased awareness of global warming and by the new technologies available. However, we have to qualify the idea that a green Enlightenment will be likely to save the planet. In reality, people have suspected for a long time—indeed, almost since the beginning of the Industrial Revolution—that this accelerated burning of fossil fuels might have harmful effects. If reactions have been slow and remain so limited even today, that is also and especially because the socioeconomic interests at stake are considerable, between countries as well as within them.[5] For the countries most affected (in particular in the global South), the attenuation of the effects of a warming climate and financing for measures to adapt to it will require a transformation of the distribution of wealth and the economic system as a whole, and this in turn will involve the development of new political and social coalitions on a global scale. The idea that there might be only winners is a dangerous and anesthetizing illusion that must be abandoned immediately.

---

4. L. Chancel, "Global Carbon Inequality in the Long Run," March 2021, WID. world. Compare L. Chancel and T. Piketty, "Carbon and Inequality: From Kyoto to Paris," November 2015, WID.world. The figures given here reflect both direct and indirect emissions (after correction for imports).

5. C. Bonneuil and J.-B. Fressoz, *L'Événement anthropocène. La Terre, l'histoire et nous* (Paris: Points, 2016); J.-B. Fressoz and F. Locher, *Les Révoltes du ciel. Une histoire du changement climatique* (Paris: Seuil, 2020).

Chinese Socialism: The Weak Points
of a Perfect Digital Dictatorship

Beyond the environmental issue, rivalries between statist, ideological powers constitute one of the main factors that might accelerate political change. Among the most crucial questions is the future of the Chinese regime, its strengths and its weaknesses. Barring an unexpected collapse, over the coming decades the People's Republic of China is likely to become the greatest economic power on the planet, even if no one can predict how soon and for how long.[6] If we compare the economic structures in force in China and in the West, the most striking difference is without any doubt the property system, and in particular the importance of private property. The share of public capital (all levels of governments and collectivities taken together) was about 70 percent in China in 1978, at the time when reforms were begun. It declined sharply during the years 1980–1990 and until the middle of the 2000s, and has been stable at around 30 percent of the national capital since then (see Figure 39).

It is striking to note that the privatization of property in China ended around 2005–2006: the balance between public and private property has hardly budged since that time. Given the very strong growth of the Chinese economy, capital obviously continues to accumulate in all its forms: new plots of land are being developed, factories and skyscrapers are being constructed, all at breakneck speed. Putting it simply, we can say that the capital being developed under public control is progressing at about the same rate as that in private hands. In this sense, China seems to be stabilizing around a struc-

---

6. Expressed in terms of parity of purchasing power, China's GDP became greater than that of the United States in 2013. However, in terms of annual national income per adult, China remains at a level only a third of that in the West: about 15,000 euros in China, as contrasted with almost 40,000 euros in Western Europe and 50,000 euros in the United States. At the current rate of convergence (5 percent per year), the gap could be filled between now and 2040–2050. China would then have a population and a GDP half again as large as the cumulative total of that of the United States and Europe.

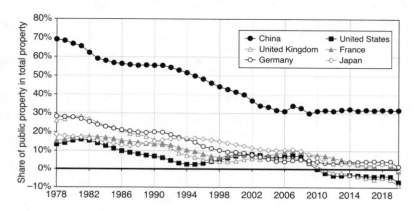

FIGURE 39. The Declining Share of Public Property, 1978–2020

The share of public property (public assets net of debt including all public collectivities, businesses, buildings, land, and financial holdings and assets) in total property (total public and private) was about 70 percent in China in 1978, and it has stabilized at around 30 percent since the middle of the 2000s. It was 15–30 percent in capitalist countries at the end of the 1970s; it was almost nil or negative in 2020. *Sources and series:* piketty.pse.ens.fr/equality

ture of property that could be described as a mixed economy: the country is no longer truly communist, but it is not completely capitalist, either, since public property represents a little more than 30 percent of the total: less than half, of course, but nonetheless a very substantial share. The fact that the Chinese state owns almost a third of everything that can be owned in the country affords it considerable opportunities for intervening in decisions as to where investments are to be made and where jobs are to be created, and for pursuing policies of regional development.

Moreover, it will be noted that this average share of about 30 percent of public capital conceals very important differences, depending on the categories of the assets involved. On the one hand, residential real estate has been almost entirely privatized. In the early 2020s, the state and companies held less than 5 percent of the residential housing stock, which became the private investment *par excellence* for Chinese

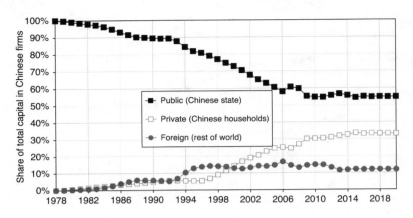

FIGURE 40. Ownership of Chinese Firms, 1978–2020
In 2020, the Chinese state (at all levels of government) held about 55 percent of the total capital of Chinese firms (listed and unlisted companies, all sizes and sectors), as compared with 33 percent for Chinese households and 12 percent for foreign investors. The latter's share has diminished since 2006 and that of Chinese households has risen, whereas the share held by the Chinese state has stabilized at around 55 percent. *Sources and series:* piketty.pse.ens.fr/equality

households that had the means, and this helped make real estate prices skyrocket, especially since opportunities for financial savings are limited and the public retirement system is underfunded. Conversely, the government currently holds around 55–60 percent of companies' total capital (including all enterprises, listed and unlisted, all sizes and all sectors taken together). This share has remained virtually unchanged since 2005–2006 and testifies to the state's maintenance of strict control over the productive system, and even an accentuation of control over the largest enterprises. We also see a significant decline of the share of business capital held by foreign investors, which is compensated by a rise of the share held by Chinese households (see Figure 40).

In addition to this mixed-economy structure and the state's strong control over enterprises, the other major characteristic of "socialism with Chinese characteristics," as the Beijing regime likes to style itself, is obviously the dominant role played by the Chinese Communist Party. In 2020, the CCP had more than 90 million members, or about 10 percent of the country's adult population. In the opinion of the regime, whose official positions are expressed daily in the *Global Times*, Chinese-style democracy is superior to the Western-style electoral supermarket because it entrusts the country's destinies to a motivated and determined avant-garde, both selected and representative of the society, and ultimately more profoundly involved in serving the common interest than is the average Western voter, who is fickle and subject to influence.[7] In practice, however, the regime increasingly resembles a perfect digital dictatorship—so perfect that no one wants to be like it. The model of deliberation within the Party is all the less convincing insofar as it leaves no trace of anything outside it, whereas conversely, everyone can see with increasing clarity the establishment of a generalized surveillance of the population on social networks, the repression of dissidents and minorities, the brutality of the electoral process in Hong Kong, and the threats made against the electoral system in Taiwan. The ability of such a regime to seduce public opinion in other countries (and not only their leaders) seems limited. We must add the sharp rise in inequalities, along with the extreme opacity that characterizes the distribution of wealth and the feeling of social injustice that flows from it, a feeling that cannot be appeased forever by dismissing a few people or putting them in prison.[8] The anticipated demographic decline and accelerated aging of the population are also going to constitute major challenges for the

---

7. The editor-in-chief of the *Global Times*, Hu Xijin, was a young student at the time of the Tiananmen Square incident in 1989, likes to remind people that it was the separatist wars in Yugoslavia that demonstrated for him the pacifying role of the Party and of the deliberations within it, along with the impossibility of leaving to electoral passions the task of making decisions as delicate as those regarding the border system or the property system. See the interview with Hu Xijin, *Le Monde*, October 15, 2017.

8. On the evolution of inequalities and Chinese data's lack of transparency, see T. Piketty, L. Yang, and G. Zucman, "Capital Accumulation, Private Property, and Rising Inequality in China, 1978–2015," *American Economic Review* 109, no. 7 (2019): 2469–2496.

regime, and in the course of the second half of the twenty-first century they may lead to the replacement of China by India as the world's primary economic power.[9]

Despite these weaknesses, Chinese socialism nonetheless has many advantages. If the Western powers persist in an outdated hypercapitalist ideology, it is not at all certain that they will succeed in limiting the growing influence of the Chinese regime. In the economic and financial domain, the Chinese state has considerable assets that far outweigh its debts, and this gives it the means to pursue ambitious policies, both domestically and internationally, particularly concerning investments in infrastructure and in the transition to new forms of energy. In contrast, it is striking to note to what point the main Western states all find themselves, in the early 2020s, in a position in which the share of public property is almost nil or even negative (see Figure 39). Having failed to balance their public accounts (which would have required them to raise tax rates for the wealthiest taxpayers), these countries have accumulated public debts, while at the same time selling off an increasing share of their public assets, so that the former have ended up slightly exceeding the latter. Let us be perfectly clear: the rich countries are rich, in the sense that private wealth has never been so great; it is only their governments that are poor. If they continue down that path, they may find themselves with increasingly negative assets, which would lead to a situation in which the holders of debt securities would possess not only the equivalent of all the public assets (buildings, schools, hospitals, infrastructures, etc.), but also a special drawing right on part of the taxes of future

---

9. India will probably see its population overtake that of China in 2028. If the country manages to surmount its very burdensome legacy of inequality and invests more in education, health care, and infrastructure, while at the same time escaping the identitarian and authoritarian excesses of the Hindu nationalists presently in power— which is far from sure—it has parliamentary, federal, and electoral institutions and a system of a free press that provide it with political foundations more robust than those of China (and far more exportable and attractive for other countries).

taxpayers.[10] And yet it would be completely possible to reduce this public debt rapidly, as these same countries did after World War II—for example, by taxing the largest private fortunes and thus giving the government some room to maneuver.[11] That involves becoming aware of the multiplicity of possible choices and the political and social mobilizations in support of them, an awareness that may, unfortunately, require a few more crises, given the ambient conservatism.

The Chinese regime has other strong points. When climatic catastrophes occur, it will have no difficulty blaming the West. More generally, China does not hesitate to remind us that it industrialized without resorting to slavery and colonialism, of which it was itself a victim. This allows China to rack up points against what is perceived by the world as the eternal arrogance of Western countries, which are always quick to lecture the whole Earth concerning justice and democracy, but prove incapable of dealing with the inequalities and discrimination that undermine them, even though they manage to come to terms with all the potentates and oligarchs from whom they benefit. On these subjects, the right response to China's statist, authoritarian socialism would be to promote a form of democratic, participatory socialism that is ecological and postcolonial, one which finally

---

10. For a recent example of this development, which is still ongoing, we can cite the project to privatize the ADP (Paris Airports) group that was adopted in 2019 by the French government. It expects this sale to bring in 8 billion euros—after having deprived itself of 5 billion per year in tax receipts by doing away with the wealth tax and progressive taxation on income from capital. It would have been simpler to transfer the property titles directly to the persons benefiting from tax decreases.

11. See Chapter 5. The value of the public assets registered in the national accounts generally amounts to between 100 and 150 percent of the national income, so that net public property becomes negative when the debt exceeds this level. It will be noted that the Western countries themselves had mixed economies during the period 1950–1980: public debt had been reduced to a minimum and public assets were large, so that the net public property represented a substantial portion (typically 20–30 percent) of the national capital. I cannot settle here the complex question of the ideal level, which depends in particular on the type of democratic governance developed in the public sector; let us simply say that it seems far better that the net public property's share in the national capital be positive but less than half, rather than that it be zero or negative.

pays attention to the global South and to all the West's inequalities and hypocrisies. Such an evolution would also make it possible to respond to the fact that neoliberalism is running out of steam, a decline that was accelerated by the financial crisis of 2008 and by the pandemic of 2020, and which can be explained more generally by the failure of Reaganism's promises to spur growth through deregulation, to the point that the middle and lower classes, who had been promised the moon, have begun to have serious doubts about globalization.[12] At first, we can certainly fear that neoliberalism might be replaced by various forms of the neonationalism incarnated by Trumpism, Brexit, and the rise of Turkish, Brazilian, and Indian nationalism, which are different political movements but all blame foreigners and diverse internal minorities for national misfortunes.[13] The failure of Trumpism nonetheless shows the limits of this political trend, which may lead to a headlong rush toward exacerbated identitarian conflicts and a new wave of fiscal-social dumping that favors the richest and the most polluting.[14] All this is hardly likely to re-

---

12. The term "neoliberalism" refers to the new form of economic liberalism in vogue all over the planet since the 1980s, as opposed to the classical economic liberalism that existed in the nineteenth century and until 1914. This idea may be useful, but on the condition that we not lose sight of the fact that this neoliberalism found a place in typical societies in the North characterized by a powerful welfare state without much relation to those before 1914, and in post-independence movement societies marked by neocolonialism in the South, in forms very different from those taken by colonialism before 1960 or before 1914. The term was introduced at a colloquium that met in Paris in 1938 and that brought together a group of liberal intellectuals (including the journalist Walter Lippmann and the economists Friedrich Hayek, Ludwig von Mises, and Wilhelm Röpke) to describe the collapse of pre-1914 liberalism and to reflect on future reconstructions. See S. Audier, *Le Colloque Lippmann. Aux origines du "néo-libéralisme"* (Lormont: Bord de l'eau, 2008); S. Audier, *Néo-libéralisme(s). Une archéologie intellectuelle* (Paris: Grasset, 2012).

13. On the structural instability of the tripartition liberalism-nationalism-socialism in the political-ideological sphere, see B. Karsenti and C. Lemieux, *Socialisme et sociologie* (Paris: Editions de l'EHESS, 2017). In short, liberalism is based on the market and on the social disembedding of the economy, nationalism replies by reifying the nation and ethno-national solidarities, whereas socialism promotes universalist emancipation through education, knowledge, and power-sharing.

14. On the way in which Brexit was financed in 2016 by hedge funds and financial lobbies demanding a new wave of deregulation and no longer limiting themselves to the

solve the challenges of the moment and seems everywhere to be likely to reinforce Chinese statist and authoritarian socialism, which also feeds on nationalism, but is based on a public authority that can give it the means to realize its ambitions, at least for a time.

From the War between Capitalisms to the Battle between Socialisms

For these different reasons, it is very possible that future ideological confrontations will be more similar to battles between forms of socialism than to the war between forms of capitalism that people often talk about. More generally, we must insist above all on the very great diversity of economic models observed around the world and throughout history, including systems that claim to adhere to capitalism or to socialism.

In this book, I have defended the possibility of a democratic and federal socialism, decentralized and participatory, ecological and multicultural, based on the extension of the welfare state and progressive taxation, power-sharing in business enterprises, postcolonial reparations, the battle against discrimination, educational equality, the carbon card, the gradual decommodification of the economy, guaranteed employment and an inheritance for all, the drastic reduction of monetary inequalities, and finally, an electoral and media system that cannot be controlled by money. These are only a few of the options: above all, I have sought to show the diversity of possible systems, and the way in which mobilizations around alternative systems have made a powerful contribution to shaping historical trajectories in the past. The debates on alternative systems and the multiple forms of socialism, which had died out for a time in the 1990s following the collapse of Soviet communism, have been revived since the crisis of 2008, and as the inegalitarian and climatic dead ends of the current

---

deregulation carried out by the European Union in the 1980s and 1990s, see M. Benquet and H. Bergeron, *La Finance autoritaire. Vers la fin du néolibéralisme* (Paris: Raisons d'agir, 2021).

system were gradually recognized. These debates and these struggles are not about to stop.

I would also like to repeat that democratic socialism, though it may seem very distant from the present world, is in reality embedded in a stream of considerable transformations achieved in the past, sometimes within a few decades. Except for a few formal similarities, the social, legal, fiscal, educational, electoral, and international institutions characterizing the authoritarian and colonial capitalism of 1910 and the mixed social-democratic economy of 1980 have little in common. If the democratic, participatory socialism described here were to be realized between now and 2050, it would be in direct continuity with this movement, and would probably not be any more different from the second model than the latter is from the first one. This reflection on economic systems is also indispensable for nourishing the dialogue between models. If Western countries, or some of them, were to abandon their habitual capitalist and nationalist postures and adopt a discourse founded on democratic socialism and an exit from neocolonialism, with major steps toward fiscal justice and sharing the tax receipts of the multinationals and billionaires all over the world, that would make it possible not only to regain credibility with regard to the global South, but also to drive Chinese authoritarian socialism into a corner in matters of transparency and democracy. On central questions such as ecology, patriarchy, and xenophobia, the truth is that at this point none of the present regimes has any particularly convincing lesson to teach others. Only a dialogue between systems and a healthy emulation might allow us to hope for some progress.

Will Money Creation Save Us?

No matter which economic model we adopt, we must finally insist on the essential role that will be played by the monetary and financial system in the coming decades. The central banks and monetary policy have assumed a decisive importance following the financial crisis of

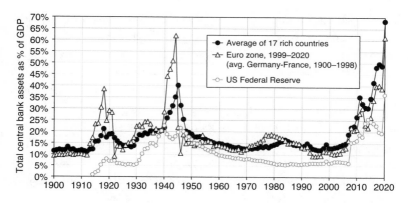

FIGURE 41. The Size of Central Banks' Balance Sheets, 1900–2020

The total assets held by the European Central Bank (ECB) rose from 11 percent of eurozone GDP on the last day of 2004 to 61 percent on the last day of 2020. The curve for 1900–1998 indicates the average of the balance sheets for the German and French central banks (with peaks of 39 percent in 1918 and 62 percent in 1944). The total assets of the Federal Reserve (created in 1913) rose from 6 percent of US GDP at the end of 2007 to 36 percent at the end of 2020.

Note: The average for rich countries includes Australia, Belgium, Canada, Denmark, Finland, France, Germany, Holland, Italy, Japan, Norway, Portugal, Spain, Sweden, Switzerland, the United Kingdom, and the United States. *Sources and series:* piketty.pse.ens.fr/equality

2008 and the pandemic crisis of 2020–2021. Specifically, the balance sheet of the world's main banks, that is, the whole of the loans they have granted and the securities they hold, has regained in a little more than ten years a level seen during the historic postwar peak (see Figure 41). In theory, nothing forbids us to go further.[15] Today, no currency is defined in relationship to gold or to a material referent: currency is above all an electronic sign on computers, which the central banks can create without limits. There are even plans to set up central bank digital currencies in the near future. Individuals would

---

15. Even before the pandemic of 2020, the balance sheets of the central banks of Switzerland and Japan exceeded 100 percent of the GDP. See T. Piketty, *Capital and Ideology* (Cambridge, MA: Belknap Press of Harvard University Press, 2020), 696–705.

have digital accounts at their country's central bank, which would permit banks to directly credit individuals' accounts, rather than routing through private banks and enterprises, as is now usually the case.[16]

The spectacular increase in monetary creation since 2008 illustrates once again to what point economic institutions are not unchanging. They are constantly redefined according to crises and power relationships, within unstable and precarious compromises. This new ease in increasing the money supply has nonetheless led to a confusion that it is important to clarify here. In short, money is an indispensable tool of economic, social, and climate policy, on the condition, however, that it is not made sacred and is put back in its place in a coherent institutional framework based especially on the welfare state, progressive taxation, parliamentary deliberation, and democratic supervision.

Let us recall first of all that the only true limit to monetary policy is inflation. So long as there is no substantial increase in consumer prices, there is no solid reason not to increase the money supply if it enables us to finance useful policies such as the struggle for full employment, a guaranteed job, the thermal insulation of buildings, or public investments in health care, education, and renewable energy. Inversely, if inflation flares up in the long term, then that means that the limits of monetary creation have been reached and that it is time to rely on other tools to mobilize resources (beginning with taxes).[17]

---

16. In addition to facilitating monetary policy, central bank digital currency could embody a genuinely public banking service, free and accessible to everyone—the exact opposite of the systems of electronic currency dreamed of by private operators (whether they are decentralized and polluting, like Bitcoin, or centralized and inegalitarian, like projects envisioned by Meta [formerly Facebook] and private banks).

17. The defenders of monetary creation in the service of guaranteed employment and the Green New Deal, like S. Kelton and P. Tcherneva, are very clear on this point. See S. Kelton, *The Deficit Myth: Modern Monetary Theory and the Birth of the People's Economy* (New York: PublicAffairs, 2020). Compare L. Randall Wray et al., "Public Service Employment: A Path to Full Employment," Research Project Report, Levy Economics Institute of Bard College, April 2018.

We must also emphasize the fact that in the event of a rapid collapse of the economy connected with a financial crisis, a pandemic, or a natural or climate catastrophe, the central banks are the only public institutions capable of reacting fast enough to avoid a spate of bankruptcies or an explosion of poverty. Fortunately, this role as lender of last resort, which had been rejected in the name of financial orthodoxy during the crisis of 1929 and led the world to the edge of the abyss, is now the object of a positive consensus, which shows that we can learn from history. The problem is that the monetary policies put in place in 2008 and 2020 continue to be inserted into a relatively conservative schema. In conclusion, the monetary weapon has been used frequently to save banks and bankers, but there is much more hesitation when it is a question of saving the planet, reducing inequalities, or relieving the public authority of the considerable debts accumulated as a result of crises and diverse bailouts and plans to jump-start the private sector.

Regarding public debts, the balance in force in the early 2020s is relatively precarious. The central banks have bought back an ever-larger share of state loans, at an interest rate that is almost zero. If the rates start to climb again, or rather *when* they begin to climb again, the interest burden will be unbearable for citizen taxpayers, and it will be necessary to implement other solutions, like the exceptional levies on private wealth that were applied after World War II. Moreover, current monetary policy poses other problems. For small savers, zero or negative interest rates are not necessarily good news. On the other hand, for those who have the means to borrow at low interest rates and to find good investments, it is possible to obtain excellent yields. In all, monetary creation and the purchase of financial securities have helped boost prices on the stock and real estate markets, and to further enrich the rich. We must add that zero interest rates constitute in large measure a new privilege for rich countries. Investors everywhere are prepared to be content with a small reward for investing their capital in safe currencies and in the debt securities of the principal Western countries (if they are not partly forced to do so by the new banking regulations), but inversely they demand high interest rates when it is a question of lending to southern countries. Rather than marveling at this miracle of zero interest rates, the rich countries would be wise to take a look into international financial cooperation, which might allow all countries to finance themselves at low rates in a time of crisis.

Generally speaking, the emergence of a new monetary tool recognized as such is a powerful factor for change: it makes it very difficult to explain to the public at large that a return to economic and financial orthodoxy is the only possible option. This tool, however, must be placed under democratic supervision. A consensus is now emerging regarding the central banks' obligation to make their balance sheets greener, indeed, to lead the movement toward durable and equitable development. This is excellent news in itself, except that this new mission will require vast democratic deliberations, in parliamentary precincts and in public forums, on the basis of detailed assessments, pro and con, that will allow us to judge the effects of the different possible monetary policies on multiple social and environmental indicators. However, the current model of the central banks is absolutely not that one: after being appointed by governments and promptly confirmed by parliaments, their leaders limit themselves to meeting behind closed doors and deciding among themselves the best way to use immense amounts of public resources.[18] Among the many highly political decisions that will have to be made, we can also mention the question of whether to postpone the repayment of certain long-term debts.[19] You can bet that many battles will have to be fought before the

---

18. See E. Monnet, *La Banque Providence. Démocratiser les banques centrales et la création monétaire* (Paris: Seuil, 2021), which proposes in particular to create a European Credit Council attached to the European Parliament. N. Dufrêne and A. Grandjean, *La Monnaie écologique* (Paris: Odile Jacob, 2020).

19. The public debts on the European Central Bank's balance sheet, for example. might be postponed by forty or fifty years without interest, or depending on the realization of climatic objectives. For public debts, as for the sums that might be credited to the accounts of private individuals, they might also be recorded on the ECB's balance sheet as a perpetual no-interest debt, which would be tantamount to canceling

central banks become a genuinely democratic tool in the service of equality.

For a Universalist Sovereignism

It is time to close our inquiry. The march toward equality is a battle whose outcome is uncertain, and not a road laid out in advance. Since the end of the eighteenth century, equality has made its way by over-turning the rules established by the regimes in power. The same will be true in the future. It would be an illusion to imagine that decisive transformations could take place if we adopt the unanimity of the countries or the social groups concerned as an untouchable principle. Each political community must be able to set the conditions for the pursuit of trade with the rest of the world, without waiting until it has reached agreement with all its partners. That is always how it has been in history: each government must, if it deems it useful, free itself from its predecessors' commitments, especially if these commitments put social harmony and the survival of the planet in danger. However, it is essential that this form of sovereignism be defined on the basis of universalist and internationalist objectives, that is, by making explicit the criteria of social, fiscal, and environmental justice that can be ap-plied to all countries in the same way.

It would be absurd to claim that such a path is easy to follow and clearly marked out: nearly everything remains to be invented. In prac-tice, this universalist sovereignism will not always be easy to distin-guish from nationalist sovereignism, which is founded on the defense of a particular civilizational identity and interests that are supposed to be homogeneous within it. In order to clearly distinguish the two approaches, we have to adhere to several strict principles. Before commit-ting to unilateral measures, it is critical to propose to other countries

---

them. In any case, it would be better to make these decisions when interest rates are zero, because conflicts between countries will break out again if rates rise in a disorga-nized way.

a model of cooperative development based on universal values and on objective, verifiable social and environmental indicators that make it possible to publicly state the extent to which different classes of income and wealth contribute to public and climatic burdens. We must also describe precisely the transnational assemblies that would ideally be entrusted with global public goods and common policies of fiscal and environmental justice. If these social-federalist proposals are not immediately adopted, the unilateral approach must still remain incentivizing and reversible.[20] Finally, the sovereignist-universalist path loses all credibility if it is not based on a constant search for credible international coalitions capable of accelerating the transition toward socialist, democratic federalism, which should remain the ultimate objective.

This kind of universalist sovereignism will also require active citizens. The social sciences can contribute to this, but it goes without saying that they will not suffice. Only powerful social mobilizations, supported by collective movements and organizations, will allow us to define common objectives and transform power relationships. By what we ask of our friends, our networks, our elected officials, our preferred media, our labor union representatives, and by our own actions and participation in collective deliberation and social movements, each of us can make socioeconomic phenomena more comprehensible and help grasp the changes that are occurring. Economic questions are too important to be left to others. Citizens' reappropriation of this knowledge is an essential stage in the battle for equality. If this book has given readers new weapons for this battle, my goal will have been fully realized.

---

20. For example, if a sovereignist-internationalist state imposes sanctions on a country that practices fiscal or climatic dumping, the latter activities must stop as soon as the country in question decides to tax the profits of multinationals or carbon emissions at the desired level. From this point of view, sectorial measures adopted without a universal basis must be forbidden, because they can easily trigger an escalation of sanctions without any constructive and objectifiable outcome.

CONTENTS IN DETAIL

LIST OF TABLES AND ILLUSTRATIONS

INDEX

Contents in Detail

Tables and Illustrations

Index

166; cotton and textile industry in, 56; education in, 81, 89, 124–126, 128, 176–178, 177*f*, 181, 195; ethnoracial discrimination in, 191, 192*f*, 195–197; foreign and colonial assets of, 143*f*; gendered discrimination in, 185; "great redistribution" in, 121, 122, 124–129, 131, 134, 135–136, 138–139; health care in, 128, 153; income inequality in, 83*f*, 153, 154*f*, 218n22; labor movement in, 126n4; military dominance of, 81; minimum wage in, 152–153; national income in, 122, 139, 140*f*, 230n6; neonationalism rise in, 236; political reforms in, 112; postslavery colonialism in, 95; progressive taxes in, 131, 131*f*, 132*f*, 134, 135–136, 136*f*, 137n19, 138–139, 140*f*, 153; property ownership in, 151–153, 151*f*, 153*f*, 231*f*; proportional taxes in, 163n7; public debt dissolution in, 148*f*; purchasing power of, 230n6; reparations by, 74–75, 80–82, 93, 195; segregation in, 81, 89, 195; slavery in, 48, 50–51, 56, 57*f*, 69, 70*f*, 80–82; taxation of capital by, 173, 174n27, 223n29; welfare state and associated taxes in, 122, 124–129
universalist sovereignism, 243–244
upper classes, 39

veterans, affirmative action for, 187n10
Villèle, Count de, 97

von Mises, Ludwig, 236n12
voting rights. *See* suffrage

wages: gendered discrimination in, 47, 185, 186*f*, 188–189; income distribution and, 45–47; inequalities of, progressive taxes reducing, 157–159; labor laws on, 102–103; minimum wage, 47, 152–153, 159; research on, 4–6; salarial socialism, 168–170
Wallerstein, Immanuel, 3, 59
Warren, Elizabeth, 223n29
Washington, George, 80
Washington Consensus, 207–208
wealth distribution: division of labor and, 9, 94; free circulation of capital and, 170–174, 203, 207, 210, 218; as heritage of slavery and colonialism, 48, 93; inequalities of, continuing, 21; reconception of, 12; research on, 4–8; resistance to changes in, 13; as social and political construct, 9–10; social parity and redistribution of, 193–196; transnational, 93–94, 215. *See also* "great redistribution"; income; progressive taxes; property ownership
Wealth of Nations (Smith), 52
wealth taxes, 163, 223n29, 235n10. *See also* levies, on private wealth
wealthy classes, 39, 42
Weber, Max, 55n6
Weeks, Samuel, 9

274 Index